SYMBOL, MYTH, AND RITUAL

Series Editor: Victor Turner

AFRICAN APOSTLES

Ritual and Conversion in
the Church of John Maranke

SYMBOL, MYTH, AND RITUAL SERIES

AFRICAN APOSTLES

Ritual and Conversion in
the Church of John Maranke

Bennetta Jules-Rosette

Cornell University Press

ITHACA AND LONDON

269.2
J94a

First published 1975 by Cornell University Press.
Published in the United Kingdom by Cornell University Press Ltd., 2–4 Brook Street, London W1Y 1AA.

m.P.

International Standard Book Number 0–8014-0846-6
Library of Congress Catalog Card Number 75-8437
Printed in the United States of America by Kingsport Press, Inc.

TO MY FAMILY

Foreword

Recently both the research and theoretical concerns of many anthropologists have once again been directed toward the role of symbols—religious, mythic, aesthetic, political, and even economic—in social and cultural processes. Whether this revival is a belated response to developments in other disciplines (psychology, ethology, philosophy, linguistics, to name only a few), or whether it reflects a return to a central concern after a period of neglect, is difficult to say. In recent field studies, anthropologists have been collecting myths and rituals in the context of social action, and improvements in anthropological field technique have produced data that are richer and more refined than heretofore; these new data have probably challenged theoreticians to provide more adequate explanatory frames. Whatever may have been the causes, there is no denying a renewed curiosity about the nature of the connections between culture, cognition, and perception, as these connections are revealed in symbolic forms.

Although excellent individual monographs and articles in symbolic anthropology or comparative symbology have recently appeared, a common focus or forum that can be provided by a topically organized series of books has not been available. The present series is intended to fill this lacuna. It is designed to include not only field monographs and theoretical and comparative studies by anthropologists, but also work by scholars in other disciplines, both scientific and humanistic. The appearance of studies in such a forum encourages emulation, and emulation can produce fruitful new theories. It is therefore our hope that the series will serve as a house of many mansions, providing hospitality for the practitioners of any discipline that has a serious and creative concern with comparative symbology. Too often, disciplines are sealed off, in sterile pedantry, from significant intellectual influences. Nevertheless, our primary aim is to bring to public attention works on ritual and myth written by anthropologists, and our readers will find a variety of strictly anthropological approaches ranging from formal analyses of systems of symbols to empathetic accounts of divinatory and initiatory rituals.

Bennetta Jules-Rosette approaches the rituals of an African independent church from an unusual standpoint. Through conversion she became a member of the Apostles of John Maranke. Her "field work," in the traditional sense, ended at that time, but by treating her own membership as a "vehicle for description" she seeks to overcome the dichotomy between commitment and detachment. To each level of sociality corresponds its own knowledge, and if one wishes to grasp a group's deepest knowledge one must commune with its members, speak its Essential We-talk (to combine the vocabularies of Martin Buber and Alfred Schutz). Reflexivity may negate immediacy, solitude may negate society, but these negations may be negated. One may observe while participating, have an objective relation to one's own subjectivity. Durkheim and Kierkegaard may yet be friends!

From this perspective Jules-Rosette sees Christianity as providing the grammar and syntax, as it were, and traditional customs the lexicon, for "symbolic combination that takes place in Apostolic reasoning and ritual" (p. 190). Traditional practices are "translated" in ways that are "neither fully nativistic nor acculturative" (p. 189), but are rather aspects of traditional culture recombined and reordered, and interdigitated with Christian imagery and thought forms—the better to communicate fundamental Christian tenets and paradigms and to interpret contemporary experience. Her travels through several central African nations among Apostles of diverse cultural and linguistic origins enabled her to perceive a "deep structure," Western in its forms of thought but vibrant with local content. Christianity and Africanity became poles of a single field of force. Ritual experience in *kerek*, "the ceremony of praise," became for Jules-Rosette the source of knowledge that transcended the opposition between watching and belonging. This knowledge, "recollected in tranquility," is the matter of her book.

VICTOR TURNER

University of Chicago

Contents

Illustrations

Preface

In their evolution, the independent churches of Africa have combined Western forms of thought with the vibrancy of non-Western cultures. This book records a personal journey toward the understanding of ritual forms and symbolic meanings in an African church, the Apostles of John Maranke. The search led me to become a member of the group. Its history and my own have merged in the descriptions.

A conversion experience enabled me to share in the vision and realities of Apostolic ceremony. For me, a vision of these realities was authoritative, but it was never the only possibility. Commitment versus objectivity created a tension in my research and descriptions, and I found no ideal midpoint between these two poles. Instead my own membership provided a vehicle for description. Throughout the book I attempt to convey the sense of participation while observing, of performance while simultaneously reflecting. Neither of the two negates the other; they mutually create the experience and meanings of ritual. For participants, the symbolism of ritual and the thought of daily life are integrally related. It is precisely through participation that we are drawn to the link between categories and action, between symbolism and ritual. This link is the topic of my study, and its discovery is always open to personal interpretation.

The process of membership, a recurrent thread in this account, relates to much more than individual conversion.

It includes any participant's ability to use a body of knowledge and symbolic thought. It also relates to an observer's fluency with that knowledge. The Apostles, like many African churches, stress the active acquiring of esoteric knowledge in ceremonies.

My investigation of ritual and symbol is divided into three parts. The first part documents the conversion experience through which I was exposed to Apostolic ritual and knowledge, the Apostles' most basic realities, from the inside. Part Two describes the ritual contexts in which Apostles participate and through which they express their most profound beliefs. These rituals are treated as aspects of natural settings, products of talk and interaction. They are also treated as settings that I began to comprehend through my participation with other Apostles. Part Three provides a perspective on change achieved by observing and participating in events in which both cultures and religious realities are in transition. It places the Apostles, and my experiences with them, not only in the context of Africa but also of a larger world.

This study of membership has been inspired by the profound vision of Harold Garfinkel. Both the works and the encouragement of Victor Turner have influenced my study of ritual performance. Talcott Parsons, my mentor for several years, has also pointed me toward an investigation of the social bases of knowledge and the importance of religion in social and cultural change.

I am particularly grateful to Renée C. Fox and Jan Vansina for introducing me to the field of African studies and to the Apostles. And I thank Haldor Heimer for the information and encouragement he provided during my stays in the West Kasai.

A number of persons have read portions of this manuscript at various stages of its development and have provided valuable insights. They include Beryl Bellman, Aaron V. Cicourel, Renée C. Fox, Harold Garfinkel, Hugh B. Mehan, Philleo Nash, Talcott Parsons, James Peacock, Gerald Platt, Melvin Pollner, Terence O. Ranger, Victor Turner, and Kangwa William. For their patient assistance and advice in the preparation of the manuscript I am grateful to Christopher Bagley, Colleen Carpenter, Edythe Hosenpud, and May Miller Sullivan.

The support of my husband, Peter Hayward, who accompanied me for the duration of the field research and whose story is only partially reflected in mine, has been invaluable. To my parents and to my daughter, Violaine, I owe special thanks for their unflagging belief in my undertaking.

Most of all, I thank the members of the Apostolic Church of John Maranke, who instructed, assisted, and took care of me in 1969 and 1971–1972. While I cannot list the names of every friend who was helpful to me, I thank leaders of congregations on their behalf: in Rhodesia, Abel and Makebi Sithole, heads of the entire church, and Baptist Lieb-Umah A. J. Fisher; in Zambia, Baptist Lieb-Umah Kangwa William and Evangelist Lieb-Umah Chisanga Luka; in Zaire, Baptist Lieb-Umah Tshiambi Luka Baptist Lieb-Umah Kasanda Vincent, Baptist Lieb-Umah Nawezi Petro, Healer Marie Tshibola, and Evangelist Lieb-Umah Tshiaba Daniel. My gratitude also extends to the families of Mutongi Kabeya Edouard and Prophet L— Tshilumbu André for their hospitality. For their tireless assistance in research, deep appreciation goes to Dinanga Jérémie, Chipipa Jacob, and Ilunga Saul.

Financial support for this study was provided by the Ford Foundation Foreign Area Fellowship Program. I received other support for various stages of field research and manuscript preparation from the Harvard University Comparative International Program, the Harvard University Department of Social Relations, the National Association of College Women, the Danforth Foundation, the Regents of the University of California, and the Academic Senate of the University of California, San Diego.

Portions of Chapter 4 originally appeared in my article "Song and Spirit," *Africa: Journal of the International African Institute* 14, 2 (1975).

BENNETTA JULES-ROSETTE

La Jolla, California

PART ONE

CONVERSION

CHAPTER 1

The Observing Participant

The whole congregation was then called the Apostle Church. They were going to keep the Sabbath, the seventh day holy and the day being Saturday. I, John, was going to give them the Holy Pascah or Passover of our Lord Jesus. These are the most important ceremonies to be observed by everyone who wants to be saved.

John Maranke

Across sub-Saharan Africa, over six thousand religious groups exist independently of the control of historic and mission churches. Among these groups is the Apostolic church of John Maranke (the Bapostolo), an indigenous Christian church. Numbering over 150,000 adherents, the Maranke Apostles have steadily journeyed northward from their Rhodesian home over the past forty years (Barrett 1968:296). Spreading as far as the Zaire Republic (former Congo-Kinshasa), they have small congregations in many Central African villages and urban centers. My first interest in the Apostles was inspired by a long-standing curiosity about African religion and the ways in which it was incorporated with Christian practice. Although my investigation may have been less difficult than that of early researchers in Africa, my experience included becoming a member of the group that I studied. While it would be unrealistic to recommend such a procedure as the basis for all ethnographic study, my membership opened a perspective and body of information that I had never imagined before. I had come with preconceived notions about the objectivity and neutrality of the observer and about the exotic rites of an African church. Instead of exotic hidden rites, I found public ceremonies that I witnessed at first with awe and confusion rather than my professed "neutrality."

The history of this book might be summarized as a gradual transition from the perspective of a participant observer to that of an observing participant. A major characteristic of this transition was a shift in my experience of events and their constancy, making it even more difficult to separate "research" from lived experience. The coherence of my early interpretations, straining toward scientific consistency, began to appear increasingly arbitrary as new experiences opened the vision of a religious world of which I had not been aware.

I spent most of the summer of 1969 in the southwestern Congo, where, an anthropologist had informed me, the Bapostolo had their largest congregations.[1] I struggled with the Tshiluba language, and the entire visit was far from my ideal conception of either a sociological or spiritual search. But I was determined to return on a second, longer, research trip. Shortly before I did so in the summer of 1971, I received a letter from some of the Apostolic leaders in Luluabourg, assuring me that they were awaiting my visit and that they were certain that I would inspire many baptisms in the United States. Skeptical about the implication that I would ever join the group, I pushed the letter aside.

I first encountered the Luluabourg Apostles on a rainy afternoon in July 1969. The dry season was just beginning, and there were still mild rains in the Kasai. An American from the local Presbyterian mission at Luluabourg had agreed to drive me several miles out of town to a retreat

[1] Following local language usage, the term Bapostolo refers to members of the Apostolic church of John Maranke in all of its subgroupings. Bapostolo is a term generally used by Zairian members, particularly those speaking Tshiluba and Congo-Kiswahili. The largely Shona-speaking Rhodesian and Zambian members refer to themselves as Vapostori or Wapostori (cf. Murphree 1969:92).

that the Ndesha congregation of the Apostles were holding in lieu of their annual Passover ceremony. Their leader was Luka Tshiambi, the owner of a local trucking business. The missionary's white Volkswagen bounced over the dirt roads, and he stopped several times to ask for directions to the Apostles' encampment. From a distance, I could see white-robed men and women circulating in a field surrounded by elephant grass and small thatch enclosures. I had read that the Apostles were Sabbatarians, who were bearded, wore white robes with red sashes, and carried canes,[2] but the sight of an encampment in which people were actually dressed and worshiping in this fashion still surprised me. It seemed like a village out of a mythical past.

The missionary introduced me to two Apostles, while others gathered curiously around to watch. One of them, smiling benignly yet with a penetrating stare, was dressed in a white shirt and a green skirtlike wrap that I later learned is called a *mutambo* and is worn under the man's white garment. Saying goodbye in Tshiluba, the missionary left. The man in the skirt led me to a small hut, where members began to question me carefully on the purpose

[2] The AIMO (Belgian Congo, Affaires Indigènes et Main-d'Oeuvres) files M-58 (1956–1959), which I had read before the pilot project, described the Apostles as wearing white robes and carrying staffs. Colonial administrators had carefully noted the biblical passages to which Apostles referred in explaining these practices. Other general ethnographic descriptions of Bapostolo ritual and doctrine are included in the following published studies: (1) Aquina (1967), in her descriptions of ritual performance, includes information that I only subsequently discovered to be misleading. The spiritual gift represented by Apostles in the insignia AP or APE was interpreted as "prophet" rather than "evangelist." Women are defined as belonging to the "lowest rank" in the church rather than as possessing a special spiritual gift. This article also stated that female prophets do not wear insignia (pp. 205–206). It is difficult to avoid making such assumptions in purely observational descriptions of ritual performance; (2) Barrett 1968: esp. 124, 176–177, 294, 296; (3) Murphree 1969: 100–110.

of my visit. They asked me how I learned about the Maranke church and whether there were Apostles of John in the United States. It did not occur to me that they would probably be well aware whether such a group existed because the church elders were fully cognizant of all of its branches. I replied in French that a professor who had visited their country had told me about the church. I said that there were churches containing the name Apostolic in the United States but that they were Pentecostal and that their members did not wear white robes.

Their questions seemed to be leading in a particular direction, yet I could make little sense of them. "What kind of baptism did you receive?" one of them inquired. "Was it by sprinkling or by immersion?" I replied that I had received baptism by immersion in a Baptist church in the United States. They stated that the Apostolic baptism by immersion "cleansed the heart" and taught people how to open their hearts. It was, they asserted, the true baptism: life came from the heart and from the Holy Spirit, which entered the heart after baptism.

Five members, who I later learned were two baptists, two evangelists, and a prophet, spoke with me for over an hour. Bilolo, a young evangelist, served as interpreter. They asked me whether I had read First Corinthians, concerning the gifts of the Spirit. I replied that I knew of it. The verse, which they read to me somewhat to my puzzlement, sounded very much like a statement of Pentecostal doctrine. At the end of the session, I was asked if I had any further questions or comments of my own. I was so struck by the contrast of this idyllic setting to anything that I had ever experienced that I asked them about their own work in everyday life to break the spell. "Of course we work. We are not unemployed (chomeurs) or lazy," an evangelist replied. "We all have trades, as that is written in the Bible." The conversation lulled, and a low, drawn out song emerged from the background. Suddenly, as if on cue, two of the members rose and left the hut. The others knelt, facing east, and began to sing.

Later I learned that no matter where an Apostle is in the encampment, if he hears the song, "Mwari Komborera Africa" (God Save Africa), he considers himself to be within the congregation and kneels to sing and pray. A short chant, which I was told was the Lord's Prayer in Tshiluba, followed the "Mwari." After the prayer, all the members disappeared except for Bilolo; this young man, a high school student, remained my interpreter for the rest of the summer, and we became close friends.

Two women appeared with plates of chicken, rice, and fried plantains. They clapped three times and retired. These claps, members explained, were in the name of the Father, the Son, and the Holy Spirit. No further blessings were performed over the food. After eating, I was escorted to the evening prayers and was seated on the north end of an aisle formed on the ground by rows of men and women, the women to my right and the men to my left. Several women stared in apparent amazement at my bared head and Western clothes, as though I had just arrived from some alien planet. They were all wearing white veils called *bitambala* with red "T's" resembling crosses, which represented cleansing through the blood of Christ and the healing and protective powers of the Holy Spirit.

Someone was preaching in a rapid staccato and flourishing a cane in the center aisle. As I listened, the interpreter showed me the appropriate passages in a French Bible. The loud preaching was interrupted at various points by songs started by both men and women. While the preaching was lively and members were quick to respond to it, there seemed to be very little further display of emotion. The ecstatic crescendoes of Western Pentecostal preaching seemed to be absent. I was so fascinated by this orderly drama and by the rhythmic flow of the Tshiluba language that I barely noticed how quickly the service passed, even though I had understood very little of what it could mean to the Apostles.

The fleeting events were registered on my tape recorder. I had also written down as many of the biblical passages as I could follow. Thereafter, in my recordings of Apostolic ceremonies, I used this same method of taping and notetaking, although my impressions of the service, called a *kerek*, varied enormously as I became more fully involved in the ritual process. From the beginning, I was awed and fascinated by the precise timing of the ceremonies and the dramatic qualities of Apostolic preaching and song.

This first field trip in 1969 was intended to be a simple exploratory study of the group that I would check against information that was already available. I had several hypotheses about the influence of religious sects on social change and about the relationship between religious and secular life. Yet my ignorance of the practices and aspirations of the Apostles made these concepts shallow. Most of this trip was actually spent learning to live in a new environment, becoming acquainted with members, and observing their main worship ceremony, the Sabbath *kerek*.

A number of research alternatives opened almost immediately. Kadima Marc, my first informant and head of the local Council of Independent Churches (Conseil Supérieur des Sacrificateurs), offered to interpret the local religious scene. After having been an Apostle for two years, he had left the church upon receiving a direct revelation from God that he should establish his own organization to consolidate the independent groups in the area. The move toward independency, I soon discovered, was quite extensive within Luluabourg alone.[3] Eighty to a hundred basi-

[3] There are several pioneering studies in the field of religious independency. Barrett indicates that the term independency first appeared

cally Christian churches outside the purview of the missions were officially registered with the local government, and dozens more thrived unofficially. Many of these groups were represented in Kadima's Council.

While Kadima had been recommended to me as an important contact, several members of the Apostolic congregation were reluctant to admit that he represented them.[4] I gradually concluded that the Apostles' reactions were related to the presence of three different Apostolic congregations in Luluabourg which, although they all called themselves Bapostolo, recognized different local leadership, though often with some overlap. The congregation of Luka Tshiambi, Eglise Apostolique de Jésus-Christ par le Prophète John Maranke, that met in Ndesha commune, was the group that I ultimately studied.[5] Another group, the Eglise Apostolique Africaine, had formed on the local level under the leadership of Tshiaba Daniel, a member of Tshiambi's congregation and also an affiliate of Kadima's Council. Toward the end of my first visit, I also learned of a third group, Eglise Apostolique au Congo, headed by

---

in a 1904 conference address delivered in South Africa, to describe churches operating outside of mission control (1968:49). The term independency has been preferred by scholars of modern indigenous Christianity in Africa to terms like syncretism, millenarism, and sectarianism which appear to have narrower connotations. The term "church," rather than "sect" or "movement," is generally employed by members of independent "church" groupings to describe their organizations. Five particularly important works which employ the framework of independency are: Barrett 1968, 1970, 1971; Hayward 1963; Sundkler 1961.

[4] Kadima Marc was recommended to me as a field contact prior to my first visit. See also Barrett 1968:74, 175, 295.

[5] This title was adopted by the Apostolic church in Luluabourg under Tshiambi's leadership between 1969 and 1970. Its resemblance to the official title of the Kimbanguist church (L'Eglise de Jésus-Christ sur la Terre par le Prophète Simon Kimbangu) is striking. For a comprehensive recent study of Kimbanguism by an African author see Banda-Mwaka 1972:3–54.

Kadiebwe Samuel, another former member of Tshiambi's larger congregation. Although I interviewed some members of this congregation on both visits, circumstances made it difficult to attend their services regularly.

On the second week of my initial visit, Kadima invited me to accompany him to the Ndesha kerek. We met at his office with Tshiaba Daniel and a member of the Apostolic Faith church. Kadima was unaware that I had previously attended the retreat service and had received an official invitation from Tshiambi to return. In this delicate situation, I decided to go alone rather than appear as an associate of the council, which was already claiming that I had come to do research on it and possibly provide financial aid. As my interest in Apostolic ritual grew, I tried to avoid political situations by remaining with Tshiambi's group.

The following week, at Tshiambi's invitation, I left the European section of town to live among the Apostles in the home of one of their prophets. This prophet, who was then twenty-seven years old, was the man in the skirt who had welcomed me at our first meeting. He lived with his family in the Katoka commune and worked at the outdoor market as a tailor of children's clothes. By coming to live under his roof as a guest of the Ndesha congregation, I had in effect defined the subject under study. I learned about the history and ritual of the Bapostolo through the Ndesha group and began to describe their practices as though they represented the Apostolic church as a whole. I believed at this time that the ceremonies that I observed contained most of the possible variations in worship practices.

My presence at the first of the services had caused a good deal of attention. On the second occasion, I was introduced as a foreign student who wanted to learn about the church. Now, when I re-examine the questions and remarks made to me, it seems clear that the Apostles had considered me a potential convert all along. Even at the first few services,

I noticed obvious ways in which my presence influenced the ceremony, although this influence was hard to evaluate.

The concept that the observer creates the reported data assumes that one filters the social world through particular capacities and conceptual frameworks. These frameworks are not under the observer's autonomous control but are built on the relationship between direct experience, descriptions that mediate experience, and occasions of observation. Through continued observation, I began to develop a repertoire of knowledge and expectations, or a common culture, that was shared with participants and created in interaction with them. Those who conduct research within familiar cultural or work settings, American sociologists in the United States, for example, already take for granted a shared language and a common cultural fluency. In my case, partial fluency in Tshiluba came only gradually, during the second phase of study. Even more difficult than developing a lingua franca for communication, however, was the critical process of gaining membership in a religious community as part of learning the purposes and experiences of ritual. This process was complex and personally absorbing.

Members gave me limited descriptions of ritual and social organization, as seen through their perspectives. These accounts usually described a particular situation. My understanding constantly shifted, for just as I felt that I was grasping a topic and its intricacies, I would witness a new event that would open another dimension of experience or ceremony to me. This piecemeal learning influenced my recording and perception of situations. In particular, my early descriptions of the ceremonies and conviction that they would not vary had been shaped by the limited number of rituals that I had witnessed and the narrowness of my interpretations.

I also received seemingly contradictory explanations of

a single event. For example, early in the research I was informed that the hymn "Kwese, Kwese" was to be interpreted literally as "Everywhere, everywhere, we see people who do not know Christ." This meant that the "Kwese, Kwese" was a hymn of proselytism. Later, I was told that the "Kwese, Kwese" provides the means by which angels are invoked to protect and watch over a ceremony.[6] The summoning hands of evangelists and baptists welcoming the angels during this hymn now began to make sense, and the entire performance acquired a new cast. For an outside observer, however, familiarity with one order of interpretation gave no clues to the others that might exist.

When I returned to the field in July 1971, I was newly married, and my husband, Peter, accompanied me. I felt that I could continue to study Apostolic ritual practices as a detached, though sympathetic, observer. But it became increasingly difficult for me to remain uncommitted and continue the work under the conditions that I had initially projected for it. Members in Luluabourg urged me to join the party of their representatives at the annual Passover ceremony. My acceptance supported their expectation that I would soon join the church. While administrators in the local city government attempted to persuade me to leave the African community and move to the European center of town, members continued to give me preliminary instruction in the doctrine and ritual of the church and anxiously asked when I would schedule my baptism. I was not ready to make either decision.

The question of which organizational unit I would study was resolved, for I had arbitrarily settled on Tshiambi's group. I had also decided to remain within the West Kasai rather than travel to other Apostolic congregations. My

---

[6] Personal instruction, Prophet Ngindu Aaron, August 1969, and Prophet Tshilumbu André, December 1971.

early difficulty in locating Apostles in Kinshasa tended to confirm this decision. The community of Apostles in Luluabourg and in the village residences of Demba Territory was the projected focus of my study.

In September 1971 the Passover mission crystallized, and I prepared to leave for Malawi. Although I had only been in Luluabourg for one month, the opportunity to witness the Passover and to visit other parts of the church intrigued me. At that time, I had attended only the Sabbath kerek and one four-day retreat, during which members had discouraged me from participating in the evening and late night services. Although I had glimpsed them at a distance, I had considered these services to be secret ceremonies representing areas of ritual that were unavailable to me as an outsider. I thought that I would understand these events if only I were permitted to see them. Peter agreed with me, and we made preparations to go.

During my trip to the Passover, I finally witnessed a full retreat ceremony complete with firewalking and all-night singing. In Malawi, partly as a result of the impact of this journey, Peter and I became members of the Apostolic church and began to receive more extensive instruction in doctrine and ritual. From this instruction grew my new understanding of the church and its ceremonies as purposeful and directly applicable to me. Explanations given to me of the times to sing and pray and of worship and healing allowed me to see ritual, not only as a collection of practices by which the flow or aesthetic character of a ceremony was maintained, but also as viable events that exerted a special influence on the daily lives of members.

On the Passover trip, I observed the Zambian and Malawian branches of the church in action and discovered that the international character of the church resulted in many regional variations in ritual performance and social organization. Songs were sung in different languages, and the repertoire of performance changed. The format of the worship service from one area to another, however, remained similar enough for visiting members to follow the ritual and communicate by the reading of biblical passages in several languages, even though a single common language was not available. In Zambia, I noticed that evangelists were much more active in the management of ritual than they had been in the Kasai area. These regional variations in language and ceremony introduced me to some of the basic differences within the church.

The period of travel was prolonged. The trip to Malawi that was to take two or three weeks stretched out into nearly three months, as we visited several congregations. Much of the information discussed throughout the book is drawn from these visits. I was certain that my research design and plans had been destroyed, for I was no longer able to continue a study of ritual in which certain styles of performance were treated as immutable. I also began to question theories of cultural syncretism that presupposed some unilinear and certain relationship between the traditional cultural background of members and the church's development. While I knew of some aspects of Central African culture, the depth of ethnographic study required to investigate cultural reflexes across a number of tribal areas seemed less rewarding than an examination of ways in which individual background and interpretations influenced each congregation's approach to the church. The variations within each ceremony relied on very subtle local adaptations of basic forms of worship.

My conception of the contexts of ritual grew broader as I acquired a background of membership understandings and learned about a field of linguistic and cultural variations within a single ritual production.[7] The study of supposedly

[7] Aquina's (1967) conclusions about the organization of ritual scenes which were, like my own, embedded in her position as an outside ob-

invariant ritual procedures and their emergence in a number of scenes of everyday life had been altered. Instead, I became more attuned to the comparative aspects of ritual format and purpose and the range of variation in the organization, pacing, and interpretation of many ceremonies.

Shortly after our return to the Congo in October, it became the Republic of Zaire, and Luluabourg was renamed Kananga. Following this change, governmental restrictions were placed on the activities of all independent churches except the Kimbanguist church.[8] Public observances were no longer allowed, and Apostolic leaders reorganized under the restrictions. My opportunity to film and record ceremonies in the Zaire virtually came to a halt by April 1972.

The prohibition of public worship drew my attention to private rituals. As early as 1969, I had been interested in the way in which Apostles were able to create ritual settings in the midst of their mundane activities. Those activities associated with prayer are called *tshijila* or, literally, "things set apart." They may be set apart by personal acts such as fasting, or by entire ceremonies. The practical organization of each ceremony is also interwoven with its spiritual interpretations.[9] In this sense, tshijila always

---

server. As an observer, one is puzzled by questions that cannot be answered within the present scope of information. Aquina (1967:206) states: "The Apostles merely state that when the Holy Spirit confers a new charisma on a man, he obtains a higher rank. I was never present at a promotion. I have observed, however, that a group of Apostles usually centers around one powerful preacher, who also holds a position of prestige in the community." Observing the conferral of a new gift at the Passover ceremony might have added new perspectives to this interpretation. I found, however, that simply witnessing the ceremony was not helpful until I had received members' accounts of it as well.

[8] République de Zaire, Ordonnance-Loi No. 71–012 of Dec. 31, 1971, recorded in *Aurore*, 620 (Jan. 20–25, 1972).

[9] Needleman (1970:30–31, 199–200) refers to esoteric religion as the spiritual teachings involved in religious practice. He distinguishes esot-

takes place in and with regard to the mundane world. For example, the prophetic examination *(keti)* conducted before each weekly ceremony appears at first to have the highly practical value of clearing persons to participate in worship. Later I saw the procedure as a way of detecting sin in members and giving advice.[10] "No one," stated one Apostle friend, "could pass through keti except a member. Only a member would understand what was said." It was only through ultimate exposure to the spiritual interpretations that keti contained that I could begin to understand them as guides to everyday conduct and life.

The Ritual Settings

The following discussion of ritual settings is based on direct explanations given to me by various Apostles and on passages from John Maranke's book, *The New Witness of the Apostles* (Maranke 1953). These are brief descriptions but they will serve as a basis for a more detailed analysis of ritual settings in later chapters. Each description was intended to have instructive value for me.

Members' Instructions

I was commanded to keep the Sabbath Holy and to avoid working on it. The day of the Sabbath was said to be Saturday. [Maranke 1953, describing experience in 1932]

---

eric religion from exoteric religion which he states may be understood as "a way of life" or the relations of religion to members' daily activities (p. 30). I would make the further qualification that on many occasions events are interpreted in an esoteric or spiritual way by members while they are cast completely differently by outsiders.

[10] Murphree (1969:102) refers to prophecy as a way of spiritually discerning sin in members.

Members' Instructions

Pray over water in a little bottle for your kerek. When you get back home, do not begin the work of the church immediately. Wait to put all your affairs in order. Then go out on *masowe* [wilderness retreat] for a whole week. The last day, pray over the water again and pray to God that He show His power in your country and that He be with you. [Lubumbashi, 1972]

Kerek is the occasion on which Apostles collectively call upon the angels and the Holy Spirit. The term kerek refers not only to this occasion as a ritual but also to the congregation itself and to the spiritual state that it attains. The word is apparently borrowed from the Afrikaans or Dutch *kerk*, meaning church. Zambian members insisted that kerek and the Scottish *kirk* were identical, while members in Rhodesia pointed out its possible Dutch origin.[11] A summons of kerek is called ("Kerek! Kerek! Kerek!"), usually by an evangelist, as a way of announcing that worship will begin. As a summons, kerek may be called prior to a full worship ceremony or during the course of song to announce that members should prepare themselves for worship.

While a number of public worship meetings may be held on weekdays, usually on Wednesdays and Fridays, the Sabbath kerek, which takes place on a Saturday afternoon, is the most important. It is stressed that Saturday, rather than Sunday, is a day of rest that should be devoted completely to worship. The meeting is held in an open field or on a hilltop, for church regulations forbid the construction of buildings as places of worship, and under normal circumstances all services are conducted outdoors. Before every occasion of worship, members remove their shoes, following God's commandments to Moses in Exodus 3:2, to show

[11] Personal communication, Jaya Festus, an Apostle of Zambia. See also Coetzee 1971:65.

that they are on holy ground. A prophetic examination for all participants, while not essential on weekdays, must open the Sabbath ceremony if a prophet is available. The meeting is also preceded by confession and is followed by a curing ceremony in which members who are ill are prayed over by the *barapi* (confirmed healers) and other members who possess the spiritual gift of healing.

Kerek follows a standard format. In the observation of over 100 kereks, I noticed that the order of presentation varied within the limits of what seemed to be a definite structure. The kerek is opened by a prophetic consultation, followed by two hymns and a congregational prayer. Then members preach and read selections from the Bible antiphonally. Preaching and reading are superseded by song, which fills gaps in the flow of the service. A final prayer and two hymns close the main service.

While I wish to deal mainly with the Sabbath kerek, there are many other variations in worship. Any meeting of Apostles may develop into a kerek, should this state be announced. Kereks held on other days may include only prayer and song. Preaching on these occasions supplements informal biblical discussions prior to the worship proper. Though public kereks, especially the Sabbath kerek, are generally led by evangelists who name the order of speakers and monitor the flow of the service, congregations in different areas may develop special procedures of their own. That every event in kerek has spiritual interpretations as well as interactional possibilities also provides for a great deal of innovation in the format.

Members' Instructions

The following are the great commandments which should be kept by everybody all the time. Every person should partake of the Holy Pascah [Passover] every year. As people should observe the Sabbath every week, so they should observe the Pascah every year at its proper time. The ceremony should be done according to its rules. No person should miss it under normal conditions. The Passover is the key of Apostleship, and nobody should dispense it. A person may then do other rituals after he has done the Pascah. In all prayers, people should raise up clean hands and look to Heaven.   [Maranke 1953, describing experience in 1932]

Members' Instructions

When you start a *musankano* [church conference], go out to the place with your prophet. Take only someone you trust, who is very just. No woman can go along. You must pray over some water and sprinkle it in a circle around the whole encampment. Build a fire and sit with him to the West and you to the East. Only you can light it. Then sing and pray that it will be a good musankano and that the Holy Spirit will come. Always begin the preaching with the passage Daniel 3, the story of Shadrach, Meshach, and Abednego. This is the most basic verse for preaching.   [Lubumbashi, December, 1971]

Kerek also occurs within two larger ritual settings: the Passover (Pascah or Pasika) and the musankano. The Passover is preceded by a week of celebration that is called the musankano of Pasika, literally gathering for the Passover.[12] In the latter, several congregations meet in a bush retreat, and the elders of these congregations hold special meetings. Each region has several paschal subdivisions, usually clustered around a single urban area that contains the largest Apostolic congregation. The baptist *Lieb-Umah,* or pastor, for that region is responsible for collecting £27 from his congregation to pay the paschal travel expenses for the church's head and to pay for gathering adequate food supplies for the weeklong musankano. Arrangements are made by the church's central committee in each region for the Passover location.

The Passover is the only sacrament of the Apostolic

[12] Murphree (1969:103–105) presents an interesting and detailed description of preparations for and events involved in the Passover ceremony in Rhodesia.

church, the only performance for which a priestly administrator is required.[13] The sacramental character of the Passover is particularly important because at that time prophets select those who are spiritually designated to hold certain "gifts," which are also offices within the church. The
conferral of these spiritual gifts is overseen by the head of
the church, originally only by John Maranke himself and
later by two of his sons. Although spiritual abilities may
be informally recognized prior to the Passover, they cannot
be confirmed outside of this celebration. Areas in which the
Passover is not given annually tend to develop difficulties
in filling leadership posts vacated by schism or shifting
membership.

The paschal ceremony consists of five main ritual parts:
(1) confession by fire: (2) keti (the prophet's gate or prophetic examination); (3) washing of each celebrant's feet; (4)
eating of the sacrament; and (5) confirmation of spiritual
gifts. All members confess their sins of the year, while
running around a bonfire. Spectators respond with advice.
Each member then passes through a straw enclosure con-
structed like a long corridor or pathway in which three or
four pairs of prophets accompanied by evangelists stand.
Once the candidate has passed through the gate for examination by each of these prophets, he enters a large central enclosure, where his feet are washed by a Lopasa
(LPZ), a member who is chosen to aid in administering
the Passover, following Christ's washing of the disciples'
feet at the Last Supper. The men then hang their staffs

[13] While the Catholic church has seven sacraments administered by
a priest, including baptism, marriage, and confession, which Apostles
do not consider as sacraments, the treatment of sacraments differs
among the Reformed or Protestant churches. Créspy (1952:35–37) states
that while faith healing may not be considered a sacrament within
various Protestant groups, it has, along with other ritual performances,
a "sacramental" character. The classification of the sacraments seems to
relate to notions of authority in the various churches discussed.

in the enclosure to indicate that they are ready to eat the sacrament, which follows as soon as most persons are cleared.

The sacrament of unleavened bread (dried cornmeal) and wine (fruit and berry extract) is prepared by twelve virgin girls selected by the female elders. It is presented to the head of the church, who wears an ephod representing the spiritual offices of the church. He and an assistant administer the Eucharist to a local committee of twelve church elders and then to male and female members, respectively. After the sacrament, prophets confirm spiritual gifts by prayer and the laying on of hands, if this has not already been done in the course of musankano. Each adult member who has received the Passover is designated to hold one of the four spiritual gifts of healing, prophecy, baptism, or preaching. Specialized gifts such as those of judges, scribes, and administrative officers are also confirmed. The paschal ceremony concludes at this point, and the musankano of Pascah disbands.

The simple musankano does not involve the ritual intensity of the Passover. The aims of this conference are the unification of various congregations for worship, instruction of members in spiritual work, and political and organizational discussions, including the arrangements for the following year's Passover. Like the Sabbath, the days of musankano are devoted to prayer and song, although semi-work activities such as clothes washing may take place on weekdays. Persons who have broken the church laws or have had disputes are judged by the *batongi* (evangelist judges). Leaders and prophets also observe the conduct and spiritual work of members during sessions of instruction and song and make recommendations for the paschal confirmation of spiritual gifts. Singing generally continues throughout the night during musankano as a form of spiritual preparation and purification. Members who sing well during this period are designated for the gift of *hari-kros* (high cross or master singer).

Members' Instructions

When you go out on masowe, you must always confess beforehand. If not, you may see monsters, and you will be frightened away.   [Lubumbashi, May 1972]

You will be much attacked by demons. Then you should put on the mutambo and go into the desert to pray. Then come back to preach and you will find it easy.   [Lusaka, July 1972]

Apostles believe that spiritual dangers can be averted by means of a wilderness retreat, or masowe. This form of prayer, patterned on Moses' spiritual experiences in the desert and Christ's solitary temptation, sustains the strong connections between personal and collective worship. On a group retreat, members are also encouraged to pray alone at a spot somewhat removed from the larger encampment. Confession must take place before masowe, or the member's life is considered to be in danger.

Members' Instructions

When you baptize a child, hold him this way. If you don't, he might slip. Then if he drowns, the government will bring you trouble. When you baptize the person and a demon comes, you box and box with him. Then when you beat him, you can put the person in the water. Otherwise, the demon can eat you. [Nyangwena, July 1972]

Only the Apostolic baptism makes the candidate a member of the church. Apostles do not accept previous Christian baptisms, even in Zionist or other independent churches, as grounds for membership. Baptism is performed by triple immersion of the candidate in the name of the Father, the Son, and the Holy Spirit and is conducted by a male member, generally one with the confirmed gift of baptism. The candidate, who is given a new biblical name, is said to undergo a part of an Apostolic conversion experience in which he "receives the Holy Spirit" and takes part in a visionary experience.

Members' Instructions

You should pray three times a night, at nine o'clock, twelve o'clock, and two o'clock. These are the best times when God is listening. Otherwise you might get Satan on the line.   [Lubumbashi, October 1971]

Ritual events that may constitute scenes in their own right are also performed privately. These semiautonomous settings are parts of kerek as well and can be seen as a preparation for the main service, particularly when performed as a sequence of a larger event. Prayer is a part of the fabric of all ritual performances. Members also gather to pray as a separate event. Group prayer is usually held for some specific purpose, such as for the sick or for the welfare of the church. Most church meetings, even those convened to discuss business, are opened and closed by prayer. Apostles view prayer as a direct and powerful form of communication and intercession with God.

Members' Instructions

If you want to learn how to prophesy, just keep saying "Imeni, Imeni" [Amen, Amen].   [Nyangwena, October 1971]

There are different kinds of prophecy. One is when you hear a little buzzing, like a mosquito, in your ear. You may see a vision or hear a voice. Another kind is when you feel a knocking in your heart.   [Lubumbashi, December 1971]

Members' Instructions

Every time before you are to do a job, you will have a dream or vision.   [Bocha, July 1972]

Prophecy is used to examine the spiritual state—past, present, and future—of each member. It includes inspiration by the Holy Spirit leading to visionary experiences and ecstatic communication. Prophets also diagnose illness and resolve disputes through their visions. Immediately before public worship, prophets perform an examination to review the conduct of all participants. The Apostle anticipates this moment when his spiritual conduct and physical state are examined, often revealing significant problems. Prophecies and prophetic examinations may also occur at any informal meeting of members. They resemble those of keti and contain a special spiritual message or advice and warnings for the person designated. At the end of kerek, public presentations of prophecies are given to the entire congregation and at times to individual members.

Members' Instructions

When you confess, start out by saying, "I put myself before God to confess." Open your hands at your sides and do not carry your staff or healing stick.   [Kananga, March 1972]

You should keep an evangelist near you at all times, so you can confess, so you can avoid any little sins.   [Kananga, March 1972]

Occasionally, the verdict of keti is that a member must confess a sin or failing. Although this confession may be faced with some apprehension, it usually takes the form of friendly counseling from one or more evangelists. Confession is performed both within and outside of kerek as an occasion of worship. The candidate volunteers or is selected by a prophet to present his transgressions before an evangelist. In the absence of other Apostles, I was informed, confession may also be "witnessed" by a tree or an inanimate object. Harboring anger, as well as personal transgressions of church laws or commandments, are subjects for confession. The evangelist renders a decision on the gravity of the transgression, and in most cases, the member is pardoned. Should the case involve unsettled disputes or accusations of witchcraft, adultery, theft, or murder, members of the central committee, other elders, or confirmed batongi are called to deliberate it in *dare* (an open place), the Apostolic court.

Members' Instructions

Q: What's the difference between curing by a young or an experienced healer?
A: The young one might have to pray for hours before he could build up the spiritual force to cure. The experienced one could do it immediately. We are all inner tubes for the Spirit, and the pump is prayer. [Lubumbashi, September 1971]

When you heal, you touch the patient's whole body. But women cannot touch the top of the head, only the side of the head. Men can touch the top of the head when they pray. [Nyangwena, October 1971]

The barapi include both male and female healers. Within the kerek ceremony, the principal time for healing is at the end of the service. One Apostle explained this form of healing by saying: "Our kerek is our hospital." Members are also healed on the spot, when they have accidents or are ill. Home healings may be conducted by barapi or by groups of elders summoned to pray for the patient. The ceremony has a prescribed format, beginning with prayers and an invocation of the healing powers of Christ and the Holy Spirit. Songs, including "I heal in the name of God in Heaven" *(Ndirapire we Mambo mudi mudenga)*, announcing that healing is done in Christ's name, are performed energetically by the healer and other members who may be present. Exorcisms are performed in much the same manner as healings, with another Apostolic chant, "Hosanna Mambo Hosanna," sung as accompaniment. In both cases, the patient's condition is considered to be caused by the intrusion of evil or demonic powers.

Members' Instructions

In Heaven you do not have to work anymore: you sing all the time. [Kananga, August 1969]

Singing is a kind of food which we give to God. [Kananga, March 1972]

You preach like a baptist, not like an evangelist. An evangelist should run around more and shout. You just stand there like this and talk softly like a baptist.

Song and preaching are the most basic features of the Sabbath kerek, although song, in particular, also accompanies prayer, masowe, healing, and baptism. Each performance of song in Apostolic ritual has a specific purpose. It may: invoke angels, begin worship, summon healing or spiritual powers, show joy of victory in the Spirit, inspire preaching, or encourage work activities. The words alone are not always indicative of the song's purpose. Certain songs are also associated with specific occasions of worship.

While preaching occurs in kerek, it also takes place, usually briefly, during more informal meetings. In that case, it does not necessarily transform the informal setting into a kerek, if that spiritual intent is absent, but rather emerges as a rehearsal for kerek preaching or as a special form of instruction and proselytizing.

These contexts have been described separately, because they are so recognized by members. They mark definite breaks in the activity of kerek and larger settings or are constitutive of them in special ways. The ritual contexts are the core features of an Apostle's religious life. That some of the settings are semiautonomous enhances their use in everyday life. By initiating them, an Apostle can turn any situation into a ritual occasion.

Although members described the spiritual base of their social organization quite early in the 1969 field trip, I discovered that their work in spiritual performance was far more complex than their descriptions suggested (Barrett 1968:177; Murphree 1969:94–100). Even though an Apostle is confirmed in a particular gift and has performed healing or prophecy, he is expected to undertake other duties both in and outside of kerek. While the evangelist has been designated with the gift of preaching, his duties also include judging cases in dare, managing the flow of kerek, presenting prophecies to other members, and seeking converts. Some of these duties are embodied in instructions that members give to each other, but many are never explicitly stated.

A case in which a prophet informed an evangelist that he was not performing his work properly because he was incapable of reading and expounding on a biblical text indicated the complexities of organizational work to me. Although persons holding different spiritual gifts conceive of these gifts as working interdependently, there were occasional disputes, such as whether preaching and its management should be the work of a baptist, as a pastor of the congregation, or of an evangelist, as a member especially gifted in preaching.

It is also taken for granted that gifts and positions involve spiritual specialization the knowledge and use of which is a central feature of membership. For example, while women may not preach publicly, they are expected to instruct new members informally. As prophetesses they also pray for the opening of kerek and perform keti, and as regular members they are expected to intervene through song during kerek to redirect male discourse.[14]

It was expectably harder for me to obtain specific accounts of conduct and events than to obtain ideal descriptions of the same activities. Many instructions took the form of ideal descriptions that could not be understood out of context. I found that I was able to extract various generalizations from events that I observed. As I became increasingly involved in gaining membership after baptism in the church, particularly in Lubumbashi, where my research efforts were spread among schismatic groups, I realized that my presence in a given community for a limited period of time thoroughly influenced my access to and view of the organization and its position in a larger society.

The Strategies of Field Research

I soon became familiar with a repertoire of ritual contexts, studying each type of ritual setting by various means: recordings, transcriptions, texts and songs, still and cinematic photography, interviews, questionnaires, and historical accounts. Tapes and photographs were presented to

[14] Cf. Aquina's (1967:210) suggestion that women are low ranking or somehow not full members. Certainly, women are not always present in the planning of ritual events. Many of the women informed me that their absence at palavers was a matter of personal preference and not a church ruling. If membership is examined as a form of religious knowledge in practice, one focuses not on complete or incomplete membership but on various perspectives for participation.

members after the ceremonies to elicit their personal impressions of ritual events. All these activities enriched my understanding of the main rituals. Often I had the most valuable insights when I left my stance as an observer and was participating as fully as possible as a member. But at these times my total involvement made it difficult to record the results of direct participation.

Throughout the fieldwork period, I used the tape recorder to gather ritual material that I generally examined descriptively rather than from a historical perspective, although both treatments were interrelated. My increased understanding of basic ritual procedures served as a point of departure for the comparative study of Apostolic ceremony in different cultural and linguistic areas. It became clear that various ritual settings constituted "working worlds" in which leaders simultaneously used practical and spiritual activities to produce a well-ordered ceremonial performance.[15] Since each act had a specific spiritual intent, it became difficult for me, as the observer, to be satisfied by merely recording a song or textual explanation without noting how it came to be presented and by whom.

My interpretations of ritual varied not only as a result of participation but also on the basis of recordings and transcriptions of events. The character of my recording also ultimately relied on my own membership, through which I focused my observations. At the beginning, my understanding of the ceremonies or songs was colored by the uneven abilities of a translator who was not an Apostle, for in 1969 my familiarity with Tshiluba was so limited that I could not transcribe my own tapes and had difficulty finding members who would do so. The translator tran-

---

[15] Schutz (1964a:226–227) refers to the working world as the realm of daily life which stands as paramount to other forms of reality or realms of existence.

scribed only those items that he could easily render into English, omitting glossolalia and background conversations. His familiarity with the language did not include the shared assumptions of group membership. Later the importance that I placed on collective accounts from members made the use of this method of interpretation unsatisfactory. In spite of these problems, I readily made generalizations about Apostolic ritual and used a documentary method or pattern-finding approach for describing members' experiences.[16] My field notes from the 1969 period were very sketchy. I had met many members but had spoken with them only briefly. My insights into ritual were based mostly on my own brief impressions rather than on explanations by Apostles. In many places, I have taken the liberty of comparing, and on occasion combining, the 1969 and the 1971-1972 field descriptions.

My first task was to learn about the basic format of the events I wished to describe. The most obvious aspects included the opening hymns and prayer and the alteration of preaching and reading. I also had an impression of keti as a separate activity or order of reality and knew that some of those who left keti were sent to confession. But why? My attempt to gain a fuller knowledge through the initial tape transcriptions was only of partial value, since one needs more than a translation of the ceremony to understand its organization and the intent of members in performing it. Without information from the members, my overall analysis of the repeated parts of each ritual depended on the literal translation of standard hymns and ceremonial formulae.

My second task was to detail the techniques of preaching and singing. I examined the tapes to isolate forms of com-

[16] Garfinkel (1959:57–59) provides a more detailed statement of the documentary method of pattern-finding in commonsense and scientific inquiry.

munication that seemed to recur in sermons and songs. By treating ritual as a repeated set of activities, each of which anticipated a particular response or continuation of an exchange,[17] I was able to examine ritual greetings, congregational responses, collaborative preaching and reading, and the integration of topics across different ritual activities. This description still overlooked much of the content of each ceremony. As far as the content and orientation of preaching and song were concerned, I was able to focus on ritual texts as moral formulations oriented toward both members and spectators. I found that the same general features of text presentation occurred across a number of different congregations and regions.

On the second field trip, I played the tapes of ceremonies and songs to members immediately after the events to discuss their reactions. Rather than make lengthy comments on the recordings, they would sing along with them, make intermittent remarks on a preacher's style or a particular song, or give a final evaluation of the day's performances. It was not until late in my second visit that the responses to playback sessions were substantially different. When members asked to hear the field recordings from 1969, they commented at length on songs that had been popular at that time and sang along, adding new variations. Even more striking were reactions to recordings of Kasaian kereks by Apostles outside of the Kasai area. Members in Lubumbashi commented on and were critical of the songs chosen for kerek, the use of so-called political songs, the use of Tshiluba for songs generally sung in Chishona, and the overall styles of presentation.

The reply sessions helped me learn song texts, as well as methods of preaching, and they opened another perspec-

[17] Goffman (1971:199–200) defines ritual similarly but distinguishes it from a fuller ceremonial process. His interest is in the ritualized aspects of human behavior in general.

tive for the study of ceremony as a process. I saw that ceremony was interpreted by the members in terms of who participated and how well they did. As to procedure, although a number of side activities might take place, the whole scene often became organized with a few overriding themes. This work of managing the ceremony relied not on standard procedures for preaching but instead on the negotiation and close timing of parts of the service and on the members' awareness of its thematic unity. A transcript that does not include these side activities presents a very different picture of the overall ritual than one that does. An excerpt will illustrate this element of negotiation in the transition between discourse and reading. This service was recorded in 1971, in Kabanana, Zambia, where the negotiation of this transitional point was handled in several languages.

Biblical reading

Member 3:	*Sema* [Kiswahili: Talk]
	(Asks reader to begin)
Member 5:	(Sings softly)
Member 7:	*Aah, pa moya* . . . [Kiswahili: Oh, but first . . .]
Member 2:	*Akaliche mfalanga, akaliche mfalanga* [Chibemba: Leave the money aside]
Reader 2:	*Nous avons le dix-* [French: We have the -teenth]
	(Standing: attempts to initiate reading)
Member 7:	. . . *pa moya* [Kiswahili: . . . but first]
Member 2:	*Baba tendayi akaliche mfalanga.* [Chibemba: Father, let's go; leave the money aside]
	(Seated in the midst of the congregation)
	C'est fini. [French: It's finished] *Balayi yonso.* [Tshiluba: Everybody read]

In this sequence, there are several side conversations during an attempt to make the transition from preaching to reading. Antiphonal reading is not achieved, and no reader

begins until Member 2, who seems to coordinate these activities, signals for the main activity to continue.

In the replay sessions, members would comment on the
oratory of the participants. When Jérémie, a young, rather
well educated member from the Kasai had read from the
Bible in French without using the oratorical intonation of
Tshiluba, he had been interrupted and asked to sit down.
His delivery was considered poor and incomprehensible.
On replay, the participants discussed this part of the service and the question of what constituted good style. A re-
strained preaching style was to be accompanied by minimal movement on the preacher's part. It was explained that
calm and physical restraint were permissible for baptists,
whose job was to give counsel, but not for evangelists, who
were supposed to inspire the congregation. Such distinctions might not have been noticed without the review of
recorded data and the immediate followup of most ritual
events. During replays, members referred to the total scene
including their recollection of its physical aspects. Body
movement was referred to if it had somehow violated accepted practice. Men generally leaned on their staffs while
waiting for the prophetic examination in kerek, although
this was never mentioned as a requirement for passing
through the line. Comments were made, however, when
speakers had leaned on their staffs excessively during
preaching or had failed to use them in leading songs.

The visual material presented similar problems to those
of the tape recordings.[18] When individual photographs
were arranged into the approximate ritual sequences in
which they had been taken, members discussed the appearance, deportment, and activities of persons photographed,

[18] Cicourel (1973:41) stresses that the interpretation of both visual and
auditory materials relies on background knowledge and assumptions
that are not available in an examination of the visual or auditory data
alone.

as well as the order in which individual incidents occurred. Showing these photographs to other Apostles living outside of the areas where they were taken produced responses different from local reactions. Members from another area tended to be less interested in the photographs as personal souvenirs and more concerned with the activities represented. Some members of the Lusaka and Lubumbashi kereks were astounded at the large congregations in Luluabourg, asking whether the picture showing a regular weekly kerek was a church conference. They picked out persons they recognized in kerek and commented on the general appearance of the spectators present. Generally, viewers quickly named and recognized ritual scenes such as keti and confession on the basis of photographs alone.

Body posture and spatial ordering are critical aspects of ritual that were, of course, excluded from the transcribed data. As a result, the recorded materials provided only a partial resource for the study of ritual practice. By using the photographs in addition to the tapes as a starting point for my questions, elusive matters that were considered important to membership were brought to light.

I introduced an interview schedule early in the final research period at the request of Luluabourg members who felt that the presence of a sociologist should be validated by some sort of concrete activity that they could recognize as "research." The questions reflected some of my earlier interests in the church's organizational structure. These included its method of diffusion across several countries, the ordering of tasks within the church, the apparent consistency of social and spiritual organization, the repeated affirmations of cure, and religious experiences which included prophecy, firewalking, and other events that for me could have only extranatural interpretations. The schedule was administered in both oral and written form. Out of 800 schedules, 205 were returned across a geographic span of three Central African cities: Luluabourg, Lubumbashi, and Lusaka. The bulk of them were administered to Tshiluba-speaking members in all these cities and either were given as oral interviews in Tshiluba or were written in French. The oral interviews often included recitations of conversions and life histories that were largely absent in the briefer written answers. In many cases, these discussions led me to a greater personal understanding of ritual. Although questions that I considered important were often the least interesting to members, even these provided topics for discussion.

All the interviews, whether oral or written, were treated by members as a form of religious discourse. In their responses to questions on ritual performance and personal experiences in the church, members strove toward a doctrinal consistency that applied to everyday life.[19] While I had expected the answers to express spiritual interpretations of events, the extent to which this occurred surprised me. Some persons even cited biblical passages to make their names, ages, and occupations appear religiously consistent.[20] In the Zaire, where the government had decreed that traditional "names of authenticity" rather than European names be employed, members would list both sets of names with an explanatory note concerning the biblical ones. A few Apostles answered both written and oral schedules or filled out the written form more than once, to assure that the information was covered "correctly" and with appro-

[19] Bittner (1963:937-938) treats this special consistency as a way of creating unity between ideology and action that is sought after and preserved by members. He asserts that all parts of a member's life must be defined as lying within the purview of an ideology.

[20] Garfinkel (1967:187) deals with the organizational background for the answering and interpreting of schedules in his study of outpatient screening. He remarks on the incompleteness of even factual information, including face-sheet questions on marital status and place of residence.

priate biblical citations. At the pastor's request, several of the schedules were checked by the church's secretary for intelligibility, literacy, and doctrinal completeness. Some members viewed the written form as an examination about the church's doctrine and wanted to know how well they had performed.

Collaboration by several Apostles during the interviews led to discussions of doctrinal and organizational matters. In one case, a small group of evangelists collaborated on their answers in a single room, while other members stood outside waiting to be interviewed. (When a healer who had not been included in the meeting answered one question differently, he was lightly ridiculed by the evangelists present. Ridicule is often used by Apostles as a means of social control.[21]) The clustering of members holding the same spiritual gift occurred in both the written and the verbal interview settings. The gathering together of those who were friends and work associates to distribute the schedules and participate in interviews gave me specific information on groupings among members over and above the questions that the schedule contained.

The linguistic issue raised some problems of translation and general comprehension, since the French and Tshiluba terms for aspects of Apostolic life did not always correspond. These difficulties were compounded when Kiswahili was introduced to supplement French questions outside of the predominantly Tshiluba-speaking area. Some of these questions were related to conceptions of church organization. For example, 'questions in which I used the words "gift" and "grade" interchangeably to describe spiritual positions, such as those of the evangelist

[21] Murphree (1969:108–109) cites ridicule as a recurrent Apostolic sanction used to bring about compliance with ritual expectations. To what extent ridicule is a Central Bantu social form rather than merely an Apostolic one is not discussed.

and prophet, were based on my implicit notion of a hierarchical structure in which some gifts were ranked higher than others. I had difficulties in translation until I understood that a "gift" such as prophecy or healing could not be interpreted as a "grade" or hierarchical rank but merely as a spiritual and organizational task. Whether or not problems of establishing an effective lingua franca were resolved, members invariably asked to substitute, add, or amend questions. None of the schedules was completed without extensive discussion. In the case of the more ambiguous questions, even verbal clarification would not have eliminated the gaps in knowledge that made it difficult for members to understand my reasons for asking them.

To supplement interviews, I used documentary data from secondary ethnographic sources and directly from the Apostles' own archives in Luluabourg and Lubumbashi.[22] Apostles' letters, personal histories, and official documents gave me new understanding of the growth and social organization of the church. The historical perspective provided a way of documenting the growth and change in individual ritual events as part of the entire group's development. The members' own conception of their history, along with their oral and written accounts of it, made immediate field situations more vivid and meaningful.[23] As a researcher, I could not possibly remain "neutral" in the face of the life histories and involvements of members.

Historical accounts also illustrated the ways in which members transferred aspects of ritual to everyday interaction, including expectations about the organization of

[22] The published and unpublished materials relating to the Apostolic church of John Maranke include: Aquina 1966, 1967; Barrett 1968; Daneel 1971; Heimer 1971a, 1971b; Lanzas and Bernard 1966; Murphree 1969.

[23] Vansina (1970:165) stresses the need for a historical theory and ethnography to remove some of the distortions of static theorizing and descriptions.

events and about the persons who were key figures in both ritual and community activities. A related area that I have approached largely through descriptive techniques is a special scrutiny and discipline that Apostles applied to everyday activities. This involved a suspension of what I perceived as ordinary expectations of logic and appropriateness in favor of spiritual and theological interpretations of events. The importance of spiritual investigation of all aspects of a member's life also pointed to the integral relationship between Apostolic ritual and its social background in a number of African societies.

All strategies of field research have been oriented toward making personal participation and membership topics of analysis rather than simply background material or fortuitous events. The participants' methods of defining ritual and other social settings have thus provided the main data informing the theory and methods of research.

CHAPTER 2

Opening the Narrow Gate

Truly, truly I say to you, we speak of what we know and bear witness to what we have seen; but you do not receive our testimony. If I told you earthly things and you did not believe, how can you believe if I tell you heavenly things?

John 3:11–12

As the Voice spoke on, the light which I had seen on the way kept shining into the house. The Voice went on to say that whoever will have sinned and would like to come back, he should come before the church and confess his sins. In this respect, a person would be saved on his death. The great judgment of the Lord is upon those who do not want to repent and confess their sins.

John Maranke

On September 21, 1971, I crossed the Malawian border and witnessed my first paschal ceremony. Through participating in these events, I was drawn into membership and began to conceive of my daily activities in terms of new religious experiences.[1] Gradually, my awareness of the importance of my own presence to the events that I was witnessing assumed a more central place in my thinking. The way in which I became a member and learned about the specific features of membership emerged as a topic of research.

For the four months that I observed Apostolic rituals as an outsider, I did not participate in the prophetic examinations and always sat in a special spot on the center of the women's side. My everyday clothes and jewelry distinguished me from the white-robed members, and constant note-taking distracted me from possible participation.

---

[1] A more analytic account of this experience, treating the implications of conversion for a sociological methodology, will appear in Johannes Fabian and Frances Harwood, eds., *The Impact of Religious Movements on Social Thought*, forthcoming.

While I did not initially ask members to answer their own questions and interpret the world for me, their inquiries baffled me.[2] It seemed impossible that I would ever understand the reasoning behind their questions or the assumptions that they were making about me.

The ceremonies that I had been unable to witness remained mysterious. I thought that they might contain the key to understanding Apostolic worship. Since my knowledge of night worship at musankano and masowe was based on brief descriptions from others, I was frustrated at not being able to see, question, and interpret the events. Early in my research, I perceived all Apostolic statements and ceremonies as maintaining boundaries between a member's way of seeing and alien perspectives. These boundaries were actually produced and reinforced by my own status as an outsider in the Apostolic community.

Leaving Luluabourg in the fall of 1971 marked a critical break with the more formal attitudes toward research and the Apostles that had been established by my 1969 visit. Shortly before departing for Malawi, I became very ill, vomiting for two days. None of my patent medicines seemed to help. When the evangelist Tshiaba saw my condition, he volunteered to pray for me. This was the first private healing ceremony that I had ever witnessed, and I had been unaware that an evangelist was empowered to perform it. Dressed in a blue robe, Tshiaba placed the Bible over a tin cup of water. He prayed slowly and quietly, then

[2] In his apprenticeship to a Yaqui shaman, Castaneda (1968:155) reached a point at which he felt that he could no longer interpret the world without his teacher's help. This need for interpretation was a point of departure for new descriptions of the religious world and presupposed a sense of the strong personal relevance of the shaman's descriptions for Castaneda. The request for and fuller reliance on members' interpretations occurred only relatively late in my study.

handed me the cup. I became nauseous and was unable to keep even the water on my stomach, but my entire body felt cleansed. A few hours later, I was able to drink tea with some other members, while they sang and prayed. This was my first experience of purposive sharing in the reality of ceremony.

Although this ceremony, despite its ambiguity, had prepared me for the possibility of other miraculous events, I was overwhelmed when I finally witnessed a night service at the Malawian Passover. The prolonged journey to the Passover assumed the form of a pilgrimage and had already begun to reshape my conceptions of the church. What had previously appeared to be arbitrary doctrine began to emerge as part of a coherent order of reality. In exchange for the assurance that I would be baptized on the following day, I was allowed to see a night ceremony. The ceremony followed the Sabbath format of prayer, singing, and preaching, with the dramatic added feature of firewalking. Smoldering coals, remaining from a blazing fire, were located at the center of the path where preaching took place. As they preached, evangelists walked through the fire, sat and rolled in it, or placed hot coals in their mouths. Women also walked through the fire as a demonstration of their spiritual purity. The fervor of the firewalkers, combined with the previous experience of healing and cleansing, reinforced my curiosity about the spiritual world of the Apostles and opened the possibilities of faith, or in terms of my status as a sociological observer, membership.

For the rest of that night, I was on the threshold of a decision and a new way of life, neither contented with my own situation nor fully ready to become an Apostle. Immediately following my baptism the next afternoon, however, the character of my instruction within the church seemed to change. I was taught for longer periods of time and began to listen to discourses and quoted passages not as abstract forms of logic but as lessons that applied directly to me. As a new order of reality opened to me, I began to seek instruction as a member rather than simply as an observer of events.[3] I discovered that members engaged in a continual process of learning whereby instructions—descriptions of how to execute a ritual performance—pointed to the organization of social scenes and ceremonies and also taught members how to construct and find their way in everyday settings. The Apostles particularly valued instruction from the church's Rhodesian source, through pilgrimages and direct contact with original members.

Shortly after the baptism, I began to notice that instructions about participation did not always coincide with what actually happened in worship. For example, the exhortation that a member should repeat the words "Amen, Amen" in order to receive a prophetic vision did not assure its presence or point to the appropriate time for attesting to it within the ceremony. While commentary on when and how to speak in specific settings was most directly helpful to me as a member, it remained opaque without basic descriptions of a ritual's intent. The explanations of specific forms of behavior for a particular occasion intensified after I joined the group, although they continued to seem arbitrary. I was told how to dress, where and how to sit, when to wash, and how to eat. No aspect of my life was outside of the scrutiny of male or female elders. No action went

[3] Schutz (1964a:36–38) speaks of the attitude of the social scientist as being that of a "mere disinterested observer of the social world," resulting from the different in purpose involved in theorizing about activities and being engaged in them. Even if involved in an activity, without a special purpose that guides ways of attending to it, the observer may be unable to see how an event is performed or interpreted by an everyday actor.

without comment, ridicule, or, occasionally, a smile of approval at some minimal mastery. Many of the notes, I took early in my membership re-emphasized what I then felt to be constant criticism but what I now see in retrospect as terse but well-meant instruction. Part of the dramatic impact of the conversion experience emerged through examining and constructing it in retrospect.

Exposure to scrutiny made me more sensitive to the progress of other members who were also learning the Apostolic way. I found that I was in no sense unique. Many parallels existed between my activities as a learner-observer and those of other members approaching the new intricacies of church doctrine and religious experience. For each new member, the conversion experience restructures basic expectations about and representations of, a previously known reality (Pearce 1971:13–14). Apostles explain the conversion experience as based on acceptance or a change of heart. The verbs *to accept* and *to believe* are both translated in Tshiluba as *kuitaba;* members often refer to themselves as *Bena Kuitabusha*—those who have accepted. Accepting Christ is interwoven with the confession of sins. Once he repents or accepts, the candidate is ready for baptism and enters a new spiritual world. This new viewpoint attempts to exclude other logical interpretations of a set of events, although the convert may be fully aware of other possibilities. Acceptance is neither permanent nor ensured by baptism, an outward symbol of conversion, for it must be constantly reinforced by fresh evaluations of emerging situations.

William James discusses certain aspects of acceptance in his description of conversion:

Some of you, I feel sure, knowing that numerous backslidings and relapses take place, make of these the apperceiving mass for the whole subject [i.e., religious conversions] and dismiss it with a pitying smile as so much "hysterics." Psychologically as well as religiously, however, this is shallow. It misses the point of interest which is not so much the duration as the nature and quality of shifts to a higher level.   [1958:205]

James further defines the conversion experience as a conscious change that may "show a human being what the high water mark of his spiritual capacity is" (1958:205). Often the experience cannot be expressed in logical and coherent terms.[4] Apostles explain this problem as part of losing one's former life in search of a more fulfilled existence. Conversion then is a reality-shaping process in which the member sheds old preconceptions in favor of new themes for, and ways of perceiving and structuring, events.[5] Acceptance may also be seen as a new way in which people think about their lives and provide existence with unifying themes. The themes of acceptance and those that the researcher extracts without the background of conversion stand in direct contrast to each other. Both sets of themes constitute closed systems with results that appeared to me to be mutually exclusive.

In my case, the initial shift from one set of interpretations to another was dramatic, resulting in a moment of

[4] In describing the enlightenment or satori experience in Zen Buddhism, Suzuki (1953:103) points out that persons who have experienced it have difficulty in expressing what they have experienced in logical and coherent terms to others. He suggests that clear characterizations of such an experience miss its depth. The conversion experience in the Apostolic church can be regarded in a similar way.

[5] Pearce (1971:13) writes: "Metanoia [conversion] restructures, to varying degrees and even for varying lengths of time, those basic representations of reality inherited from the past. On those representations we base our notions or concepts of what is real. In turn, our notions of what is real direct our perceptual apparatus, that network of senses that tells us what we feel, hear, see, and so on. This is not a simple subjective maneuver but a reality-shaping procedure."

shock in which even the physical terms of existence seemed to alter.[6] Apostles handle these changes symbolically in the baptismal ceremony. Each ceremony also seems to intensify a spiritual order of reality, making a definite transition from the concerns of everyday life to those of a life beyond. Activities in a spiritual world require a new and special alertness, although, perhaps, a very different awareness from that of everyday life. As a candidate on the threshold of membership, I was discovering a potential point of access to that awareness. This does not mean that every ceremony entailed a specific shock that completely altered my attention to the world. Instead, once the specific intent of certain rituals became known to me, the possibility of attaining multiple forms of awareness and flowing easily from one to another emerged.

Acceptance is also built upon restrictions of the sort that I experienced in the intensive monitoring of my behavior after baptism. These restrictions reinforced the rejection of worldly concerns that Apostles term tshijila (holiness or purity); by this they subject themselves and others to rigorous spiritual discipline and scrutiny. A holy man *(muntu wa tshijila)* fasts frequently, observes sexual abstinence at specific times, and withdraws for prayer to a wilderness retreat. Certain aspects of ceremony are associated with holiness as an order of reality and a way of life. The "Kwese, Kwese," for example, is viewed as a holy song *(musambo wa tshijila)* with respect to both the vision of angels that it inspires and the religious obligations that it

---

[6] Schutz (1964a:231) argues that mundane existence is the paramount reality against which all other experiences in the world must be seen. Passage from one form of existence to another is described as involving a "specific shock" whereby the boundaries of one realm of experience become apparent. In some cases, this model of shifts in experience may be applicable to our discussion, but an awareness of shifts and a point of change are presupposed.

places on members by distinguishing them from the people and affairs of the mundane world.

These spiritual reinterpretations of reality include changes in conceptions of time, space, and social relationships. Ceremonial time becomes the time that it takes to experience a performance, including absorption in chants through which Apostles assert that they obtain a glimpse of Heaven, bypassing the standard time and reality orientations of mundane interaction. The place of prayer, similarly, comes to be seen as a new Jerusalem, a protected Heaven on earth endowed with this timeless quality. Social relationships are transformed in this spirit world in which unity of purpose attunes members to a new order of existence. Practical activities are then regarded as indicators of the spiritual, and interactions seen in the light of their ritual intent. While an outsider treats speaking in tongues as merely a chimerical reaction, members are aware of how it is inspired and approach it as a form of spiritual witnessing.

Those who have accepted refer to themselves as witnesses of the Holy Spirit and the voice of God. The manifestations of acceptance usually occur in prophetic visions or inspired acts of singing and curing. Every member is expected to have such visionary experiences, and to my knowledge, most reported that they did. These experiences were similar to the complex dreams recorded in John Maranke's own revelations. Members also gave numerous accounts of extraordinary experiences connected with baptism. Prebaptismal visions of light and of renewed bodies and spirits were presented by members as "omens" and part of their reason for joining. The following accounts of baptismal callings were given by John Maranke and by Apostles interviewed in the Zaire:

At midnight, I was bound by a vertigo. I saw a tall man who wore white linen and a garment. His clothes were snow white. This man commanded me to follow him. He led to the east, where there were two doors on a temple. The one door was to the south and the other to the west. There was also a window on the western side, and through it I saw a pool of water outside. There were beautiful flowers surrounding the pool. I replied that I had seen it, and the man went on to tell me that the name of the pool was Jordan, the name of the pool in which people are baptized.

He told me that he was the priest of the Jordan and that at the end of June, he was coming to baptize me. He also said that I was going to receive the Holy Ghost. A big congregation was I going to make and would call it the Apostle Church. On that day, I was going to be baptized and given a new name.   [Maranke, 1953, describing experience in 1932]

Before baptism John experienced many visions through which he claimed to recognize and demonstrate to others his status as a chosen messenger of God. During this period, he performed extraordinary feats, preached, and prayed for prolonged periods of time. James (1958:186) suggests that such visions and feats might be regarded as one aspect of the "subconscious incubation and maturation of motives" by which a potential convert gradually prepares for a major conceptual and emotional change. The change in motive or intent is also marked by a change in sense of self or identity symbolized in the receiving of a new name of the day of baptism. This name not only emphasizes the member's new spiritual obligations, it also establishes his position in a community of believers. Apostles with the same biblical name have a bond of kinship analogous to the tie existing between the namesake (Tshiluba: *shakena*) and his partner in traditional Lulua practice.[7]

[7] The Tshiluba term means "namesake." A friend or relative of the parent may choose to name the child after him. The relationship of the shakena to the child is much like that of the godparent to the godchild in American society. The term may also be used among any persons who have the same name, who view themselves as brothers or sisters having a special bond. Among Apostles, this relationship creates a special personal and spiritual bond.

One night, I had a vision. I saw Apostles moving up and down the clouds like Jacob's ladder. A voice asked me, 'Do you know how long it takes an elephant to bear its young?' I said 'No.' The voice asked again for the antelope and for other animals, if I knew how long it took to bear their children. I said 'No.' The voice told me to believe in Jesus and become an Apostle, because I did not know about the things of the world. [A prophet, Lubumba-shi, 1972]

This account reconstructs a vision that led a member to baptism. In order to interpret the vision as a valid set of instructions, the member acknowledges its divine charac-ter and consults a prophet as an intermediary and transla-tor of the experience. Relating a visionary or ecstatic ex-perience is as important as the experience itself. Members also regard a course of action ultimately pursued as sensible in retrospect by virtue of the initial visionary instructions. Single events emerge as signs, pointing to an inevitable spiritual outcome.

I remained outside of the church for seven years, while my hus-band was baptized. I already knew all of the rules of the church and could prepare all the foods properly. I kept my children away from medicines, as my husband instructed. Then we went to a village to visit my husband's family. It was always difficult for me to stay at this village because the relatives pestered me about becoming an Apostle. My own parents were opposed to this idea.
While we were in the village, my husband became very ill with a stomach disease. The prophet said that he could be cured only if I were baptized. I agreed that the Apostles could baptize my body but they would not have my soul. When I approached the water and reluctantly entered it, a snake appeared out of no-where. The baptist hit the snake and broke it in two pieces with his staff. I then said, go ahead. Baptize both my soul and my body. I was finally baptized.   [A female healer, Lubumbashi, 1972]

This spiritual account of baptism reflects the personal conflict that preceded it. Prior to her conversion, Esthere had outwardly conformed to an Apostolic life without spiritual acceptance. This period was also one of "subconscious incubation," during which she learned Apostolic forms of interpretation through example and participation. Even though what could be interpreted as a sign, the illness, appeared at the time of baptism, Esthere did not accept it as a reason for her personal change. Only the snake, emerging as an immediate personal danger and taken to be a sign of her own dual nature, convinced the woman to accept a spiritual order of reality as meaningful for her.[8]

Each of these accounts points to a shift from one form of communication to another. The shifts are of two kinds: those that are sudden and visionary and those resulting from a background of instruction and indoctrination. Once the transition has been made from one order of reality to another, concepts that were illusory appear as integrated into the fabric of the new reality.

Apostles consider their spiritual experiences authoritative and irreversible, facts that cannot be refuted by argument or rhetoric.[9] These experiences are part of the refocusing of a member's view of his life's progression. Straightforward questions about miracles or unusual experiences out of the context of this personal reshaping yielded little commentary from members. Even before my own baptism, I had already begun to interview members about their conversion experiences. I had expected dramatic answers, but I actually received terse responses, subtly embedded in Apostolic doctrine and belief and in

[8] The use of fear to induce a shift in perception from the personal application of one order of reality to direct experience is not uncommon. Castaneda (1971:41) emphasizes this technique as a part of his apprenticeship. Castaneda was frightened by the threat of another sorcerer to use his spiritual skills in self-defense.

[9] Suzuki (1953:104) also stresses this final and irrefutable character of new insights as a feature of the Zen satori or enlightenment experience. This term seems applicable to Apostolic conversion as well.

personal history. On occasion, my direct questions about visionary experiences even met with suspicion and distrust, for some members assumed that I had little background to understand what they said and would misuse it.

The following interview responses will illustrate some individual reactions to inquiries about conversion.

Q: Who gave you the news about this church?
R: The Holy Spirit itself showed me the Apostles praying in my house twice. Acts 9:3–6.
Q: Was this person an Apostle?
R: No, it was the Spirit of God.
Q: Why did you question him about the church?
R: No, I accepted abruptly because it is the Spirit of God.
Q: How did you feel at this time?
R: Because when the Spirit of God descended on me and chased the demons, I felt good. The sickness was over.
Q: When did this happen?
R: In 1971, when I was baptized.
Q: Why did you become a member of this church?
R: By the will of God. Jeremiah 31:3. [The passage reads: "The Lord appeared to him from afar. I have loved you with an everlasting love; therefore I have continued new faithfulness to you."]   [An evangelist, Lusaka, 1972]

This Apostle's answers actually provided spiritual instructions about his conversion. Although he recognized the influence of individual Apostles on his conversion, explaining that they had exhorted him to stop frequenting bars and brothels, he stoutly asserted that it was the Spirit of God and not another member who had caused his conversion. After the interview, he described himself as a former lover of dance music and alcohol, who had been both curious about and insolent toward these Apostles. In the description of his abrupt conversion, however, he mentioned only that the Spirit of God chased the demons and healed him.

Q: Who gave you the news about the church?
R: John Maranke.
Q: Was this person an Apostle?
R: Yes.
Q: Why did you ask him about the church?
R: To know where this same church came from.
Q: How did you feel at this time?
R: At that time we felt feelings of the Holy Spirit.
Q: When did this happen?
R: That happened in 1953.
Q: Why did you become a member of this church?
R: To be unified with the church. [An evangelist, Lubumbashi, 1972]

Q: Who gave you the news about this church?
R: I gave it to you so you can adore God and your Savior Jesus.
Q: Was this person an Apostle?
R: Yes, he was an Apostle.
Q: Why did you ask him about the church?
R: Because he spoke to me about enjoying God.
Q: How did you feel at this time?
R: I had joy to see.
Q: When did this happen?
R: In 1957.
Q: Why did you become a member of this church?
R: To accept, God gave me that. [A prophet, Lubumbashi, 1972]

Both men gave spiritual interpretations of the conversion experience. In the first interview, it is feasible, but not likely, that John Maranke spoke to the member in person. The answer to the first question made the following questions seem absurd unless interpreted spiritually, admitting a reality other than that anticipated by the questions themselves. Obviously, Maranke was an Apostle and the church came from Rhodesia. But the member was concerned with its spiritual justification. In the next set of questions, the member turned the question into a request for assistance, answering that he introduced me, the interviewer, to the baptism to adore Jesus. Within the doctrinal terminology, he also replied that he joined the church "to accept."

Women gave substantially different answers to conversion questions than men. They were more concerned with questions of faith healing, the alleviation of female disorders, and the mysticism of eternal life.

Q: Who gave you the news about this church?
R: They told me that if you enter this church, you will die like everyone but it is to search for the hidden life in Christ.
Q: Was this person an Apostle?
R: They were all Apostles.
Q: Why did you ask them about the church?
R: I asked them because I was pregnant, and they told me to pray God always.
Q: How did you feel at this time?
R: I saw that their words were true, because I had six births without remedies.
Q: When did this happen?
R: This came by prayer after the faithfulness of the Holy Spirit.
Q: Why did you become a member of this church?
R: I became a member of this church to know the commandments of God, then to wait for the hidden life in Christ.   [A healer, Kananga, 1972]

The answers had two main themes: a spiritual search and physical cures through faith, without recourse to medicines. The cures convinced the candidate to continue her spiritual search. Like the others interviewed, this member was less concerned with revealing who introduced her to the church at a specific time than she was with interpreting her conversion in terms of present spiritual progress. These answers also presumed knowledge about esoteric and doctrinal matters on my part, which I have used freely in interpreting the responses.

Q: Who gave you the news about this church?

R: The first person that I saw was a mama. It was Mama Ngalula Ruth. Ngalula Ruth.

Q: What did she say?

R: She informed me about the church, that it was a good church. And first, since we have lots of cares, sickness, and frequent the hospital she said to us, that if you enter our church, all that you spend of silver and go take medicines, that has no importance, and you will see for yourself how God helps us.

Q: Was this person an Apostle?

R: She is an Apostle up to the present.

Q: When did this happen?

R: 'Seventy.

Q: How did you feel at this time?

R: At that time, my desire was to enter this church. If one dies in this church, I shall die too; if one stays alive, I shall stay alive.   [A healer, Kananga, 1972]

These responses resembled many others. Even when members did answer with respect to specific precipitating events, dates, and persons, their relevance was often difficult to determine. Did the dates refer to an actual baptism, a spiritual visitation, or a church confirmation? Interpreting these conversion experiences relied on far more information than the questions themselves indicated, including some familiarity with the doctrine, spiritual purpose, and lives of the persons involved.

Conversion and new ways of perceiving the world are not possible, I learned, without suspending previous assumptions about what is normal and logical.[10] Suspension

10 This process of suspension can be discussed in terms of a phenomenological epoché or active suspension of one order of reality in favor of another. In discussing the attitude of the scientist or theorist, Husserl (1970:135) describes this suspension as a "withholding of the natural, naive validities and general validities already in effect" for everyday life.

of assumptions does not always imply new beliefs. A new understanding emerges only gradually from previous interpretations. Not only were conversion and baptism new experiences, they were events that had never been deeply meaningful to me. I had no way of giving these incidents any lasting symbolic or personal importance. Before baptism, a dream was simply that, perhaps frightening or pleasurable but certainly not a prophetic sign or warning. After conversion, every dream and imagining became a potential message integrated into a new order of reality. Both present and past dreams influenced daily experiences as focal parts of a spiritual world. Church prophets encouraged me to recast past events in terms of images predicting them. Once the baptism took place, the conflict between opposing forms of interpretation did not stop, and in certain cases it deepened as my knowledge of spiritual explanations evolved against the background of new situations or old forms of reasoning.

When asked what their baptism involved, a member of a South African Zionist church merely replied: "We baptize people by dipping them thrice in the water and let them confess their sins; after that we give them white uniforms and teach them the word of God and let them understand. Amen" (Sundkler 1961:208).

In many ways, my own baptism in the Apostolic church was a perfunctory and simple event. As a child, I had joined the Baptist church and had been immersed in a small pool under the altar. The physical experience of baptism was not alien to me, but the possibility of undergoing a new spiritual experience was frightening. Friends in America had warned that I would never learn anything about the Apostolic church without becoming a member of it: the larger question was whether membership would simply serve as a tool for me as a researcher, or whether I would reach a point of abandon where the experience for its own sake would become more important than reflection on it.

My growing interest in the church's teachings made membership increasingly attractive. Sincerity was not an issue, for I would never have considered joining without belief. I simply had no idea what belief was. Most convincing in my decision to join was the absolute certainty of the Apostles whom I encountered that I would ultimately join them, that I had, in fact, been sent on a spiritual mission for that purpose. One member informed me, after the fact, that my baptism had been predicted as early as 1942 by John himself, as part of a larger prophecy about the church's expansion to Europe and America.

Like Esthere, I had learned and consciously reflected on the Apostolic way of life by living among members. I was already learning Apostolic songs, following dietary laws, and associating largely with members of the Apostolic community in each town that I visited. But before the Malawi trip the obligations of membership were not binding upon me, and I could shift out of the frame of reference of the Apostolic community without confession, guilt, or direct spiritual scrutiny.

Apostles stress that while a member may seek some approval from other members, it is essential to remain withdrawn from the outside world and abandon the necessity for its consensus. Leaving Luluabourg in September 1971 had meant the possibility of abandoning such consensus without full and immediate knowledge of the new forms of validation that would take its place. Peter and I were to travel with the evangelist Tshiaba, who, now reunited with Tshiambi's kerek, would also represent the church's West Kasai wing. The leaders' underlying assumption was that the three of us would cross-check each other and collectively present a reliable version of Rhodesia's judgment on the Congolese church. Tshiaba had left the Kasai several days prior to our departure and was to meet us in Lubumbashi.

The downtown area of Lubumbashi, though small, was

quite built up with shops and resembled a European town. I wondered where Apostles would be likely to live in such a place. On the following day, while we were applying for visas at the Zambian consulate, Tshiaba suddenly appeared, and we began to make joint plans for the journey to Malawi. We left the consulate with Tshiaba and quickly removed our luggage from the European hotel where we had spent the night. This marked my final stay in a European section of town for a long time to come and the beginning of a new and stronger bond with the Apostles.

The taxi took us about four miles from Lubumbashi to a suburban commune called Katuba. Except for the tremendous numbers of people, this commune seemed more "rural" than "urban." The dirt streets, lined with open sewers, were a flocking ground for geese, mangy goats, and stray dogs and provided a sharp contrast with the more sedate European section. A new and rapidly growing community, created in 1957 as a suburb for urban African workers (Minon 1960:2ff), Katuba is the seat of the Apostolic church in Lubumbashi, the location of several Bapostolo congregations, and the base for two paschal centers.

We went to a small house with boarded windows. Inside sat a man wearing dark glasses who seemed to be nearly blind. Although he appeared elderly, he moved with agility to greet the three of us and motioned us to sit around his table. He was Nawezi Petro, the church's first Congolese member. Tshiaba translated his Kiswahili into French, insisting on referring to him throughout as "the old Nawezi" and "the papa." After greeting us as his children, Nawezi went to one of the backrooms and pulled out an old newspaper article dated August 1970, stating that officials had put a stop to a meeting of six hundred Apostles in the bush and were holding two church representatives responsible. Nawezi proudly pointed to his name, declaring that he had been unjustly arrested for church matters sixteen times, under both the colonial and later governments.

Tshiaba nodded his head, acknowledging that Nawezi had indeed suffered, and they then dismissed me to arrange my room and baggage. Nawezi and his wife made us feel very much at home, and I adjusted to the house immediately. This was fortunate, for I was eventually to spend nearly three months living there, receiving much of my Apostolic instruction behind closed shutters at Nawezi's table.

On the following day, I left with Peter and Tshiaba for Kitwe, Zambia. Nawezi had given us a letter to Abel Sithole, John's son, requesting the Passover in the Zaire along with political assistance in unifying the Lubumbashi congregations. The short journey to the Zambian border was direct, but once we crossed the border, transportation became more difficult. It took several hours to reach Kitwe by a combination of taxis, from which we were expelled at odd points, small buses, and trucks. Once there, the journey to Lusaka, where we were to meet other Apostles, still remained. For over seven hours, we remained at a dusty stop in Kitwe. Many of those waiting were old and seemed quite ill; their incessant coughing made the wait seem interminable. Tshiaba introduced me to a man whom he claimed was a Kitwe Apostle, despite the fact that he was clean shaven and had teeth that were neatly filed into sharp points. After conversing with the Apostle, Tshiaba talked to me constantly of the church history, old Nawezi, and the beauty of the Passover. It was hard to listen, and taking notes, as constructive as that might have been, was out of the question.

The next morning we arrived in Lusaka. Tshiaba took us to a community several miles out of town, Marrapodi suburb, where most of the Zairian Apostles live. French and Tshiluba were spoken, and the life of the Kasai seemed to be extended to Zambia. We went to a modest house much like Nawezi's where we met another church elder, Kadima Alphonse. Tshiaba explained that Kadima and

Nawezi had worked together in the early days of the church and that Kadima had also just arrived from Lubumbashi to join us on the journey to the Passover. I thought it strange not to met Kadima in Lubumbashi, until I later discovered that he had broken with Nawezi and established his own congregation. It was the Sabbath eve, and the day passed quickly in discussion. Kadima showed us British magazines containing photographs of the Apostles, and Tshiaba explained the healing and guiding powers of the angels who, he said, were mentioned by name in the Bible. Tshiaba remarked that Kadima was an important elder, whose memory of past events and of the Bible was impeccable.

The next day I witnessed my first Zambian Sabbath service and, in fact, the first full kerek since leaving Luluabourg. I was surprised that Tshiaba was so well known to the Zambian congregation. He was able to introduce Kasaian songs into the service smoothly, with good response, although some of the local members did not understand Tshiluba. At the close of the service, those going to Malawi were selected and formally announced. The head evangelist, Luka Chisanga, who was going, chose the evangelist Mrogodo and his wife, from Ndola, and Jaya Festus, a Zambian evangelist, to accompany the Zairian group. At the last moment, the evangelist Kabangu Luka, representing yet another Lubumbashi congregation, added himself to the crew.

On Sunday afternoon, we packed into the back of Mr. Mrogodo's truck, which had a canvas canopy resembling a covered wagon with small slits on the side, making it possible to view the road. Because of passport and currency difficulties, the Zairians feared that they would not be able to cross the border. They began to see the crossing as a spiritual test, a keti within everyday life, and Kadima asserted that he would cross regardless of what happened. He recalled the colonial days, when everyone was able to cross the border without papers, and was sure that something similar would happen this time. The others laughed.

When we reached the border, the Zairians were indeed told to return to Zambia, for their papers were not in order. As Americans, Peter and I were well received, and the Zambians were allowed to cross on British passports. The Zairian group bade us farewell, and Tshiaba reminded us to deliver Nawezi's and Tshiambi's messages to Abel Sithole. He stressed that we were the only first-hand witnesses to represent the Zairian branches of the church. I continued on to Malawi, feeling that I had been strangely chosen for a special mission that I was not particularly suited to fulfill.

As we drove to Blantyre, the capital of Malawi, the Apostles sang heartily for hours. Singing was not only a way of passing the time, it invoked and sustained a spiritual order of reality that the members shared. The forcefulness of their singing reminded me of my status as an outsider and made me realize that I would inevitably have to face the question of baptism. Tshiaba had already told me to remove all jewelry except my watch, but I had not liked his presumption of my baptism and had stubbornly refused. By the evening of our third consecutive day of travel, we reached Blantyre and found the paschal site with the help of the local police, who seemed quite friendly toward the Apostles. It was well past nine o'clock, and we were exhausted from travel. The Malawian Apostles, both men and women, swarmed around the truck and greeted the Zambians warmly, giving them the kiss of membership. While some of the women approached and hugged me too, the men pushed them away, warning that we were pagans. At first, it was decided that neither Peter nor I would be allowed to leave the truck until the following morning, when not Abel but his younger brother Makebi would arrive to administer the Passover.

It was extremely cold, and the prospect of staying on the

truck one more night was grim. During a brief palaver (informal meeting), the Zambians explained that we had come to represent the Congolese congregations whose leaders were not able to cross the border. Thereafter, we were always introduced as "Congolese" or "from the Congo." On condition that we would either be baptized or leave in the morning, we were allowed to stay in the paschal encampment overnight, I on the women's side and Peter on the men's. As we parted, a Malawian evangelist informed me that he expected to see us clothed as members, ready to receive the Passover, if we were still in the encampment at noon. Mr. Mrogodo stated that if we were baptized, there would be "one Zambia, one nation," paraphrasing Zambia's political slogan. If not, we would apparently have to find our own transportation back to the border. The choice was difficult, but the decision had become obvious—baptism.

Walking barefoot over the cold ground, I found the shelter assigned me. I was to stay with two women, Mama Ida Mrogodo, the wife of the evangelist traveling with us, and Mama Esthere, a Rhodesian prophetess who lived in Blantyre. I unrolled my belongings, wrapped a blanket around myself, and crouched in the corner of the hut. Outside, the women sang and laughed and seemed to be imitating the preaching styles of the men. Mama Ida and the prophetess put on white robes and immediately prepared to leave for the kerek beginning in the center of the encampment. I remained huddled in the corner, expecting to be treated like an outcast who would not be allowed to worship with the members or witness their mysterious night rites, but they looked back and told me to join them.

The ground was cold, hard, and full of brambles, which the other women did not seem to notice. We sat in the last row of the women's side, away from the fire. The Apostles' white robes glistened. An evangelist preached and members sang fervently. The chanting became more intense as the evangelist began walking through the campfire and others joined him. They walked through several times, with no visible harm to themselves or their robes, handled the coals, and even ate them. All the while, Mama Ida Mrogodo was shouting, "Amen! Amen!" She seemed to be in a state of trance. From an almost silent traveling companion, she had become a vocal medium. Once the closing hymn was sung, the two women guided me back to the hut to sleep and returned to the all-night singing. I regretted going back to the hut, for I had hoped that the key to Apostolic ritual would be revealed to me that very night. I felt that I had once more been excluded from something secret but was too tired to worry about it.

Early the following morning, I was told that my husband had consented to baptism, and I was asked for my decision. I also agreed but was uncertain about the implications of the baptism. When Peter passed me in the encampment, he said he "felt like a fish in a snare with no choices to make." The baptism was scheduled for two o'clock, since Makebi was to arrive later in the afternoon. At noon, Mr. Mrogodo came to the women's side of the encampment, consisting of a rough semicircle of huts in the western part of the paschal clearing, facing the kerek area and the straw Passover enclosure. The evangelist announced, "You must prepare to be baptized. Take off your good clothes and put on some dirty ones so that they won't be damaged. Your husband says that he knows what to do." He volunteered his wife's help in these matters.

Since I had never witnessed a baptismal ceremony before, I had no idea of what to expect beyond the evangelist's terse direction. To my surprise, I was given very little instruction by his wife, or by any of the other women. I was puzzled when Mama Ida continued preparing lunch and arranging the hut as if nothing were going to happen.

The men had brought back two chickens, and she requested my help in plucking them, but I was of little assistance.

By one-thirty, Mama Ida had still made no move to help or instruct me, and I could not understand how mundane activities would be more important than a great event such as a new baptism. Mama Ida said with a smile, "The Daddies must eat." I was unable to understand Chinyanza, and most of the women, including Mama Ida, spoke only broken English, if any. As a result, I sat in the hut alone and waited for someone to summon me, while the other women worked and ate. Finally, Mama Ida came in to eat with me. Afterward, she told me to remove all of my jewelry and to put on a simple wrap. I parted reluctantly with my wedding ring, earrings, and other pieces of jewelry that I valued, leaving them in a small plastic box in the hut. I had a flash of resentment, feeling that I had been put through a "degradation ceremony." That I was already being instructed in ways of detaching myself from worldly concerns did not occur to me.

When I had dressed, I sat alone looking at the straw wall of the enclosure, while the other two women sharing the hut with me finished cleaning after the meal. Suddenly, as I watched the wall, a radiant six-pointed star appeared. It seemed filled in on two corners with red patches and on the others with white, blue, and yellow patches. The outline of the star was a shiny copper. Momentarily, this star, about five feet in width, was vividly present, flashing three times like a neon sign. Then it disappeared. A few minutes later, Mama Esthere, the prophetess, came and instructed me briefly. "Now you are becoming an Apostle," she said. "You cannot wear jewelry. Apostles take no medicines. No medicines. You cannot go dancing or drink beer." She did not say anything else. I longed to know more, but this was the sort of instruction that I was to receive repeatedly in the future.

Mama Ida then accompanied me to the procession of white-robed Apostles that had formed in the middle of the camp, directly across from the hut. In the line behind me was another woman who was also a baptismal candidate. Gradually, the line turned southeast toward the baptismal pond. When I did not see my husband among the other men, I thought that perhaps he had changed his mind. He emerged from his hut briefly and again returned to it. Finally he joined the line, and the progression to the "Jordan" began. This particular Jordan was a very small natural pool in which oil and industrial wastes had been deposited. The oil glistened on the water and beaded in various places, reminding me that we were actually not far from the commercial center of Blantyre.

On the way to the river, the members sang "Hosanna." A group of men leading the line started the song, which passed back through the women's section almost serially, like a private message. Each person sang a different part of the song as the line moved with singleminded intent toward the river. At the river, members lined themselves on the banks of the pool, women on the left, men on the right, and the three candidates in the middle, with a prophet and a baptismal evangelist.

The prophet began the work of finding new names for the candidates through prayer. An evangelist stood beside him, prayed, and shook his head, as if in assent. Then the prophet whispered a name to my husband, a name that was inaudible to me. I later learned that it was David. The prophet resumed his prayer and whispered to me that my new name was Maria. I did not react. The woman behind me was mistakenly given the name of Jacopo (Jacob). The evangelist corrected the prophet and told him that he would have to ask again for a woman's name. This time, he received Elizabeth.

In the company of the evangelist, the three of us were led to the water, where we squatted precariously on the ledge. The prophet took my husband's wedding ring and threw it to a member of the crowd. The others had already begun to sing the "Kwese, Kwese." The baptist started to clear away the oil with his staff, then jumped into the pool. Peter was led in first. The baptist whispered something to him and immersed him three times, holding his head down with the right hand. I later discovered that in all baptisms, males, both old and young, are immersed before females as a sign of accord with the true Spirit of God. The three dippings were performed in the name of the Father, the Son, and the Holy Spirit. When he emerged on the other side (the candidate enters on the west and emerges on the east side of the pool), David was greeted by a small group of Apostles, each of whom kissed him three times: the kiss of membership for which he was now eligible.

My head scarf was thrown to the same member who had received my husband's ring, and I was led to the water. As I entered the water with the evangelist, I trembled. The baptist, who took my hand, whispered that I should not be afraid and instructed me to close my eyes when under water. I was immersed three times, and when I climbed out of the water, I again saw the copper star. On the other side of the pool, I was met by Mama Esthere and Mama Ida, who both kissed me. The women led me about ten yards from the river and under the cover of some bushes gave me some dry clothes. A little later, I changed into a plain green Apostolic garment belonging to Mama Ida. All clothes worn by members on retreat must be in solid colors, unmarred by prints or designs. Most of my own were not suitable for the musankano. With my new clothes and name, I began to blend in with many of the women. I was one among many Apostolic Marias and a potential healer.

As I left the water, I turned back briefly to see Elizabeth enter, but I was taken away before I could watch her baptism. After returning to the hut, I glimpsed the star once more, with strange, illegible letters under it. An encompassing voice that was not loud yet seemed to fill all of the space said: "Go to the Jews," three times. This experience was later interpreted as a prophecy by a baptist, who explained it, citing Matthew 10:5 in which Christ charges the Apostles to begin preaching among "the lost sheep of Israel." Once the star faded away, three bottles of medicine stood before me as if glued to the wall. One was large and black, with a white skull and crossbones emblazoned on the front. Another was red, smaller, also with a skull and crossbones. The smallest bottle was white, without the skull and crossbones. A voice said that I was not to touch the first two bottles that contained manmade medicines, but only the third, very small, clear bottle filled with oil and water.

I barely had time to compose myself and absorb these visions when Mama Ida entered the hut with Peter's oil-stained clothes and sent me to the edge of the encampment with a bucket of water to wash them. Hardly noticing the clothes, I went through the motions of washing them in an elated, almost dazed state. The sky, which was already bright, seemed almost fluorescent. Unable to remove the oil stains, I washed the clothes quickly, splashing water on the ground. Peter felt that the stains, which remained on his shirt for several months after the baptism, represented the sins of a past life. For me, the personal implications of the baptism were impossible to determine. The comparison of present and past lives was ambiguous: I was uncertain about my obligations and how I would be able to sustain the promise of a new spiritual life.

The chickens that we had plucked roasted on the fire as the sun set. I had been told to prepare for the Passover celebration that evening but did not know what to expect. Still in a dazed state, I went with Mama Ida to take tea to the elders' enclosure, where I glimpsed Makebi, who asked me about my journey. Mama Ida motioned me to kneel and seemed embarrassed when I did not. Once we returned to the hut, Mama Ida gave me her white veil, although she had no spare robe. With the priest, his assistants, and the Zambian entourage, we left for another Passover site about eight miles from the encampment where some of the members met and kissed me. I was then led to a large fire. Within moments, everyone began to run around the fire. I was walled in between the crowd, three persons deep, and the fire. Suddenly I was pushed toward the fire, and I jumped quickly across it, literally to save body and soul. I was not burned and had no idea how other Apostles might have interpreted it if I had fallen. Two days later I found out that members had been shouting their year's sins around the fire—the prepaschal confession—to an audience of advisers. Persons who fell into the fire and were burned, as I nearly was, were considered to be in sin. If they walked across the fire unscathed, they were assessed to be in a state of purity and were ready to partake of the sacrament. Similar rituals have been recorded in other African churches.[11]

As the crowd dispersed, I moved to the women's keti, where women with children strapped to their backs pushed furiously toward the straw barrier surrounding the priest's table. After I had been standing at the gate for a few moments, jostled by the crowd, a paschal assistant ar-

[11] Crawford (1967:233–234) points out the similarity of Apostolic rituals involving fire to those of other independent churches in Central Africa, but he erroneously equates confession around the fire among the Rhodesian Apostles with a traditional fire ordeal. Andersson (1958:219) asserts that firewalking as a test of a member's moral character and righteousness was prevalent among independent churches and prophetic movements in the Lower Congo from 1920 to 1930.

Plate 1. Prophets' gate. Before receiving the Passover, members are examined as they pass through this gate. (Paschal enclosure, Blantyre, Malawi, 1971)

rived and took me for an interview with Makebi Sithole. Makebi and his secretary seemed to analyze the letters we had brought in a jocular fashion, aware of unstated contradictions that Peter and I were not. After leaving Makebi's hut, I entered a circle of members who had already passed through the prophetic gate. At this time, I did not pass through the gate myself. Those who had already passed were separated from the others by red cloth partitions that I later learned symbolized the awesomeness and the purification of the sacrament. The members who had been admitted sang as they waited for Makebi to emerge. As the singing continued, they filed past the Lopasa or paschal organizer who washed their feet and quickly wiped them dry. Then they resumed their places in the semicircle

Plate 2. Table where sacrament is administered. After passing through the gate, members enter the central enclosure where their feet are washed. They file past this table to receive the sacrament. (Paschal enclosure, Blantyre, Malawi, 1971)

around the paschal table to wait for Makebi. The continuous singing created a spiritual atmosphere that easily made me forget how cold and late it was.

Dramatically, Makebi, accompanied by his evangelist, stepped out in a white robe and head covering to present the sacrament. The twelve members of the local Central Committee sat at a long bench and partook of the dried cornmeal and fruit juice by lamplight. Then the others followed, regardless of gift or grade, the men first and then the women. As each member filed past the table, he took a piece of the bread from a dish in front of Makebi and drank the juice or "wine" from a silver chalice that the evangelist wiped off and refilled for each person.

After everyone had taken the sacrament, members of the Committee of Twelve and the Zambian head evangelist, Luka Chisanga, pushed the crowd back and began to signal about fifty persons by name. Although I had moved to the side with some other women, I was called to join them. We were lined in men's and women's rows, each person facing the group of prophets at the front of the line. Four prophets circulated, laying hands on members' heads and casting off the women's veils as they did so. Fervent chanting formed a background for all of these activities. As each person was touched, the managing evangelist shouted his newly confirmed gift for all to hear. After all persons had been confirmed, Mama Ida, who had become a prophetess, and I, now a healer, returned with our group to the encampment.

Members were busily preparing for Makebi's return to administer a second Passover at our encampment. Although it was already well past midnight, groups of night singers enlivened every part of the encampment. The night fires and songs sustained the feeling of transcendence created by the ceremony itself. Mama Ida and I returned to the paschal enclosure. Explaining to the prophets that we had already participated in the earlier Passover, we were allowed to enter. There were far fewer members here, since many had already gone to the other site, and they passed rapidly through the footwashing and the paschal line. We again ate the sacrament and moved to the side of the enclosure to watch the confirmations. The entire ceremony had been absorbing. In a single day, I had entered into a new realm of Apostolic life and had eaten the sacrament, an event for which other members often waited years.

As an Apostle, I had become thoroughly subject to the many consequences of membership. It was reiterated that acceptance was always a voluntary act. I recalled that in a sermon, one member had stated: "Who wants to join us will do so deliberately, so does whoever wants to quit. We do not have any strings attached to our faith."

Deliberate acceptance in my case consisted of a commitment to new possibilities and guidelines for life without knowing specifically what these might entail. Only when I returned to Zambia did I begin to receive more specific instruction in the purposes of baptism, principles of conduct, and the performance of ceremonies and songs. Some of the lessons involved direct Bible study, learning through parables, demonstration, and performance. Lengthy explanations were seldom given beforehand. The severest form of teaching consisted of direct attempts to modify behavior.

For me, one of the most difficult customs to learn was the ritual practice, observed with particular scruple in Zambia, of kneeling to all male members in a stylized fashion. This is observed most strictly on first meeting a man and on the musankano retreat where a woman must kneel when speaking to any man, including her own husband. The more considerate men also knelt at this time. The only way in which I could master this was to remind myself that I was honoring the Spirit of God in each man and to remember that women also kneeled to one another. Wherever possible, I compromised with a curtsy.

After my baptism, the Zairian prophet Ilunga told me that I need not worry about the rules of conduct, since it was not a matter of individual will to follow them but only the result of the acceptance and guidance of the Holy Spirit. Once the decision was made to become devoted to Christ and the Spirit, conscious reflection on each activity became a hindrance. Of course, conscious reflection and questioning are central parts of the ethnographer's task and appeared both desirable and unavoidable for myself and for the other new members that I had seen. But a tension developed between reflection and participation.

Two days after the baptism, I received lengthy biblical

instruction from Kangwa William, the Lieb-Umah baptist at the Nyangwena farm, about sixty miles from Lusaka, Zambia. He began by explaining the importance of the Bible and how it should be used. "You cannot understand the Bible without seeing the miracles first. You saw those things at the Pasika. Walking on fire, eating fire, healing, and prophecy. Now you know. You would not believe these things if someone had told them to you, would you? No. You must first see these things for yourself." He continued, "If you follow the commandments, you will enter Heaven. If not, you will burn in Hell, but the fire will never consume you, and you will be in agony. The flesh is separate from the soul. The flesh will die and will eventually disappear. The soul dies and inherits eternal life if you keep the commandments." He stopped and considered the fate of those who do not accept. "The entire world will be destroyed. But those who follow the commandments will inherit eternal life." He added, "Evil deeds bring bad blood."

The rest of the session consisted of the citation of a number of biblical passages intended to illustrate examples of life in the Spirit. Each passage was explained briefly, and I was asked whether I really understood it or not. "Understand" meant the ability to use the passage, apply its teachings, and commit it to memory. Romans 11:7–8 was used to explain that the Holy Spirit and not simply the laws of religious practice were the full promise of the Apostles. James 5:13–20 supported faith healing and prayer for the ill by the elders of the church. Amos 1:3 was cited to warn against unnatural intervention in any illness. The passages were regarded as subject to interpretation for any life situation that Apostles would encounter.

Although I had previously been aware of some ways in which each aspect of Apostolic life was explained and justified in sermons, I had not given too much attention to biblical discussion intended for personal use. The selection of passages did not have an apparent order and seemed to be based on what was appropriate for the occasion. I gradually discovered that certain passages were used to convey basic teachings. Often Mark 16:15, concerning the spiritual gifts, was presented first to the newcomer and used as a way of interpreting other biblical passages in terms of the spiritual responsibility of Apostolic membership. While my initial instruction contained a variety of passages, at certain meetings only one epistle or one of the Gospels might be read extensively. All passages had a moral and instructive intent, but specific instructions were relevant to the situation at different times. Passages used for general evangelism were occasionally different from those that had to be mastered in depth as part of the total process of membership.

In addition to biblical instruction, prophecy and the diagnosis of illness provide personal guidelines. The prophet reinterprets the world for the candidate and leads him to the spiritual re-examination of his actions. In diagnosing illness and suffering of all kinds, the prophet teaches these methods to other members. While the member can use a limited form of diagnosis for self-analysis, the method of diagnosis itself is assumed to be a gift of grace and cannot be fully transmitted from one member to another. One Apostle discussed suffering as follows:

Are these things happening to you because of your sins? Is it because God is tempting you? Or what is the cause? After you have found out where disaster is coming from, then you will know how to get rid of it. [A baptist, Luluabourg, 1969]

Suffering is considered to come from many sources, including those not within the member's control, such as sorcery and witchcraft. The individual's reaction to suffering is a major consideration. If he is angered or frustrated, the forces of evil are said to have gained control over the situation. Once the cause of suffering is determined and publicly announced, the diagnosis is generally accepted. The instruction received after baptism is specifically calculated to warn members against temptation and provide them with spiritual protection.

Since it was the Sabbath eve, after our period of instruction we went to evening prayer. Not having a robe, I wore the plain dress in which I had been baptized, with Mama Ida's white head covering. Our new apprenticeship continued publicly, through prophetic testimonies at the close of kerek. Peter and I were requested to stand. If we agreed that the prophecies presented were correct, we were asked to say "Amen" and make no further comments. Were the candidate to reject the prophecy, he did so at his own risk, knowing that the impact of a false rejection would fall upon him. This seems to follow the form of a traditional Shona adjudication (Holleman 1969:216–224).

The prophetess began by stating that Peter had two friends, one slim and young, the other taller and somewhat older. She predicted that these friends would stand against him in matters concerning the church. When asked if he had such friends, my husband first replied that he thought so, later saying that he was certain of it. Then the prophetess asked if he had been ill with appendicitis. Peter replied, "Amen." He later stated that the scar had become painful again. She warned that the scar would open up soon and that he might die if he did not watch his conduct and remain within the commandments of the Bible and of the church. She advised him to have a bottle of holy water blessed by the baptist who had instructed us earlier and to drink it regularly. I later regarded this advice not merely as a prediction but also as a way of assuring commitment to the church.

Perhaps the most convincing part of this prophecy concerned the immediate situation. The prophetess asked whether my husband had some hidden bottles of medicine. He replied, "Amen." "These bottles," she stated, "should be burned immediately by an evangelist." We hesitated to give up the medicines completely. The evangelist, who later confiscated them from our luggage, remarked that he had no idea that we had them with us, boasting that only an Apostolic prophet could have discovered them. The prophetess turned to me. She informed me that my blood was impure and that I was to be given holy water to drink. The elders of the church were told to pray for me to remove the sickness in my blood. Although the full impact of this prophecy was not yet clear to me, I said "Amen," still awed by the discovery of the medicines. Later illnesses, combined with further prophecies after my return to the Zaire, made me recall and confirm what she had said.

On the whole, the directness and clarity of these prophecies reinforced my acceptance of a new order of reality. As time passed, I became even more absorbed in the Apostolic community. I did not realize how total this involvement was becoming until I took a short trip to Lusaka several days after the baptism. There I was so shocked to see the style of life portrayed in European and American magazines that I was certain that I would never return to the West. None of these images would have seemed the least bit remarkable to me before.

The week following the baptism ended in a series of confession and curing ceremonies that continued to expand my knowledge. Through these ceremonies, I discovered the importance of "speaking out" (kureva), the public confession of difficulties and transgressions by each member.[12] Bengt Sundkler found similar ceremonies that he

12 Aquina (1967:211) stresses that the Apostles avoid the traditional Chishona term kudura, which means to recite a charm or to confess one's

termed purification rites to be at the heart of ritual practices in South African Zionist churches (1961:201–214, 228–234). They included severe practices, such as pummeling candidates with holy sticks, reimmersing the offender in a river or stream after he had eaten unclean food, and inducing vomiting with mixtures of holy water to exorcise demons. In the case of major transgressions, reimmersion is also found in the Apostolic church. But on the whole, confession outside of kerek is combined with arbitrating disputes and curing illness.

The return to Zambia threw me into daily situations which tested my newly acquired beliefs. Three days before our baptism, I had witnessed a case of confession involving two mothers and their children. The case was still unresolved when we returned from Malawi. All four had been ill, and prophets had attributed the illnesses to hidden sins. The case had been referred to evangelists for confession and later given back to the prophets and healers. The first of the mothers was a young member of the head evangelist's family, and the second was his senior wife.

The younger mother first appeared in kerek to confess that her child was suffering from stomach pains and diarrhea. She did not feel that she was at fault but insisted that she was vulnerable to the attacks of demons. She also confessed that she had been angry with her husband. That evening, members sang and prayed over the young woman's child, but no improvement was noticeable. The senior wife, who had not confessed in kerek, also brought in her child to be prayed over by the elders. Her husband was among those praying and encouraged her to confess. I could hear the mothers' voices chanting between the chil-

desires through incantation and is used in divination. Instead, they refer to "speaking out" their transgressions and use the term *kureva* or *kurerura*, "to speak out or to denounce," which is also used by Shona Catholics to mean "to confess."

dren's cries as healing ceremonies continued throughout the night.

On the following morning, a group of elders met to discuss the younger woman's illness. The senior wife was also summoned and complained that both she and her child were still ill. The young mother was given an ultimatum to confess all of her hidden sins and request forgiveness for her anger. The evangelist and the prophet placed their staffs on the floor in front of her and told her to cross the staffs if she found their verdict to be just. There was a long pause. She did not cross the staffs. The senior wife, who was not asked to confess, sat comforting her child. After the younger mother's refusal, singing and praying for both children went on for about half an hour and continued intermittently throughout the day.

Several days later, the children's illness became acute. The senior wife's child developed a high fever and could not eat. The curing ceremonies continued over the next three days, but attempts at confession were abandoned. Every ten to fifteen minutes, the mothers could be heard in some part of the house, singing over their children. Prophets skilled in diagnosis were summoned. It was rumored that the illness was "caused" not just by the mothers but by all four parents, who were in sin, including the evangelist. There was mutual criticism among the persons involved, but no further public confession was initiated. Diagnosis was also terminated, and very soon, the senior wife's child died. The younger mother's child remained weak but seemed to be recovering. The child's death, however, did not cause the members to lose their faith in the healing process. The senior wife later became a prophetess because of her ability to diagnose illness, although she had not been able to prevent it in this case.

Only through membership was I able to participate in the healing sessions at length. This allowed me to see how

Apostles developed spiritual explanations and techniques of cure and involved me directly as a singer and witness. It was most difficult for me to accept the child's death as the inevitable outcome of spiritual interpretations. Children seemed the most vulnerable to illness and were the least able to present their confession in an Apostolic sense. Even though diagnosis and confession did provide the entire Apostolic community with a way of making the world meaningful and of working through misfortune, such explanations still appeared arbitrary to me at the time.

Resistance and questions were expected during my transition from an outsider to an Apostle. Members claimed that such reactions were not rare, and I was to witness them at subsequent baptismal ceremonies. The candidate's necessity to cling to one form of interpretation in the face of another is not merely rhetorical; it is based on life options. This consideration is built into the immediacy of Apostolic instruction. The new member gradually learns to characterize the world differently, often separating himself from family and friends to do so. This separation, spiritually described by Apostles as an inner protection, is also a physical separation from the world in Apostolic family and community units that are more or less insulated. One speaker expressed the spiritual dimensions of this separation in the following way:

If you throw something with bad intention [i.e., malice or sorcery] it will never reach me. This is true. The only one to achieve such an act is he who is here with me. If one of you tries it, he will notice that I am very far away.   [Demba, 1969]

As has been stressed, living within the commandments is considered to protect members from sorcery (evil intentions) and illness and give them the promise of eternal life. The outsider, however, is still considered vulnerable, since the world of the impure and the profane is still invisible as such to him. Even the established member must be reminded of appropriate and effective ways to interpret new situations through prophecy, confession, and evangelical advice. Maintaining membership has meant the intertwining of spiritual principles with each aspect of daily life. The Apostles with whom I lived created and remained faithful to their membership by evaluating their actions as a community of believers.

The most immediate result of baptism, about which I had long been very curious, was learning a vocabulary of membership that provided a new personal and social scrutiny of my behavior. These instructions for a new life were gradually revealed, ambiguous and subject to variation, each time members discussed them with me. The certainty of members in applying a religious morality to their behavior under all circumstances, while impressive, often seemed arbitrary to me even after I joined. The critical transition for me was that from an outside observer looking for general descriptions of the church and its worship to that of a full member for whom all descriptions had their own personal implications and sense of urgency.

PART TWO

RITUAL CONTEXTS

CHAPTER 3

The Management of Ritual Settings

There came to me a very short man who had two books in his hands. He had the one in his right hand and the other in his left hand. When he had come to where I sat, he gave me the book that was in his right hand. Although the book was in a new language, and besides the fact that I had not yet gone to school, I managed to read it. When the man found out that I could read from his book, he told me that I had been blessed for ever. I was further told that I could inherit Eternal Life. Amen.

John Maranke

Membership gave me a new vocabulary with which to share in and develop my reactions to ritual, but it was difficult to pinpoint exactly how it altered my assumptions. Once I gained entry into a ceremony and mastered its performance, I had difficulty reflecting on how that mastery was attained. I knew, however, that membership allowed me to see ways in which I was guided through ritual events and the subtle movements and cues that were basic to the structure of ceremony.

Participating in and describing the weekly Sabbath ceremony became essential to the understanding of Apostolic life. This ceremony is a dramatic and vigorous expression of faith that contains all of the basic features of Apostolic ritual organization. The ceremonies are staged events, and in order to participate in them, one must understand the relationships of their parts and how they are rearranged on different occasions. Management of ritual refers to its performance, background knowledge about an activity's structure, and overall consideration of the flow of the event.[1] Membership also enabled me to recognize the free-

[1] In some studies of interaction (Goffman 1959:51–53, 208; 1967:176–177),

dom that Apostles employed in negotiating the features of each performance within the bounds of a few prearranged activities.[2]

The format and purpose of kerek can be recognized by all members, while specific content is highly variable. As I participated more fully in ceremonies, I was able to detect the multiple meanings of each performance and their relationship to specific settings. The basic Sabbath kerek with all of its formal components allows for open innovation and a highly participatory form of involvement, especially for those who share in its spiritual purpose. Kerek is a ceremony of praise, intended to invoke the angels and the Holy Spirit to be present with and strengthen members. It is also a time of confession and cure, during which members express their personal triumphs and grievances to the community. Each kerek has three distinctive components: prayer, preaching, and hymns and songs of praise. A unique religious totality is developed when people from a number of language groups read a single biblical passage during the course of a ceremony.

Several months in the Kasai had given me fixed ideas about the features of Apostolic worship. I knew that prophecy and confession took place immediately before the

management has been treated as largely interpersonal control of emotion and expression. The organization of a larger scene, for example a ceremony, is then examined in relation to and as a product of the personal presentation. Other approaches (Garfinkel 1967:118–127) have used the concept of "management" to delineate basic procedures that persons use in the overall process of negotiating and structuring social scenes. This approach makes it possible to examine various aspects of a social performance in terms of the ways in which persons reason about their environment.

[2] This contrasts with Parsons' (1955:56) suggestion that the process of internalization establishes "an organized pattern of meanings which the external object has acquired" and that the meaning of parts of a setting may thus be predetermined and capable of only minor variations in some cases.

core parts of the main worship event. I had always assumed that these parts of the ceremony were performed away from the area set aside for preaching but observed that confession took place before the entire congregation in Zambia. The basic format of a sung prelude followed by two standard hymns and a prayer seemed a constant for all full worship ceremonies. But as I discovered during the period of governmental surveillance in Zaire, even these elements of format could be abbreviated and modified. The opening hymns and prayer are followed by preaching and song, which constitute the core elements of kerek and are often referred to in themselves as "kerek." Preaching is antiphonal and alternates with the recitation of biblical passages by either appointed or volunteer readers. Songs are freely interspersed between preaching and reading. After three or four speakers have preached, each with the intervening readings and songs, the whole congregation prays aloud. A closing hymn ends this portion of kerek. Members assume less formal sitting positions as they listen to prophetic testimonies and announcements. A parting song draws the gathering to a close. Following preaching and song, the semiautonomous curing ceremony already mentioned is held apart from the main worship area. (Excerpts from the ceremony and a more detailed description of the kerek's basic format are presented in Appendix A.)

Each public expression following the opening hymns is considered a form of preaching in a special mode. Sermons, songs, reading, sermon interruptions, and audience participation are all forms of "preaching." In this sense, the main speaker's position is on a par with that of others, and he expects his activities to be complemented by theirs. The negotiation of competing parts of the ceremony is based on this acceptance of multiple forms of preaching. No member has exclusive claims to the floor, and almost any act of participation, if it wins collective support or attention, can

Plate 3. Opening prayer. The Lord's Prayer is recited rapidly in the kneeling position before each worship service. (Kerek, Kananga, Zaire, 1972)

be made a legitimate and focal performance. The drama and the confusion that often characterize kerek arise from these competing claims, especially when different congregational and language subgroups share in the performance.

While kerek may be seen as a curative rite and a time of instruction for members, it is also oriented toward presenting the gospel to spectators.[3] To Apostles, God and the Holy Spirit are witnessed in kerek and each of its performances has a consequent importance. The symbolic progression of kerek sustains a spiritual order of reality. This

[3] The sense of the word *instruction* is multiple. It refers both to moral instructions and spiritual messages and to instructions about how a ceremony should be performed. In this sense, we might refer to instructions as metacommunications, discussed in detail by Bateson (1972:188–189), or messages about the messages directly presented in sermons and songs.

Plate 4. Preaching and reading. Preaching and reading are performed collaboratively with careful attention to pacing and style. (Kerek, Kananga, Zaire, 1972)

progression consists of the welcoming of the angels and the Spirit, the witnessing of their power, and their departure. The force of the spiritual visitations remains during the curing ceremony and is sustained by prayer in all of the week's activities. For nonmembers, the spiritual order of reality is largely absent, and they do not share in its invocation. The very summons of "kerek" separates them from this reality, while it draws members into its awareness.

The distinction between orders of reality and perception available to members and outsiders is also sustained on the level of instruction, the message of kerek. Nonmembers are criticized for the error of their ways and challenged to join. Members are exhorted to keep the commandments that they have already accepted and enter into a spiritual world through song. Apostles claim that the spiritual world of song is not accessible to those without purity of heart, that is, those who have not converted. Although all instruction in kerek is public, the esoteric nature of what is intended for members is considered to be preserved by virtue of their qualifications to hear it. The close timing of the parts of the service and its oratorical presentation are similarly thought to be possible only through spiritual inspiration and in turn facilitate the attainment of spiritual states for members. Participants also evaluate oratory in aesthetic terms and treat the entire performance of kerek as an art.

Apostles recognize that kerek has a bounded structure, and they expect the basic parts of the full ceremony to recur each time. But in smaller biweekly meetings and curing ceremonies, as long as songs of prayer are sung, oratory and discussion may be minimal. In the full kerek, both the semiautonomous and core events are part of the ceremony's symbolism. As members are examined by prophets, they file into the place of prayer with men to the east, the symbolic area in which Christ is to return, and women to the west. The men and women sit in rows facing each other, leaving open a middle aisle for preaching. The use of a ritual path for sacred words and actions is not limited to the Bapostolo. It appears in the ceremony of other independent churches and in many traditional African settings for spirit invocation. The Ndembu and Tonga groups of Zambia refer to ritual symbols as trailblazers or pathfinders (Chindembu: *kujikijila*—to blaze a trail, to make a symbol; Tonga: *kunjila*—to enter a path or the body of a person by spiritual intrusion).[4] The construction of sacred enclosures, such as those used at the Passover and

[4] These etymologies are found in Turner (1969:15) and Colson (1969:70). The importance of a path recurs in African ritual. The Tshiluba term for path is *njila*, which may bear some etymological relationship to tshijila, or holiness. Apostles refer to the Bible as the *Mukanda wa njila*, or the passport to Heaven.

symbolically in the aisle, are also common features of West and Central African rituals. Such enclosures separate both spiritual and human outsiders from those participating directly in the activities.[5]

Songs are also integral to the progression of kerek and maintain an atmosphere of worship before the opening of the service and during its course. Once most members are seated, a baptist, often but not necessarily the head of the congregation, opens the main service with the two standard hymns that lead directly into a rapid recitation of the Lord's Prayer. The opening songs are almost always sung in Chishona, John Maranke's language, just as they were composed. The preaching that follows is introduced by an evangelist, who presents the schedule of speakers. Although this schedule is fixed, others may interrupt to introduce a "small word" or commentary on the assigned speaker's discourse. In this way, an open-ended pattern for the alternation of topics is created. The sermons are brief, based on biblical topics that the speaker explains in terms of Apostolic doctrine. Each speaker selects a reader to present verses collaboratively, line by line in an antiphonal manner. As the reader recites the verse, the preacher expands upon it, repeating either the entire verse or key words and phrases.

Apostolic sermons are rich in metaphor and moral instruction. Each metaphor suggests a specific form of conduct for members.[6] For example, "we are written of Christ's blood" instructs the Apostles to follow biblical

[5] Littlejohn (1967:331–347) points out that some African groups such as the Temne build most enclosures including their houses to shut out "bush-demons." The construction of ceremonial enclosures among the Apostles might be regarded from similar premises.

[6] Fernandez (1972:54–55) suggests that preaching in a number of independent churches is rich in metaphor and that these metaphors have "performative implications." That is, they contain instructions about the performance of ceremony and directives about the lives of members.

commandments and to be sacrificed to Christ. Features of each situation suggest different ways of applying such instructions. The cadence of preaching is sustained by "interruptions" of song that result in its intensification and acceleration. Although not prescheduled, the songs pick up and elaborate on themes of preaching. The ceremony is performed so that gaps or pauses are generally filled, producing a continual flow of sound. Except at moments when women initiate songs, members are always in motion in the center aisle, creating a dramatic visual effect.

The open-ended character of the service allows for audience response and participation in the form of greetings and song interruptions. Speakers periodically greet the entire congregation, which replies collectively. These greetings serve to encourage participation, to punctuate or organize short sections of discourse, and to emphasize points made in speaking. Although there are moments, including these greetings, at which members expect pauses or shifts of activity, each shift is negotiated among the participants. An attempted initiation of song or preaching during the course of the current activity may be vetoed. Yet alternation of speakers and activities is expected to occur smoothly, particularly in practiced transitions between speakers and readers. Where a definite transition in the activities occurs, there is a change in the topic presented and in the intensity of the ceremony. Songs also redirect the subject and may themselves be transformed into chants. Sustaining topics through different parts of the kerek is a method of creating a central theme of worship that members can use as a way of anticipating and referring to other parts of the service, controlling them as they emerge.

Members segment the ceremony by interspersing short periods of discourse and song, generally lasting from two to five minutes in length. The segment that follows another is decided spontaneously, and several combinations may occur. Periods of singing and preaching may last for several sequences. Each preaching episode is marked by rhetorical greetings, and its topics are developed consistently, so that it resembles a "paragraph" of discourse. Segments of singing may delay discourse as they gradually become a sustained chant.

Another procedure implicitly used to assure the alternation of activities in kerek is a rank-ordering of participants so that the younger or less experienced speakers preach first. [7] Song interruptions follow a similar ranking pattern when speakers are interrupted for song, often by close friends of their own age. The ranking pattern is not constant, however, since more spontaneous responses tend to occur as the service progresses, with speakers and readers jumping up to insert comments or passages.

Throughout the service, members are involved in open response, rapid pacing, and picking up cues.[8] Collective attention to pacing is an important way of balancing parts of the ritual and maintaining the integration of topics and themes across its segments.

The ceremony can also be examined in terms of proce-

[7] Albert (1964:35–54) presents a model for rank-ordered speech based on status, age, caste, sex, and other sources of taboos among the Burundi. In applying a similar model to Apostolic speech, the order of speaking would rely on a system of social organization which would have to be assumed as fairly explicit across tribal groups or made available within the church's own organization. However, among Apostles, with the possible exception of the pastor's position, the relationship between social status and speech events varied greatly from one situation to another.

[8] Pacing is an important feature of Apostolic ceremonies. It is used here to mean short-range timing over a two- to five-minute part of the ritual. These units of ritual are generally uninterrupted parts of preaching and song which remain topically consistent. Members treat pacing as central to the meaning of ritual. Schegloff (1968:1084) notes the importance of pacing in his analysis of a summons-answer sequence in ordinary conversation.

dures that maintain the flow and assure that topics are explained to an audience of both Apostles and outsiders. These techniques are rhetorical and rely on establishing an overall pacing for the service.[9]

Metaphor. Using metaphor, the speaker exhorts members of the congregation to set a moral example for the community and to commit themselves to the work of God. The metaphor simultaneously describes and creates a specific social reality:

Bapostolo, life to you. (Response.) Now this is for you Apostles. Are you written in Christ's blood? Everyone is watching your everyday language, your life. They are reading you night and day. Do you prove blood written or not? People can convert their hearts by observing and imitating you.

Overlapped antiphony. This style of presentation is used in both preaching and song and, in preaching, contributes to its musical qualities. In this case, the speaker repeats the reader's verse without elaboration. A fuller explanation of the social and spiritual context of the passage occurs once the collaborative reading is completed. This rapid speech absorbs the listener and helps to create a spiritual state through its chantlike tones.

Reader: Get up
Speaker: —Get up
Reader: —illuminate
Speaker: —illuminate
Reader: —because the darkness will cover the earth
Speaker: —because the darkness will cover the
Reader: —and everybody but Jehovah will rise among you
Speaker: —earth and everybody but Jehovah will rise among
Reader: —and His glory be manifested—
Speaker: —you and His glory be manifested. . . .

[9] Close timing of kerek tapes indicates that these preaching and singing segments were rarely violated without criticism or comment when the full worship ceremony was performed.

Reference to prior parts of the service. Speakers integrate the themes previously introduced into their own sermons with slightly varying implications. They also reflect and comment on songs, characterizing both the ceremony itself and the persons singing:

Bapostolo, life to you. (Response.) Looking at how we sing, it is not necessary that I do the Gospel. I do the Gospel because I feel sorry for you. You got this Gospel at no cost, therefore you should propagate it free of cost. If we stood here and sang all day without saying anything to you, you would not realize what we are doing.

Preaching as moral formulation. Speakers address the congregation ("we") and the spectators to whom they are preaching ("they," "you") with direct moral formulations and recommendations for conduct:

Life to you Apostles. (Response.) Be aware that Judas was among the Apostles of Christ. Life to you Apostles. (Response.) But the church of Jesus Christ did not die. People did not reject the church because Judas, being a traitor of the Lord, was one of the Apostles. But if people saw me commit adultery, they would say our church is no good. If they saw me drink alcohol, they would say our church is no good.

Several other techniques are used to unite parts of the service and to maintain continuity within a single activity. By direct elaboration on the song text, it is integrated with preaching; topics are changed, and the speaker may reject song in favor of continued preaching. Once initiated, songs may also be used as a form of preaching, with each verse presenting instructions about a biblical topic. Songs also provide accounts of a holy way of life and instruct members in its attainment. Like the sermon, the song refers to and improvises upon a specific biblical passage to explain its relevance, as in the following example:

Read Hosea four at verse eleven and you'll see
See the desire to smoke and drink, they've lost the thought
    of God
People come to the drum of life
    Jerusalem in Heaven near the Father. . . .

This song uses a biblical verse to explain prohibitions against smoking and drinking, contrasting these activities with seeking God and salvation.

Now I wish to devote special attention to a particular Sabbath service that was held on an Apostolic cooperative farm at Kabanana, about three miles from Lusaka. The main sermon was given in English and was designed to convince me, as a newcomer, to accept the baptism of the Apostles. Although it was one of the few sermons that I heard given in a European language, neither its style nor its content was exceptional for this congregation. While it was specifically directed toward the foreign visitors, the sermon was still intended to keep the attention of members and provide them with moral and spiritual teachings. As a result, it was necessary to read the Bible in the major languages spoken by the congregation: Tshiluba-Kasai, Chishona, Chindembu, Chibemba, and Kiswahili. The actual presence of members of a certain ethnic or language group is not always necessary for such reading. In Lubumbashi, the Bible was regularly read in Lingala, for which there were no first language speakers present, as well as in Tshiluba-Kasai, Tshina Lunda and Chindembu, although nearly all persons present spoke fluent Kiswahili, and many used it as a lingua franca at home. Nyalongo's sermon is of interest analytically, for it was then that I first became aware of how members made use of the basic format of kerek and handled competing aspects of ritual in different languages. For Apostles, what initially appeared to me as baffling and momentarily chaotic exchanges had a special message—the universality of the Bible and the spiritual unity of worshipers from different backgrounds.

The reading of the Bible in a certain language initiates the translation of Christian precepts into the terms of that culture.[10] The particulars of worship are translated into a member's natural language, into the conceptual forms in which he privately thinks on most occasions, so that in addition to using a common language for worship, persons would often pray and perform ritual in their original tongue. In response to my questions, members replied that they did not consider a single language the "language of God," although one member said that Hebrew was a language of God, and others told me that God had spoken to them in their own tongue. A more prevalent belief was that God could speak every language, or in one case, that the language of God "resembled the thoughts of men everywhere." [11] This contrasts with the belief in other independent churches that the language of the founder is sacred.

The use of multiple languages was not the only distinguishing feature of the Kabanana ceremony. Its modifica-

[10] Barrett (1968:127–131) stresses the importance of vernacular versions of the Scriptures for the growth of independent churches. In fact, he contends that vernacular Scriptures are a critical causal factor in the growth of independency. He states (p. 127): "Through these Scriptures God, Africans perceived, was addressing them in the vernacular in which was enshrined the soul of their people; but a large portion of the missionary force still had not learned the vernacular and addressed them in foreign tongues. The vernacular scriptures therefore provided an independent standard of reference which African Christians were required to seize on."

[11] Some independent churches make the claim that the language in which their ceremonies are performed is sacred. While the Apostles of Maranke use Chishona in most of their rituals, they do not make this assertion. A closely related church, the Apostolic church of John Masowe, founded in Rusape, Rhodesia, does assert that Chishona is the original language of the people of God and of mankind. For brief discussions of the church of John Masowe or Hosannas, see Sundkler 1961: 323–325; Daneel 1971:339; Kileff 1973.

tion of what I had taken to be the standard format of kerek in the Kasai was remarkable. This ceremony was conducted by a much smaller group than those I had witnessed in 1969 and early 1971, with more informal, personalized styles of preaching and singing. In dealing with the English sermon, I shall focus on the ways in which it was presented as a performance rather than on the standard format and repeated speaking techniques used.

Each occasion of performance introduces an element of variation on the basic format or code of ritual that allows participants to recognize a particular performance as meaningful and effective. This variation is at the core of the managed aspect of ritual.[12] It is through the balancing and negotiation of different language and expressive forms that kerek continues. The forms of expression used and the topics introduced directly reflect upon the ceremonial context. Not only are verbal forms subject to modification for each performance, the physical arrangement of kerek and the ritual movements of members also vary. Management consists of introducing new activities so that they fit into the recognizable format and segments of kerek.

When we arrived at Kabanana in the company of the Congolese group, many men and women seemed to be milling around in the dry, thorn-filled field near Luka Chisanga's house. Two prophets had separated themselves from the group and had gone farther into the field to pray. As they prayed, they moved their staffs together in the shape of a "V." Men and women stood in a single line behind them for the prophetic examination, since there were not enough members to warrant separation of the sexes. Al-

[12] This variation points to the indexical properties of a ritual performance. That is, each part of the ritual refers to or indexes the performance as a whole. The indexical features of ritual stand in contrast to basic aspects of its format. For a discussion of indexicality, see also Garfinkel and Sacks 1970:348–350.

though not yet baptized, Peter and I were instructed to join the line with them. For the first time we were exposed to keti as participants, but neither of us was given a personal prophecy. Once members had been examined, several were sent to confess before a group of evangelists seated within the congregation.

The public confession allowed me to hear the topics and resolutions of disputes in a way that would not have been possible in the Kasaian ceremony. A woman confessed in Kiswahili to having fought with her husband over money. Her husband was brought in, and she asked forgiveness of him. Luka Chisanga, the Zambian head evangelist, handled her case. Then two Kasaian women confessed in Tshiluba that they had had several disputes over the proper time to serve their husbands tea. Their case was settled by a young Luba evangelist, who told them that although the time for tea was unimportant, fighting was a sin. Following his direction, they knelt, shook hands, kissed each other and returned to their seats. A young girl then confessed very softly in Chibemba and was followed by an older man who presented his case in Chishona. Both cases were judged by a Zambian evangelist. Confession took place in several languages and was judged by members of the appropriate subgroups within the kerek rather than by a single group of evangelists.

Preaching was also performed collaboratively by members of various subgroups. While its order was already preset by Luka Chisanga, preaching was interrupted frequently and in diverse languages by the interjections of ritual leaders. The negotiation of biblical passages and the languages in which they were to be read was prolonged. Readers interacted more competitively than in the Kasaian congregations. This very difference enabled me to learn more about the initiation of reading in general as a managed ceremonial event. The overall result of the rela-

Plate 5. Confession. Before each Sabbath ceremony, members confess to a group of evangelists. In this case, confession is performed within the place of worship. (Kerek, Lusaka, Zambia, 1971)

tionship between ceremonial activities and format in the Zambian congregation gave an initial impression of open and informal worship with more latitude for individual variations in both performance and doctrinal interpretation. The theme of informality recurred in my field notes for that day:

September 18, 1971: Demeanor was much more informal throughout the service. No posture check was done, and a lot of shifting around, talking by members and personal exchanges took place. Much of this had to do with the intimate setting, with a great deal of amusement, playing around with the multiple languages, with bantering about the fact that Tshiluba and French readers both kept trying to read first. There were also large and developed interruptions that seemed out of place in the small setting.

Plate 6. Another member confesses. Evangelists listen and give counsel. (Kerek, Lusaka, Zambia, 1971)

Nearly every song began as a straight interruption. T. began one simultaneously with a woman, then let her go on. When he did a song in Tshiluba later, it was his same one, which he for the most part taught to the congregation. His was the best rendition.

Since Nyalongo's sermon was in English, I was able to follow it more closely than usual, despite some difficulties with his accent and expressions. His English renditions seemed to make other members all the more anxious to read passages in both African and European languages. The members from Zambia were especially selected to preach by the head evangelist and represented the indigenous congregation. At the same time, Zairian members, also regular participants in the local kerek, were given equal opportunity for expression as the ceremony progressed. Rather than ranking preachers, the evangelist intervened to assure that each reader would begin at the same biblical verse and read passages of equal length.

Nyalongo's own background influenced his sermon. He had been a Catholic, and after completing primary school, he had intended to go to seminary. About this time, he had become very ill with no apparent cause. After visiting several traditional *nganga* (healers), he was told that seven ancestor spirits were pursuing him. All the spirits wanted him to become a nganga, but for some reason he was unable to accept their invitation. English doctors were also unable to cure him. He was then told about the Apostolic church and its healing ministry. He traveled to Rhodesia, where he joined the church and affirmed that he was healed, although his doubts about the church did not disappear immediately.

Nyalongo was embarrassed about shaving his head and began to grow his beard only gradually. His doubts began to recede when he witnessed three signs predicted by an Apostolic prophet. First, he was spiritually guided to resurrect a child who had been dead well over three days. Timidly, he began to pray over the child without full hope that he could succeed. By performing as a mysterious voice had instructed, Nyalongo asserted that he brought the infant back to life. The second sign took place when he returned to Zambia: the Holy Spirit requested him to walk on fire, which he did without pain. On the third occasion, he healed his own child of a deadly illness simply by touching her. It was apparently on the basis of these miracles that Nyalongo assumed many of the healing responsibilities in the Kabanana congregation.

These miraculous events had, according to Nyalongo, reduced his resistance to the Apostles and their strict regulations. His faith was further reinforced by a series of visions that conclusively led him to the church. In these visions, he was taken to several churches, and a special message was revealed in each. Members of the Catholic church appeared as a group of children playing with "mud" money. The Seventh Day Adventists were a joyful group celebrating a wedding. In their midst, Nyalongo stated that he had seen a woman "jiving." The Salvation Army appeared as a very intelligent group reading the Bible. But they were also very proud and vain. After all of these churches had appeared to him, an angel emerged and declared: "There are already 9,999 churches, and one more is needed to make 10,000. You must rush to join the 10,000th." At this point Nyalongo awoke, convinced that he had found the fulfillment of his visions in the Apostolic church.

It is with this certitude that Nyalongo preached, dramatically providing for us an account of John Maranke's spiritual ancestry and of the church's miracles. To do this, he began with the story of Mary and Joseph's flight into Egypt, a journey that is believed by the Apostles to have established a sacred inheritance for the entire continent. This story is also integral to John Maranke's spiritual ancestry, for John is believed to be a descendant of Chakazunkano, the man who hosted the Holy Family in Egypt. Apostles state that Chakazunkano's son was washed in the bath water left by the infant Jesus and was thereby healed and became the sanctified ancestor of an African church. Nyalongo began his sermon with this account:

Joseph, be flee from here, go right into Africa. That's where Egypt is. That's where He was kept for at least three years, after which He was to go back to Palestine to preach His own people. *Runyararo kune Apostol* [Peace to you Apostles]. (Response.) [13]

[13] This is a Chishona greeting which allows for congregational response. Rhetorical greetings are used in Apostolic ritual to punctuate preaching, reinitiate it, or complete it. Different greetings are used according to the region and the speaker's language.

The sermon then turned from the topic of Christ's own baptism in the Jordan to that of his apostles and followers. At this point, the biblical reading was announced, and an initial attempt was made to recite it. Nyalongo introduced a single standard reading, Mark 16:15. This passage is often used to present the themes and miracles of the church to potential members and to broach the topics of baptism and conversion. The passage was read over the course of the ceremony by four persons in French, Chibemba, Tshiluba, and English. The four readers and the evangelist Luka Chisanga, who were important figures in the social organization of the church, also became major influences in my ultimate conversion. They made a special effort to insure that I had "understood" the biblical message. Reading was conducted in the local oratorical style that was used for both European and African languages. Some readers remained seated, and all read from their respective positions in the congregation.

Nyalongo: *Runyararo kune Apostol.* (Response.) If you could see a person or any other Christian taking his own foundation, not taking the dename—the designation of Jesus, we exactly, we know exactly that the chap is astray. That's why we see most of our people being immersed, not immersed but spread with some water on their forehead. What's the reason? Where did they take such a—It's too stupid otherwise, I would say so. There are so many people who have had educated. But you could see him being sprinted some water on the forehead. What is the main reason?

Member 1: (Glossolalia) *hff hu baptizwe ho*

Nyalongo: There is no one who could explain to me in the way of Jesus Christ. There is no short way. You must follow the example. You could look my chapter: Mark 16, verse 15. But wait—

Member 2:   —*Vese Mako* . . .

Nyalongo: But wait. I wish I could proceed on bit by bit so that if I reach such a period, I could then tell to read, you see. But now I want to keep on emphasizing, you see, what is the churchism of the Apostolic people.

As Nyalongo preached, cold wind blew dust against our clothing. The women shivered, and children huddled closer to us. Ezekiel (Member 1), a Muluba, began to speak in tongues, apparently in response to Nyalongo's question about the baptism. The word "baptizwe" could be discerned amidst the muffled sounds of his shouting. Nyalongo continued to preach, barely pausing to acknowledge the interruption. A message that many could understand seemed more important to him than the private "tongues."

Ezekiel's "tongues" could also be interpreted as a challenge to redirect the ceremony. As Nyalongo continued to preach, he named the biblical verse that formed the core of his message. Luka Chisanga, asserting his strategic position as a manager of the ceremony, that is, someone able to "negotiate" the rights of speakers, started to name the chapter in a laconic fashion. He did this for the benefit of the congregation and with the intent of selecting a particular reader rather than beginning himself. Prepared for the eventuality that reading would begin immediately, Nyalongo extended his turn by interjecting "But wait." The congregation acknowledged his right to continue preaching and to signal the reading of the verse himself. He spoke of the baptism of Jesus and the symbols associated with it, emphasizing the importance of experiencing baptism, in contrast to learning about it from books. In conclusion, he stressed that baptism made a member humble rather than haughty.

Apostolic preachers often prolong their turns in order to inform readers of the verse to be read in advance, giving them time to find the passage and allowing for a smooth transition to reading. The second portion of Nyalongo's sermon was again pitched at the outsiders ("people who have had educated"), as was the long personal discussion of his own conversion that followed the kerek. Although similar to that of evangelists observed in other kereks, Luka's position as a manager in a multilingual situation was even more critical. His knowledge of English and several African languages gave him an essential tool for mediation. The kerek continued with a rich interplay of different languages as shown by the following transcribed excerpts. Out of a congregation of about sixty men and women, fully ten to fifteen members were interacting in at least five identifiable languages, some of which were intelligible only to a few of those participating.[14]

The negotiation of reading began as follows:

Nyalongo: . . . to ask for a thing you are re– requesting. *Runyararo kune Apostol.* [Chishona: Peace be with you, Apostles] (Response.) Book.
Member 2: All right.
Member 3: *Naro?* [Cannot translate]
Reader 1: *Tudi ne mukanda wa Mako*—[Tshiluba: We have the book of Mark]
Member 2: *Ah, baba. Umuka.* [Tshiluba: Father, get out]
Member 3: *Kunitefu*—[Cannot translate]
Member 4: *Nanku*—[inaudible] [Tshiluba: Like this]
Member 3: *Sema*—[Kiswahili: Speak]
Member 5: (Sings softly)

[14] Examining texts in an entire performance is quite different from analyzing a speech exchange between two persons. The occurrence of address, interruptions, and the initiation of speech have a definite shape for two-party activities that does not always remain once more persons become involved. Schegloff suggests that we may distinguish between those activities requiring a minimum number of participants and those which have a maximum number. Once four persons are involved, separate conversations within a larger conversation are more feasible. For the first point, see Schegloff 1968:1088, 1094.

Nyalongo signaled a reader as he finished by simply using the word "book." Luka (Member 2) did not regard this
statement as sufficient and again took the floor to negotiate
the selection of readers. His affirmation of "All right" suggested that a reader could begin. Ezekiel, whose earlier
outburst of tongues had interrupted Nyalongo's well-
paced English speech, began to read in Tshiluba. Although
he was quick, Luka lost no time in suggesting to him that
his reading was inappropriate and that he should wait for
a later slot. Once Ezekiel was told to "get out" of the reading, the entire exchange lost direction and momentum as
several members attempted to figure out what was needed.
One member even used the vacant slot to initiate a song,
but others did not respond. Exactly how and why the
decision was made that Ezekiel did not have the right to
begin reading is unclear. The decision may have been related to his status, both as an unconfirmed evangelist
and as a Kasaian whose place was not to "host" the kerek,
or to the subsequent decision to begin with a European
language. Luka used both English and Tshiluba in this exchange and was supported by a member speaking in
Kiswahili in an attempt to lead back into the sequence of
reading.

In an earlier discussion of methods in Chapter 1, the
segment following the song interruption was introduced.
It is crucial to the exchange, since it involved Luka in a side
discussion with a member who had just arrived. They discussed financial matters in Kiswahili, while a second
Kasaian reader, the baptist Eli, initiated Bible reading in
French. This interjection, like the earlier song, was abor-
tive. Only when Luka, in his capacity as manager, returned
to the central activities, could the ceremony go forward and
some resolution be achieved. Eli seems to have inadvert-
antly cited the verse inappropriately by starting to announce it as sixteen. The intense competition for the floor

made it impossible for him to continue without Luka's signal of approval.

Even after Luka had stopped talking, several side conversations wove in and out of the central discussion, while the Kasaian reader attempted to begin his passage in French and was again interrupted. Both he and the Tshiluba reader were now prepared to begin. Luka then chose a third Chibemba reader without discussion. No one was elected to read in Kiswahili, leaving only the matter of a possible reading in English. The choice of Jaya as the final reader, with the full approval of Luka and others, terminated this particular negotiated segment of the ceremony.

Member 2: *Alisema Jaya.* [Kiswahili: He said Jaya]
Member 12: *Jaya ne mubi.* [Tshiluba: Jaya has a sin]
Member 2: *To. Ya. Yaya Festo.* [Tshiluba: No. Go on. Jaya Festus]
Member 12: *Yah.*

The necessity for Luka to select a reader was clearly established by these interchanges. He had modified the standard expectation of reader selection by the preacher, thereby making the entire process of reading a prolonged and problematic ceremonial sequence. A Tshiluba speaker raised the question that Jaya, a Zambian, might be "in sin" and therefore unable to read. Once it was determined that he was not in sin, the full recitations began with the approval of Luka and of his Zambian friends.

Reader 2: *L'Evangile selon Saint Marc*—[French: The Gospel according to Saint Mark]
Member 11: *We, sombela.* [Chibemba or Tshiluba (aside to a child): You, sit down there] . . .
Reader 2: —*Chapitre sieze, versée quinze*—[French: Chapter sixteen, verse fifteen]
Member 14: *Uh huh.*
Member 12: *Yah.*

Reader 2: *L'entête* [i.e., *la lettre-en-tête*] *dit: Apparaissement aux onze. Quinze.* [French: The heading says: Appearance to the eleven. Fifteen]

In this exchange, two members approved of the chapter citation, helping to insure that reading might proceed without further pause. The exchange was followed by readings of the entire verse in French, Chibemba, Tshiluba, and English, after which the preacher continued his sermon. Possibly the English rendition appeared last because as a European language it was considered to duplicate the French. The important point is that Luka, as manager, was able to direct members into an order of readers representing the major languages of the congregation and spectators, including two (French and English) that were not ordinarily used in kerek. Only once this arrangement was successfully handled could the regular antiphonal pattern of speaking and reading that characterizes kerek be introduced.

When the performative components of ceremony are examined in detail, the variations peculiar to each situation emerge as important aspects of the event. Although these variations cannot serve to define a wide variety of rituals, they demonstrate the flexibility of the actual ceremony even where a single text or activity is already prescribed. In examining the choice of readers in this brief sequence, it is difficult to discover basic principles that members used consistently to guide the pacing and performance of ritual. But the ways in which segments were signaled and negotiated in this service emerged as a special process in comparison to ceremonies that I had already witnessed. The following conclusions are plausible, although all seem partial:

1. Readers were selected in the order that they stood or otherwise indicated their availability.

2. Readers were selected on the basis of the language most intelligible to guests or outsiders, to be followed first by a local language reader, and then by others.

3. Readers were selected on the basis of rank-order or seniority within the church.

4. Readers were selected according to other personal or ascriptive criteria.

5. Readers were selected purely on the basis of the occasional insertions and control of the managing evangelist.

While all these factors seemed important at some point, the process of management never could have taken place solely through the efforts of the managing evangelist. It involved the recognition and cooperation of all members. The flexibility of ceremony would seem to stem from members' abilities to introduce variations upon the commonly known, formal features of ritual that can be recognized and acted upon whenever they occur. Within the space of a few minutes, children "play kerek," reproducing its openers, hymns, and a condensed ritual format.

The management of events is only part of a ceremony's variations. Moral recommendations are intertwined with instructions about performance that members use to interpret the event itself. Apostles conceive of their work as did their founder John Maranke: "Go and preach to all people in all countries, teaching them not to commit adultery, they should not steal, not to covet and that they should not be easily angered (Maranke 1953:12). Members believe that these commandments cannot be followed by personal effort alone but only through help from the Holy Spirit. Nyalongo, like other evangelists, stressed that the Holy Spirit becomes accessible to members of the community only through baptism by triple immersion that sets them apart from others. The baptism is considered to be validated by miraculous events like those Nyalongo considered to be turning points of his life.

The baptism and the gifts of the Spirit are also considered to be a symbol or designation of membership. Nyalongo explains:

If you could see a person or any Christian taking his own foundation, not taking the dename—the designation of Jesus, we exactly, we know exactly that the chap is astray. . . .

But now I want to keep on emphasizing, you see, what is the churchism of the Apostolic people. Now as it was in such, you see, here to show some examples, the moment He left the River Jordan, that's when He went to Ainon where He baptized again to show *the symbol* [emphasis supplied.] [Kabanana, Zambia, 1971]

A similar belief in the symbolism of the Holy Spirit was presented in an earlier sermon in the Kasai.

The epistle verse goes on saying that the fifth angel went and preached to crowds where he chose multitudes of people that he set as symbols. This symbol is what we came here for. This symbol is the Holy Ghost. We got it. Do not join us because you are after wealth but because you want to get this symbol. [Demba Territory, 1969]

Nyalongo explained that following Paul's admonition to the Corinthians, all spiritual gifts must be made evident as religious work for the community. Yet the source of inspiration was in the Holy Spirit, the community's ultimate symbol, and in the particular symbols transmitted through dreams and inspirations. At a critical juncture, Nyalongo had nearly convinced me that the impact of these inspirations could be brought directly into daily life and even result in the resurrection of a child. Baptism would allow me to share in these gifts of healing and prophecy and to understand preaching and prayer differently. The gifts are spiritual options open to all members rather than sacraments to be performed on special occasions by a limited group. Since they emerge through and yet are distinct from the ritual occasions on which they are presented, one must examine the content of ritual along with its managed performance.

When Nyalongo discussed spiritual achievements such as firewalking, visions, and cures, he cited the state of purity of the participants or, in the case of failure, their state of sin. At the time, he was particularly perplexed by the illnesses of the two Zambian children whose cases were discussed earlier. He viewed these cases as blocked by a failure to confess and to assess the right relation of all the participants to God. Such assessments would have to be made on the basis of known practical facts (such as the week's activities of the patients) and on esoteric grounds by prophets able to assess a candidate's spiritual purity. This discernment is linked to prayer and to the spiritual state of the seer himself. Nyalongo did not cast his previous miracles into doubt, however, as a result of the problems then facing the Apostolic community. Instead, he stressed the ways in which baptism symbolically separated Apostles from outsiders and strengthened them.

Nyalongo's sermon had also reflected this symbolic division between Apostles and outsiders. Apostles were humble and unlettered; outsiders were rich, proud, and educated. Apostles worshiped to please God and to invoke the presence of the Holy Spirit. They watched their attitudes to avoid sin; outsiders walked in sin. Apostles as singers worshiped only God; outsiders "jived." Each of Nyalongo's definitions, each explanation transposing vision into a social reality, had moral implications for ways in which Apostles handled their contact with other members of the community so as to maintain spiritual and ritual distinctiveness. Nyalongo's sermon and discussion stressed that salvation through Christ is a major preoccupation of Apostles, particularly salvation in accordance with the visionary message that John Maranke brought to Central Africa. Through examining the performance of ritual, a basis for linking spiritual aims and states to ceremony as a form of collective communication can be established. These considerations are central to the content of worship and influence ways in which ritual themes are sustained in ceremony as a feature of broader social life. At the close of kerek, Nyalongo continued to discuss theological points with us until late in the evening. Tshiaba and Kadima remained with us, occasionally listening in, as they planned the impending journey to Malawi.

CHAPTER 4

Song and Spirit

Many thousands of angels were playing harps. They had also all sorts of musical instruments. There also sat in space some elders who played harps. They were sitting crosslegged and were singing a new song. I had not heard this song, and even today I cannot imitate it.

John Maranke

Before I joined the church, the songs that I heard in ceremony were aesthetically pleasing, but I was unable to conceive of them as intentional acts oriented toward spiritual ends. The words of the songs, apart from a ceremonial context, revealed little to me. If the words of a song suggested that it was intended for evangelism, I was unable to discern that it could also be used for spiritual invocation. Only through participation could I enter into the states that those songs evoked and simultaneously created. Through participation, I observed that songs are purposeful courses of action through which Apostles attempt to bring about a state of inner unity and peace. Yet the most forceful validations of my conclusions were based on my own acceptance of these states as possible and meaningful experiences.

The analysis of music introduced here will focus on song as a managed event in ceremony, particularly the Sabbath kerek, and on song as an intentional act that provides a thematic unity for kerek worship.[1] With the exception of standard Chishona hymns, these songs are drawn largely from the Kananga congregation and are sung in Tshiluba-Kasai. In addition to the hymns that are integral to a ritual's standard format, members are aware of the silences

---

[1] Bellman (1974:4–10) stresses in his discussion of Kpelle secret societies that the members' location of intended meanings is essential to the performance of ritual.

and slots that are appropriate for song initiation and improvisations in kerek. Occasions for song are not synonymous, however, with the ecstatic states reached in singing.

Singing as a Managed Activity

The absence of an announced format for most events in kerek distinguishes it from Western ceremonies. Although speakers are preannounced, the relationship between speaking and song is not determined before their performance. The successive ordering of singing, preaching, and Bible reading relies solely on judgments by members as to when to shift the focus of the ceremony from one set of activities to another. These judgments are crucial to the flow of the event, since, with few exceptions, most activities in kerek do not have a prescribed "end." An event is finished simply by the advent of a succeeding activity.

With the exception of the standard hymns, singing in kerek is viewed as a form of preaching for which special spiritual preparation is necessary. The standard songs, always led by a baptist, presuppose his ability to serve as a spiritual example for other singers. Unlike songs found in the midst of kerek, only the opening hymns, "Kwese, Kwese" (Everywhere, Everywhere), and "Mwari Komborera Africa" (God Save Africa), and the closing hymns, "Pa Ku Denga" (In Heaven) and "Ndo Famba" (Our Prayer is Ended), are sung at fixed points in the service. In contrast to the other songs, which are highly variable, these hymns have a single tune and text with a fixed verse structure that remains constant whenever sung, although they vary to some extent on a regional basis. Since they do not vary internally and do follow in a fixed order with relation to each other and to the service as a whole, these hymns structure the format of kerek and are boundaries for its segments of song and preaching.

The initiation of the "Kwese, Kwese" by a baptist begins the service as a spiritually protected occasion. It is part of

a series of spiritual invocations that precede the announce-
ment of speakers and preaching. At the close of the service,
a benediction by the final speaker cues participants to face
east and pray for personal redemption as a way of witnessing Christ's return. The congregation then stands to sing
the "Pa Ku Denga," also led by a baptist. This hymn,
spiritually interpreted as bidding the angels farewell, tells
of the joys of Heaven and parallels the "Kwese, Kwese" as
a spiritual boundary in the service. The "Pa Ku Denga"
initiates the concluding prophecies, testimonies, and announcements after which the "Ndo Famba" marks the
close of the preaching portion of kerek. The concluding
curing ceremony is characterized by its own songs that are
used differently from those found either in the opening or
in the progression of kerek.

The baptist leads the opening and closing hymns while
standing in the congregation, in contrast to song leaders
who conduct and move freely in the aisle. The baptist is
not necessarily specialized in singing and may even be a
"poor" singer in terms of setting the pitch for the congregation. The point is that the congregation follows his lead to
open the service. Unlike the songs and hymns sung while
seated, the "Mwari" is sung in a position of prayer (kneeling, facing east, arms extended, palms upward) and has
been referred to as prayer.[2] The congregation sings the "Pa
Ku Denga" standing and facing inward, and a benediction
immediately follows.

The hymns are sung slowly and have stanzas and re-
frains as in Western hymnody. The "Pa Ku Denga" is
taken from the Chishona Methodist hymnal, while the
"Mwari" is a revision of another Methodist hymn, "Ishe

[2] Murphree (1969:102) recounts that before the Lord's Prayer is said,
a prayer is recited congregationally with the members facing east. It is
almost certain that in this case he is referring to the "Mwari Komborera," which precedes preaching in each kerek, although his description
is ambiguous.

Komborera Africa," considered by many Rhodesians as the African national anthem. Before John Maranke changed the words to apply to Africa's spiritual plight, the "Mwari" was sung by Apostles as "God Save Israel." Members say that this song means that Africans will be spiritual leaders but certainly not the only people to be saved. Apart from its position in the format, the "Mwari" has a key spiritual meaning, since it is used to invoke the Holy Spirit to the place of prayer.

Only one other song has no change in its words or time of presentation. This is the "Alleluia" prelude sung before each sermon as a way of purifying the speaker. As each speaker is seated, the one to follow stands and sings the prelude, which the congregation meets with the sung response of "Amen." Apart from the opening and closing portions of kerek, the time when songs appear is not governed by overall considerations of unity for the ceremony, nor is there a prescribed number. Although chanting and continuous singing are more likely to take place later in the service, members do not expect a given song to occur at a specified time. On the 1969 field trip, I tended to regard spacing merely in terms of the temporal progression of the service. As a member, however, I came to consider the overall distribution of songs less important than the close pacing of parts in which the participants were immediately involved.

The first song to be sung during each sermon is introduced once the speaker has presented his initial topic and before the first verse is read. These songs are often initiated by the maharikros of each congregation, who have a large repertoire.[3] Succeeding songs begin just after the an-

[3] Murphree (1969:99n.) records *harikros* (pl. *maharikros)* as *Hakrios* and claims that it resembles the Greek word for "hilltop" or possibly "goddess of the citadel." Aquina (1967:206) transcribes the letters as "Ahkls" or "Harkos," conceivably exactly as they were written on the uniforms of members. Apostles stated that the term meant "high cross," or singers who had attained a high standing, and traced it only to the English language.

nouncement of verses, allowing the readers time to find the passage. The "coherence factor" that seems to be consistently recognized is that singing, whenever it takes place, follows speech without an appreciable gap in time. This factor does not determine what will be sung or the length of time allowed for singing. In this way, the ceremony is maintained as a continual flow of sound of which the components are negotiable.

The appropriate time to sing appears through the implicit claim made by members that it is right and proper to sing. These claims resemble the assertions of the right to speak made by readers in concert with the ritual manager in the Kabanana kerek. They may be negotiated or rejected, until a tacit agreement is established among coparticipants allowing song to begin. The congregation also uses song to redirect the ceremony by shifting activities and by intensifying those activities on a spiritual plane at a given point, implying that the speaker has either finished his discourse or has gone on long enough for the moment. This redirection into song may be interpreted as a spiritual act. While the maharikros are acknowledged to have a special gift of song, all members are capable of inspired singing and of participating in the spiritual states thereby created.

Song initiations are regarded as open claims that can be supported, accepted, contested, or enforced by other members in various ways. Depending on the circumstances, the members use the open-ended structure of ceremony as a mutual resource for its performance in whatever form it takes.[4] When singing begins, a faint opening verse can be heard from a member seated in the congregation. On most occasions, only a few voices join the first response. By the second chorus, others join in harmony. It may take several

---

[4] The description of alternate strategies in a time-bound situation and their consequences has been discussed in Pollner's (1970) analysis of courtroom interaction.

verses before the full congregation participates in the
chorus. If the song leader is a man, he sings the second
verse, then walks to the aisle, where he conducts with his
staff to raise an energetic response. If songs are initiated
by women, a similar pattern is followed, as first other
women and then both sexes participate. Regardless of who
initiates a tune, only its gradual acceptance qualifies the
moment as one for song.

Once the song has been accepted, it passes through several phases of intensification. The verses may begin
roughly, with members coming in on choruses at slightly
different times. Certain members will then distinguish
themselves as informal song leaders by singing louder and
slightly faster than others or through glossolalia and yodeling. In noting the transition from a song, "Sodom and
Gomorrah" (see Appendix A), to a chant, "Mambo Wa Ku
Denga," I was able to identify seven phases of intensification of which members appeared to be aware during the
course of singing.

1. The song is initiated.
2. The attack of the chorus becomes unified.
3. Song leaders place increasing emphasis on phrase accents and syncopation.
4. Song leaders, followed by the congregation, begin to
draw out verses, creating a dramatic tension that spurs the
congregation to louder and more fervent expression.
5. Glossolalia stirs singers to become more intensely absorbed in song.
6. Yodeling creates a similar effect, when it is interspersed with song.
7. A plateau is reached in singing by the gradual transition to chanting created by the repetition of verse and
musical phrases and increasing syncopation.

These features, which I noted on one occasion, occur
frequently in Apostolic music. While the dynamics of sing-

ing are socially organized, their effects upon members are those of deepening involvement in a subjective experience.[5] Members described the state of song as one of ineffable joy and compared it with Heaven. They viewed its production, however, as a negotiable social event initiated by a song leader to be followed by the congregation. Beginning a song is a voluntary act, since song leaders are ordinarily not assigned except in very large kereks, where their appointment by ritual managers ensures that several members will have a chance to sing. Even assigned song leaders choose the moment to begin singing, barring rare cases where the speaker calls for song. Ordinarily, no attempt is made by the speaker to regain control of the service, whether the singing was designated by him or not. The strength and volume of song result in part from the leader's efforts to rouse a strong response on the refrain. The initial transition from speaking to singing is smooth and immediate, once the song leader's claim is accepted. The main ceremonial activity is transferred to song as smoothly as it is from speakers to readers.

In cases where the transfer between the speaker and the reader breaks down, as it did in the Kabanana excerpt, the attempt to maintain rapid transitions and a continuous texture in the ceremony is especially evident. On different occasions, when for some reason the reader could not begin immediately, a silence of several seconds developed. These gaps were filled by others who volunteered songs that went on well past the time when arrangements for the next reading episode had been settled. In the earlier excerpt, when Luka prolonged a gap between speaking and reading, one member sang softly to himself, although no action was taken to lead the congregation in song.

[5] Cf. Ronald Shor's (1972:239–267) discussion of hypnosis both as a socially managed setting and one in which the subject loses his grip on a generalized reality orientation.

Plate 7. Preaching. Preaching in the Apostolic kerek is performed antiphonally and alternates with singing initiated by the congregation. (Kerek, Kananga, Zaire, 1972)

When there is no pause and a song is begun spontaneously in the midst of a sermon, the initiator finds it difficult to gain momentum for singing, although the speaker expects to cede to such interjection. To ensure that his song is acknowledged, the initiator may begin in the brief pause between one sentence and another so that the pause may be thought of as the end of a section of discourse. Interruptions also occur in the middle of a statement before the preacher reaches a stopping point. In either case, the song's survival depends upon the speaker's decision to accept it by stopping either to listen or to join in the singing. From the speaker's perspective, the song may be an unwanted interruption. From the singer's perspective, it may be intended to enliven or change the direction of discourse. In addition to this order of intentionality, the song has

Plate 8. Singing, men's side. Singing is considered part of the members' spiritual work. (Kerek, Kananga, Zaire, 1972)

spiritual themes that emerge through its content and performance.

The elegance of close timing that is continuously sought by members does not necessarily apply to beginning song. Its initiation may also simply override a speaker who continues preaching during the first verses. A speaker who wishes to enforce his control of the service and continue preaching demonstrates a similar sense of timing when he interrupts the singer. He may continue his sermon immediately after a verse and before the chorus or show by his actions during the verse that he intends to initiate preaching. In some cases, the fact that only a few members usually enter on the first chorus makes it easier for him to continue, since the majority of the congregation may be waiting to see whether the song will actually gain momentum. If the song is not contested, the second response generally brings in the whole congregation; if the speaker counters with further preaching, the members who are preparing to sing can adroitly keep silent without challenging the mainstage activity.

At times the initiator quickly recognizes that the preacher has no intention of stopping and brings the song to a halt. This act results in an overlap of preaching and singing. On other occasions the congregation responds strongly from the start, and the speaker's attempt to veto song may be ignored if he does not have the finesse or authority to counterinject speech at the right moment. Gifted singers are often more readily followed than others when they initiate well-known songs. In another strategy used to regain the floor, speakers resume the sermon after two or three song verses so that the song is not so much rejected as ended. Just as a hearty song can effectively terminate a sermon, ending a song is regularly a speaker's prerogative. On one such occasion, the speaker said, "We are happy to praise the Lord, but first let us read something." He thus allowed for a short song rather than none at all.

The management of song reflects its development as a "lived within" experience embedded in the subjective time of singers. Subjective or internal time flows with melody and with the phases of song's intensification. It relies upon rhythm (objective musical time) but is separate from it.[6] Songs are thus experienced individually and expressed as collective experiences in the objective time of the group's rhythm. Although it can be thought of separately, the actual rhythmic structure of songs in kerek is simultaneously lived within as it is produced by singers. A codified version of the complete song with a fixed number of verses or a

[6] For a further elaboration of the distinction between objective and subjective time, see Husserl 1964:22–27; Gurwitsch 1964:322–325.

single tune is not available at any point as it is in Western music. The music created is part of "the flux of experience in inner time" made possible by the direct communication and intensification of musical themes among participants. Through musical interaction, members are able to convey subtle harmonic patterns without a score. Furthermore, certain interjections, such as glossolalia and yodeling, express rising enthusiasm in the group and press members to sing more closely or move toward chanting. Changes in tone, tempo, and volume are also involved in this intensification.

The sharing of a flux of experience and the internal as opposed to the objective uses of musical time characterize not only Apostolic song but collective music-making in general. For example, in the context of composed Western music, Alfred Schutz writes:

This sharing of the other's flux of experience in inner time, this living through a vivid present in common, constitute what we called in our opening paragraphs the mutual tuning-in relationship, the experience of the "We" which is at the foundation of all musical communication. The peculiarity of the musical process of communication consists in the essentially polythetic character of the communicated content, that is to say, in the fact that both the flux of the musical events and the activities by which they are communicated, belong to the dimension of inner time. [1964b:173]

Schutz stresses that music is a form of social interaction based on the experience and development of a shared relationship. For Apostles, this relationship is implicit in membership and in the progression of ritual as well as in the song itself. Through chanting, Apostles communicate the internal progression of song and its accompanying spiritual states collectively. Apostles know what an entire song should sound like musically and what is needed to sing it as it should sound. Individual singers select appropriate times to sing based on their knowledge of the rhythmic structure of the entire piece. They find places within this structure and communicate them to others as ways to sing. In particular, gaps in the tune appear as opportunities to sing in counterrhythms.[7] The spiritual effect of this continuous singing is to ensure, as one member stated, that God hears each member's voice. Singing, he added, is a way of building up credit toward salvation and is noted in Heaven.

As a result of the implicit knowledge contained in Apostolic music, it is difficult for the outside listener to hear the parts and intent of the music. The maintenance of the rhythm depends on the auditory and eye-to-eye contact with which the performers cue each other as the congregation continues the rhythm established by the leader in song and in body motion. The song's complementary parts increase its rhythmic possibilities. Many variations are conventional and are expected from one song to another. But each selection always contains slight variations, giving the performance its unique rhythmic and spiritual character. For example, the same words and tune may be sung on two different occasions with different rhythmic variations (in 4/4 and 6/8 time or in simple and dotted rhythm). Even the most conventional variations, constituting what a Western listener would call "the tune" itself, appear in new forms through slight changes that affect the overall rhythmic pattern of the song as it passes through different verses. A few high, stressed notes may serve as the tune on one verse, while the next may use notes in a complicated pattern.

The tendency to fill out the tune with variations can lead to singing in which neither a leader nor a verse-chorus

[7] This practice is known in traditional Shona music as *Kubvumira* or *Kudzadisa* (answering, trusting, joining in singing) (Garfias n.d.).

structure can be distinguished. This blending usually marks the attainment of a state of spiritual fervor and is characterized by increased tempo. Each of the variations is a tune in itself, for which members devise new parts. Apostles do not learn these songs as single tunes but as sets of improvised parts that together create the whole song.

When Apostles sing alone, they sing melodies that can be fit into the harmonic texture of group singing rather than tunes that independently "summarize" the musical thought. They anticipate the addition of other parts. Often, when singing alone, men will change their voices to a higher pitch in imitation of women's voices. In large kereks, a polyphony results from harmonic interaction that creates the impression of the continuous sound alluded to above. The congregation develops the force of a song through its harmonic possibilities, singing some songs with one or two parts and others with eight or more. Although to one Western listener who was not able to distinguish these parts, the songs appeared to have no melody and no harmony, for the most part, the harmonies that emerge use a Western major scale.[8]

Singers and Leaders of Song

The initiation of sung events is also based upon the status of the singer. Song interjections are frequently carried out by women who lead selections while seated. Some, but not all, of these women are maharikros who rehearse their selections together prior to the ceremony. This is the only time that women control the flow of the ceremony. The frequency with which their injections are accepted consti-

[8] While many Apostolic hymns use simple major harmonies, others have more traditional features that vary regionally. For example, some Kasaian songs have pentatonic tunes while Zambian ones do not. Jones (1969:224–227) notes a similar feature in the respective local musical traditions.

tutes a "right to interrupt" that may be upheld over song
initiations by men. As maharikros, these women cannot
evangelize publicly but can use their song interjections as
a form of preaching. Interrupting an evangelist, Sara sang
of domestic problems and warned men not to beat their
wives. Maria sang original Chishona songs from Rhodesia,
competing with an evangelist who attempted to initiate
similar songs, correcting his wording and pronunciation.
Eva redirected the service in song, suggesting a change in
the topic of preaching from the social to the personal difficulties of baptism. The expectation that women will
check a poor speaker provides the impetus for each one to
keep discourse lively and interesting.

Sung sermons are expected and encouraged from
women. The speakers in turn comment upon the quality
of women's participation. Whether they are maharikros or
not, those women who are particularly strong in the gifts
of grace are treated with deference when they interrupt
and give moral instruction through song. Consideration
and encouragement are given to all singers, however, including children. As female-initiated songs draw to a close,
rather than allow them to finish abruptly, men may help
by adding verses.

The physical location of singers in kerek also influences
their musical performance. Women may have difficulty in
sustaining songs, for they must introduce verses from a
seated position that may be far from the sacred path. Small
groups sitting together initiate vocal lines and develop
song variations in common. A women's subgroup in the
Kananga congregation often rehearsed and sang in unison
in kerek as a single group of song leaders. New variations
in song spread from the small groups of singers to the
congregation as a whole, from women to men and back
again. Ordinarily, however, one hears distinctly only those
people sitting nearby. The emergence of choral parts is not

Plate 9. Women seated in kerek. Women and men sit apart, denoting holiness. (Kerek, Kananga, Zaire, 1972)

arbitrary. It takes place through the mutual adoption of choral themes by subgroups in kerek and by the duplication of individual voices from each part of the congregation. When I sang in kerek, I found that whatever note I chose to sing on was already occupied by other singers so that I was singing the same part with different members of the congregation as the variations shifted. As I became increasingly absorbed in the singing, I reflected less on following a single subgroup's variations and instead moved more freely among melodies, harmonies, and rhythms.

The status of song leaders is also established through ceremonial and interactional settings outside of kerek. The maharikros earn their titles through intensive singing in musankano. They are responsible for song leading in retreat and in conference settings where they sing for several

Plate 10. Singing, women's side. Women initiate many of the songs and use them as a form of preaching. (Kerek, Kananga, Zaire, 1972)

hours at a time. This singing is a background for intensive exorcism and curing ceremonies. Young members vie for selection as maharikros by testing their expertise in these sessions and use the occasions to meet other young people. Small circles are formed spontaneously at retreat during the free hours between kereks, so that music forms a continuous background to the entire conference setting. The groups of young people circulate night and day, singing for a while in each section of both the men's and women's sides of the encampment.

Although these song leaders hold a special place in kerek, the balance of activities between speaking and song is generally of greater concern than the achievements of a particular singer. Alternation between speaking and song is paralleled in other parts of the service by antiphonal exegesis in preaching and the responsive greetings between the speakers and the congregation. It is likely that this balance has some cultural grounding in patterns of speech and their sequencing in traditional usage.[9] Through alternation, each part of a ritual ensures participation in some form for all members and provides a means for shifting smoothly into the following activity. This alternation also gives the entire ceremony a rhythmic structure that is modified by the shifting relationships between its parts.

The leader-response format is used by Apostles in virtually all of their songs. Lomax characterizes this format in his description of the "African Gardener Style":

[It is] a style of overlapped antiphony which singles out a strong, dominant leader. In overlapped antiphony, we encounter a symbol of one of the universals of African life, the yea-saying, responsorial, and seldom silent village council of elders. In musical overlap, the chorus sings its part independently and responsorially during a portion of the song leader's section. Thus, there is a constant supportive and complementary vocal reaction to every new line the song leader produces.[10]

Even the opening and closing hymns, which do not make use of a responsorial method as such, rely on the leader-response format to initiate each verse and refrain. The leader gives out the first word, and the rest of the stanza serves as a response. The songs that follow the opening hymns are sung in overlapped antiphony rather than in a simple call-response pattern. Song leaders accompany the

[9] For our purposes, Sacks Jefferson and Schegloff's (1975:1–5) approach to turn-taking in the ordering of conversation and interaction as a whole can be profitably combined with Albert's description of status-ranking as basic to organizing African speech patterns, since both techniques are used in Apostolic preaching and song.

[10] See Lomax 1970:193. The practice of responsive singing is described in Chishona as *Kuteererana* (listening to each other) or *Kudaira* (answering) (Garfias n.d.).

congregation for part of the chorus, often overlapping the congregation's entrance to and exit from song. During the verses, the members sing or hum short rhythmic phrases supportively. Unlike the close but distinct pacing between preaching and song in which events follow each other immediately in their own rhythms, overlap emphasizes the common time structure in which both leader and chorus sing together. Chants for prayer and cure are not performed in overlapped antiphony but in unison after the leader begins each verse.

Tune and Text Variations

To sustain songs, members continually add new musical and textual materials. Once a song is begun, new verses may be introduced during the course of singing, and rhythmic variations take place from a commonly known base of possibilities. Another method for creating variations in rhythm and content in song is the direct use of the tonal features of speech. The long and short syllables and high and low tones of speech already have a musicality of their own that is preserved with little change in many tunes, and members use them freely as a base of improvisation.

Song: *Lekelayi machumba, luayi, tuyayi mudi Nzambi.*

Speech: *Lekelayi machumba, luayi, tuyayi mudi Nzambi.*
         [Stop wavering, come, let's go to God]

While songs draw on previously established verses and rehearsed ways of singing, new versions may always be used.[11] Personal style influences the approach to song texts,

[11] Zimmerman and Pollner's (1970:80–113) description of the occasioned corpus in which elements of a situation are assembled as the situation emerges could also be applied to the use of musical variations in song and the development of innovative text and tune combinations.

tunes, and their harmonies. The style of singing creates a basic pattern for phrasing, rhythm, and congregational response. The use of speech patterns in new texts, while a source of innovation and change, also indicates definite patterns for incorporating new verses into songs for the experienced singer. As a new member, I was often surprised to hear the same texts sung to different melodies.[12] This difference was particularly noticeable when I visited other congregations and made it difficult to follow "songs" that I had already learned, thinking that they could not possibly change. This appearance of familiar songs with new tunes was one of the striking features of the Kabanana kerek. Not only melody varied. Altered texts would often be inserted into what I assumed was the "original" or real song so that only some small refrain or fraction of the song, as I had so carefully learned it, remained. Ultimately, I could no longer assume that there was a "real" or original text or tune.

Textual Variations

Be aware that the ten races of earth will inherit Heaven
Be aware that the ten races of humanity will inherit Heaven
  (Sung together)

You who are asleep, get up, you will miss Heaven
You who are sleeping in alcohol, you will miss Heaven
  (Sung together)

The angels in Heaven sing Hosanna
The angels near to God sing Hosanna
The angels near to God in Jerusalem
Our resting place is near to God in Jerusalem
  (Not sung together)

[12] Kilson (1971) presents a large collection of ritual variations on the song texts used in West African divination.

Variations in Tunes

The example below may be compared with the one on the following page.

"I put my heart in God" [13]

L: Leader   C: Chorus

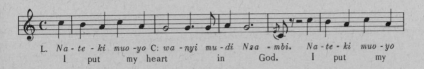

L. Na - te - ki muo -yo C: wa -nyi mu - di Nʒa - mbi.   Na - te - ki muo - yo
I   put   my heart   in   God.   I   put   my

wa - nyi mu - di Nʒa - mbi.   Na - te - ki muo -yo   wa - nyi.
heart   in   God.   I   put   my heart.

Several tunes have variable texts that do not follow in fixed sequence but may be sung at any point, once the tune is introduced. These free-floating verses make the elicitation of unified "songs" and song texts from members a difficult and incomplete process apart from performance. When asked whether they would write down the words of their songs in French or what the words of "Sodom and Gomorrah" were, members gave no answer or laughed at the questions. Finally they produced a three-page document that listed the verses of several songs sequentially,

[13] These transcriptions are idealizations that single out a dominant vocal line as the tune in the Western sense and do not describe the variations from verse to verse, although the relative time value and pitch are fairly represented. These idealizations illustrate the similarity between different songs. It is questionable whether members employ any such conception of a single dominant melody. Even when singing alone, they assume the contributions of other singers to complete the musical texture. Foss (1973:39–67) compares methods of transcription in Anglo-American folk music and proposes a more detailed form of transcription based on Béla Bartok's method. Such a fuller transcription of Apostolic singing would have to include at least four to six parts in most songs.

without reference to the tunes to which they belonged or how they should be sung. Instead of a set of verses belonging to the song "Sodom and Gomorrah," the list I received contained "typical" verses that might be sung in the future; actually they represented only one more combination among many, and the verses were never sung exactly as transcribed. On four occasions when I recorded and transcribed the "Sodom and Gomorrah" chorus, it was sung, in close variants of the same tune, but none of the verses were, to my knowledge, sung on more than one occasion.[14] This free textual variation, often based on biblical verses, while unique in this form to the Apostolic church, also resembles singing in other African churches that have developed their own musical styles and collections of new songs (Sundkler 1961:193–198, 282–285).

"Earth is Sodom and Gomorrah" (See Appendix A)

L: Leader   C: Chorus

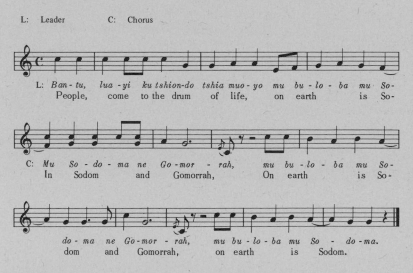

L: *Ban - tu,   lua - yi   ku tshion-do   tshia muo - yo   mu   bu - lo - ba   mu   So-*
  People,   come   to the drum   of   life,   on   earth   is   So-

C: *Mu   So - do - ma   ne   Go - mor   -   rah,   mu   bu - lo - ba   mu   So-*
  In   Sodom   and   Gomorrah,   On   earth   is   So-

do - ma   ne   Go-mor - rah,   mu   bu - lo - ba   mu   So   -   do - ma.
  dom   and   Gomorrah,   on   earth   is   Sodom.

[14] Further versions of this song and other Apostolic song texts have been recorded by Heimer (1970:456–457) and by Lanzas and Bernard (1966:215–216).

Apostles, however, unlike some other African churches, exclude dancing and musical instruments, which are considered worldly and to cause evil. Only the voice is held to be suitable for praising God. Although they do not dance, Apostles sway rhythmically as they sing and imitate drums and trumpets with their voices and hands (a technique called *ngoma*). The tape recorder, though called by the name for the traditional finger piano *(tshisanji)*, is not considered outside the rule and is used by members to record kerek and replay songs in separate sessions.

By now, it may be concluded that the treatments of text in songs and sermons are similar. The "lessons" given to members also come from direct participation in the song as a congregational effort. Like the content of preaching, the content of song is generally viewed as beyond refutation. A possible exception arises when individually composed songs appear with basic themes and tunes that are particular to a given congregation and contain its history. In this case, a song may be sung in praise of God or for storytelling purposes rather than as a form of preaching.

Apostles use songs to warn nonmembers of the danger to their souls. They look forward to the hope of Heaven and back to the sinfulness of the earth. Each song contains a characterization of the community of believers or of outsiders. The following excerpts show some of the perspectives through which membership appears. These messages are relevant as specific instructions to members about how to conduct their lives. They were not sung at one time, but were drawn from a number of different occasions.

"We" Verses

> Our joy is in the Spirit of God
> We are the light come from the Father

Our God has been announced to us by St. John in the
temple
We are pilgrims, we are pilgrims
We are not baptized from the cup
We are sons of Heaven

Other verses address the recipient of the word directly,
whether the person is a member or not. Calls to obey the
law and predictions about finding grace appear in "you"
references.

"You" Verses

You who wish to pray, pray from this moment on
You who are taught how to sing will inherit Heaven
You who are asleep, get up, you will miss Heaven
You who are staying because of drinking, you will miss
Heaven
God is good to worship so you go to Heaven
Please sing out all your sins
Your time has come
Watch after yourselves
Love each other like you like yourself
This Holy Spirit, if you don't have it, you don't enter into
God's Heaven
Beware, do not say that you did not know
Cigarette smoking and alcohol keep you from God.

While "we" represents the confidence of members in an
achieved salvation and refers to the collectivity of singers,
"you" expresses the plan of bringing moral instruction to
the outsiders who are as yet unsaved and to those members
of the church who need spiritual encouragement. From the
singer's perspective, all need the Word, for outsiders are
potential members, and members themselves may become
lost. "You" is thus a broad term addressing whoever can
hear himself as a recipient of the message. On the other
hand, "they" is used rhetorically to refer to all outsiders
who refuse to hear the Word and to Apostles who neglect

Christian teachings. Other verses present parables or point to the act of singing itself and the position of the saved as singers.

"They" Verses:

> We told them, Lord, they refused
> The people have eyes; they have no ears
> The people look but they do not see
> They refused Jesus, the Jews
> Light shone on those who believed
> Those who walk in light shall judge the world
> He loves those who keep His laws

Apostles as Singers

> Please sing out all your sins
> It is time to sing for our Lord
> It is time to sing for Jesus
> We sing and ask for grace
> Today's throne is to sing

The preceding verses instruct Apostles how to conduct singing. They describe singing as an act of devotion and an integral part of the holy life. They provide ways for developing shifting emphases on biblical topics. One prophet described the holy city as a place where the saved sing all the time, relieved of work and trouble. The identification of Apostles as the flock of God and kerek as part of the holy city is intensified in repeated chants such as "God in Heaven" that often terminate song verses. While each verse of a song has a rhetorical force that influences the topics and direction of preaching, the song chants allow participants to sing as the saints and members of the heavenly city. They no longer sing about adoration but instead strive to imitate angels' voices. The words of the songs drop away, leaving the music itself as a direct expression of relationship with God and the angels. After such intensity, the shift back to preaching is usually made vigorously, often with repeated greetings that prolong the enthusiasm of the congregational response.

Chanting and Spiritual States

Chants are special types of songs, reliant on subjective changes in members' perceptions of ritual contexts. While they may last for fifteen to twenty minutes in objective time, their import is in establishing a collective orientation to the words of the chant in order to achieve spiritual transcendence. It is simple to recognize and understand a trance-chant state while one is experiencing it, but difficult to transmit it in a convincing way outside of the sung medium itself.[15] Members assert that chanting as a powerful ritual vehicle is possible only after they have confessed their sins. The relationship between confession and song is commonly accepted by members and is their way of conceptualizing good singing (cf. Schutz 1964a:7–10). Therefore, to understand what members are doing when they sing, one must have a notion of the preparation for song that extends beyond its observed management.

As songs develop into chants they become highly repetitious, and the use of textual material decreases. Members either maintain the tune at a steady level or intensify it through glossolalia, rising pitch, and increasing syncopation. This intensification draws the member's entire body into the act of singing and has a compelling effect on the congregation. If the song flags, more vigorous members or the song leader will attempt to restore it by more energetic and closely timed singing. The spiritual quality of this singing brings the entire group into a state of collective fervor, reached through the mutual cuing to chant.

The work of restoration and encouragement plays a large part in the ability of members on retreat to sing for

[15] Cf. Tart 1972 for descriptions of various trance states.

hours at a time. The individual singer becomes completely absorbed in the act of singing. Once more vigorous singing is achieved, the chorus is transformed from a loose collection of voices, still heard individually, to a cohesive group of voices heard as a whole. Responses become increasingly coordinated through repetition, strong accents are more highly stressed, and the tune becomes tighter, without pauses or gaps. Often the parts become fixed as the chant settles into complete repetition. On other occasions new forms and variations arise spontaneously from the midst of the congregation and from the song leaders. Although this type of chanting is highly valued, it is not always produced in kerek. When members achieve this state, they explain that they have done so by virtue of their purity of heart in preparation for song. It is this chantlike character of songs that Murphree refers to as the hypnotic quality of Apostolic singing and that draws the congregation toward a spiritual order of reality (cf. Schutz 1964a:12).

While the state of ecstasy attained during song is characterized by the close participation of members, Apostles do not evaluate "good singing" in exclusively interactional terms. Not only the strength of the performance, but the very words and variations, are considered to be the work of the Holy Spirit. Although moral formulations in each song are addressed to a definite audience, members consider themselves primarily to be singing to God. They describe singing as "a sort of food we give to God." The power of this sacrifice to purify the singer when used properly is repeatedly stressed. New members are specifically instructed not to sing along with secular songs and popular music and must even confess if they do so. Singing along with dance hall or "bar" music is regarded as particularly sinful, involving a loss of spiritual energies.

For Apostles, singing is a form of spiritual witness and ushers the comfort of the Holy Spirit into all of those occasions where spiritual guidance is sought. Gestures such as waving the head or crying out "Amen! Jesu!" and other confessions of Christ mark the presence of the Holy Spirit and indicate subjective changes in the experiences of believers.

For me an outsider, the transition to chanting, though audible, had no special meaning. I merely heard it as a transition from one song leader to another or as a seemingly endless repetition. As a member, however, I learned that chants such as "God in Heaven" were intended to place members in a heavenly state and, indeed, in a heaven on earth. The chant created its own separate reality. It was not possible to create and enter this reality without being spiritually prepared for its restfulness. Members maintained church laws and avoided anger not only as a path to grace but also as an essential preparation for good singing. As an outsider, this seemed illogical to me. My participation as a member meant I had to master this preparation and comprehend a song's spiritual intent in order to listen to and produce it. Apostolic songs became intelligible for me as witnessed and lived-in performances through my own participation. Through membership and specifically through song-chants as intentional acts, spiritual realities were opened to me as ways of reflecting upon ritual and social interaction.

CHAPTER 5

Substance and Style

On laying a man's hands on the one baptized, the people were going to receive the gifts of the Holy Ghost. If I laid my hands upon anybody so that he could prophesy, it was done and likewise to those I wanted to be Evangelists. Some were given the power to heal the sick and to perform wonders.

John Maranke

Although the compelling quality of kerek for both members and outsiders may overshadow smaller scenes of worship, it is only one of the many ritual performances in which Apostles engage. A view of these other scenes is essential for understanding the importance of religion to the lives of members. Much of the practiced ease with which kerek is performed follows from the participation of families and other groups in these smaller events. Women develop and exercise their most direct leadership outside of the Sabbath ceremony. The spiritual interpretations of the social order presented outside of kerek make ritual and integral part of Apostolic life that continually reinforces the faith of members.[1]

When I returned to Zambia as a new member, I became acutely aware of the connections that other Apostles drew between social and ritual events. My behavior was evaluated in and with respect to ceremony. These evaluations influenced the type and extent of participation open to me. On a daily basis, I was engaged in a series of important events outside of kerek. I began to rely increasingly on my own participation to interpret each new setting.[2] I saw the

[1] This assumption basically follows Durkheim's (1965:59–61) definition of a church as a moral community bound together both by rituals and by all of the aspects of a life that members share.

[2] Pollner (1970:95–99) stresses that the interpretation of a setting relies

development and consequences of these scenes as personal and ritual events. As I rehearsed songs with other women, participated in and observed palavers (informal meetings), prophecies, and healing ceremonies and subjected myself to personal confessions, I mastered the vocabulary of Apostolic worship and learned about the direct relevance of daily events to all ceremonial performances. At the Malawi paschal ceremony, I had not even known that the "fire ordeal" was a form of confession. A few weeks later, the soul searching invoked by keti and confession had transformed the routines of daily life into spiritual elections and tests.

Both with respect to their performance and on a personal basis, the semiautonomous events of confession, curing, prophecy, instruction sessions, and palavers are linked to kerek. The Sabbath ceremony also provides the background and model for another category of ritual events: baptisms, funerals, and confirmations in high ecclesiastical office. On the other hand, confession and prophecy, which have an entirely different format from the rest of Sabbath worship, are specifically intended to prepare the candidate for participation in the rest of kerek, regardless of when they take place.

The Palaver

The palaver *(tshilumbu)* is not only a ceremonial event, it also indicates a special order of religious reality. "To have a palaver" indicates that an Apostle has a private discussion of doctrine, a particular religiously relevant dispute or a matter of common concern to take up with other members.

---

on the immediate work of recognizing and assembling its components. This process is continuous and cannot always be generalized from one setting to another. Instead, the particulars of each setting are organized in terms of their appearance rather than retrieved from a larger set of elements.

The palaver itself, like the kerek, may assume an extended form, in this case a meeting, with its own ceremonial organization. It may also consist of a single case to be adjudicated before elders or with peer members. Full palavers are scheduled regularly before each kerek and are sometimes convened after the service to evaluate sermons and songs and to discuss ongoing matters.[3] The palaver is a pivotal event, mediating between ceremony and daily life, for it is the arena in which secular and organizational matters are aired in conversation. Instruction sessions in which doctrine is applied to secular affairs qualify as a subset of palavers and the same rank order of speakers that appears in kerek is established and used. Thus, the palaver both influences and reflects the organization of preaching and the forms of interactional leadership that take place in other ceremonies. As in kerek, those with the greatest authority generally present the final arguments.[4]

While women do participate, both as onlookers and, in some cases, as decision makers, the palaver is far more central to the male Apostle's universe. The male leader presents the topics and determines the ordering of speakers and, from one perspective, it is largely through palavers that he gains an instrumental sense of membership. Before baptism, I was given the position of a "ritual male" as a visitor in palaver and was encouraged to introduce topics

[3] Although my presence with a tape recorder did influence the recording of songs and replay of tape recordings directly following the service, these palavers were not simply interview settings created by the researcher. In Zaire and Zambia they were often held as prolongations of after-church discussion and informal meetings of members to discuss the week's activities and the church service.

[4] The determination of speech order by status and other social consideration that may be external to the speech event itself is proposed by Albert (1964:35–54). She argues that class, sex, and age determine the sequential ordering of interruptions or of a speaker's opinion in indicating that another should follow him by question or remark.

in much the same way as young men present tales of their travels. Once I became a member, my presence was still welcomed as a silent onlooker, unless "women's palavers" were introduced, in which case my opinions were solicited. Although they took the form of a business meeting, all of the palavers that I attended started and ended with collective prayers, which presented an unresolved ceremonial problem, since separation of the sexes to the east and west is generally observed in prayer, while the seating arrangement in the meeting might be mixed.

The personnel is by no means constant. Subdivisions within the church such as baptists, prophets, healers, or the Committee of Twelve convened palavers relevant to their activities. These meetings mixed administrative business with instruction in specialized activities for those of each spiritual gift. In these cases, female healers and prophets rarely initiated their own palavers. The "healers' palaver" generally referred exclusively to men, while women were expected to meet in song and sewing groups. Spontaneous palavers also developed from an encounter of members without status specialization. These palavers could include women but only occasionally did. Unlike informal discussions, however, palavers are usually scheduled events with preselected participants and an established agenda.

Once the palaver is convened, new topics interact with knowledge of social organization in determining the order of speakers. Speakers who are regarded as knowledgeable are invited to present information first, regardless of their status in a hierarchy. They are generally questioned by the elders or the organizational leaders and respond in uninterrupted periods of talk. Curiously, the oratorical pattern of palaver speech is more linear and less tolerant of interruption and repetition than that of the sermon format used within kerek. It would seem that members have applied some elements of traditional speech patterns and criteria to the preselection of speakers in an Apostolic setting. Respect for elders, "rank," the length of discourse, and postures and gestures accompanying it are part of the criteria.

Although the influence of tacitly recognized forms of seniority is by no means uniform, its resemblance to the influence of prearranged rules determining the selection of speakers in more hierarchical societies (for example among the Barundi) is striking (Albert 1964:35–54). Shona Apostles continue to observe some of the elaborate greetings and speaking rules associated with traditional kingship in ordinary conversation and palavers.[5] Potential distinctions for participation on the basis of insignia of office (maka) and perceived status are disavowed as inherently hierarchical by members and are not always operative.[6]

Spiritual distinctions have a subtle influence in palaver. The Apostles believe that no member should overtly use authority to achieve a special status.[7] Active responsibility, not aggression, is rewarded. In addition to seniority and interactional leadership, members recognize two distinct divisions of office: grades or ranks (mianza) and gifts of the Spirit (bipedi). The spiritual gifts are designated in terms of works of healing, evangelism, prophecy, and baptism. Members do not recognize these gifts as hierarchically ordered and are embarrassed by the suggestion that they

[5] Martin (1971:114) reports the same practice in another Shona independent church. Vamatenga, the leader of the Mai Chaza church is treated as a direct representative of Mwari (God), as were traditional chiefs, and can only be addressed in indirect discourse through a speaker.

[6] Murphree (1969:96–97) found Apostolic leaders reluctant to classify themselves in terms of rank-ordering. This reluctance also appeared in my own interviews.

[7] Murphree (1969:97) states: "The Vapostori say as the Swazi do, 'No man should put himself forward,' and one is reminded by their practice of what the Kriges say concerning the Lovedu search for power: 'Such power is sought in normality, equanimity, and maturity.' "

Apostolic *maka* or insignia of office

AP   APE

Evangelist
Junior Grade   Senior Grade
APE: Apostolic Preacher Evangelist

MTN

Mutongi (Judge)
(Evangelist)

MR   MRP

(Healer)
Junior Grade   Senior Grade
MPR: Munganga Rapa Preacher
(Doctor Healer Preacher)

AM   AMS

Mabarani (Scribe)
Junior Grade   Senior Grade
(Evangelist)

LPZ

Lopasa (Passover Attendant)
(Baptist)

Prophet
Junior Grade   Senior Grade

HARIKROS

Harikros (High Cross)
Master Singer

Baptist
Junior Grade   Senior Grade

L-
Third

L-U
Second

LIEB-UMAH
First

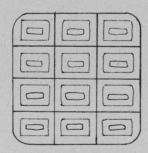

The Twelve Maka
Worn by John Maranke and his son Abel

Administrative Ranks
Lieb-Umah: Leader of the Community
or He Who Speaks With God

might be.[8] Members explained that ranking refers to the position of Lieb-Umah, which may be roughly rendered as priest or member of a congregation's Central Committee. This position is derived from a sacred word Lieb-Umah (pronounced rabba-umah) that John Maranke received in a prophetic revelation. I was told that the sense of this word is "he who speaks with God." There are other possible derivations and incidental meanings of the word, including rabbi or the Hebrew *rabba* and *ummah* (community). Its similarity to the Islamic term *ummat* (religious community) may indicate an Arabic influence.[9]

The Lieb-Umah rank bestowed by the church during the Passover is divided into three grades: full Lieb-Umah, L-U and L-. The members hold this rank in conjunction with a spiritual gift and constitute a Committee of Twelve for each local congregation. They do not attempt to form a special élite or demand deferential treatment, but exercise leadership without ostentation. In the absence of a Lieb-Umah within a local community, the baptist or persons with designated gifts may do the administrative work and guide the congregation as a whole. When a Lieb-Umah is called in for consultation on an individual case, his special spiritual and administrative abilities are respected. While the Lieb-Umah organizes many of the palavers and is a major participant in kerek, other ritual managers and administrative appointees may be delegated to carry out the ceremonies. Whether or not they have confirmed spiritual gifts, these managers become interactional leaders across

[8] Murphree (1969:174) argues, on the other hand, that bipedi are hierarchically ordered, viz., baptists, evangelists, prophets, and healers.

[9] Murphree (1969:99–100) and Heimer (1971:245) both note the interesting discrepancy between the accepted spelling and the pronunciation of Lieb-Umah. Both also note the possible Semitic origin of the words. While these speculations are interesting, they do not touch upon the position of the Lieb-Umah in the Apostolic organization.

ritual settings and are key figures in kerek and curings as well as palavers. As a result of their presence, an informal discussion may be elevated to a palaver. Thus, those most active in palaver and kerek are not necessarily officially recognized organizational leaders. This makes the observation of leadership in ceremony a complex problem.[10] Before baptism, I was able to recognize and interpret some of the cues involved in the organization of palavers and to tie them to members' assessments of social status. These assessments were not particularly relevant to me, since my participation in palaver was an exceptional event for members. The following excerpt from my early field notes marks the interplay of status and speaking format in palaver:

Formal speaking among members of the inner circle begins in a counter-clockwise direction from the head pastor. Guests may be called upon to make preliminary comments of both an introductory and a substantive nature. On this occasion, they are addressed by their titles and are usually asked direct questions about their personal welfare and impressions of the setting. For the first round, guests are given little time to answer such questions. A speaker is questioned where his strength is presumed to lie.

A question provides an opportunity for the guest to account for his presence at the meeting, but this is generally quite brief. A member already knows why he has been invited. The first cycle allows members to present their tales, problems, and plans in a preliminary way. Accounts given during this period may be condensed and presented to the baptist. [I was referring to translation here.] While the head pastor is the hub of the communications nexus, he does not attempt to monitor time, content, and responses to sequenced talk.   [Kananga, August 1969]

[10] See Jules-Rosette 1974a, where a distinction is made between charismatic powers of leadership and institutionally recognized powers of office as they are manifested in ceremonial and informal interactions.

I had been called upon by the head baptist to explain the marvels of American science. "Is it true," he asked, that a man can be sent to the moon? If so, is he not likely to meet God there?" Discussions followed by younger men about technological marvels that they had encountered in their travels. Only after these topics were summarized by the head baptist could an order of business be introduced.

In prekerek palavers, the order of speakers would parallel that to come in the ceremony with some selection and rehearsal of the major passages to be read. Preacher-reader coordination was important and was discussed in palavers. As evident in the Kabanana case, a delicate problem concerned whether or not the managing evangelist had the prerogative to intervene in the ordering of kerek and the readers' presentations. If the kerek was the domain of the baptist, who was considered responsible for its members, then infringement by the evangelist would be out of order. On the other hand, if the evangelist was charged with all matters of preaching, the organization and staging of ceremony were primarily his responsibility. Different conventions were involved, depending on the precedent that one regional congregation claimed to establish as opposed to another. In the West Kasai, the baptist Lieb-Umah was regarded as the major ceremonial leader able to delegate the responsibility of organizing kerek to junior members. Others argued that the original Rhodesian pattern favored an evangelist-centered kerek. Both views pointed to the importance of the speaking format as a guideline to ritual performance in kerek and palaver.

When public worship was no longer possible in the Kasai area, palaver assumed the status of a Sabbath ceremony. Its ceremonial aspects were stressed, while the outward appearance of informal discussion made the setting less conspicuous than a full kerek. Alternate singing and prayer following a masowe format were interspersed with other ritual activities, providing a ceremonial occasion in the absence of the Sabbath kerek. The following excerpt is taken from such a palaver held in a baptist's yard on the Sabbath. A "pre-Sabbath" discussion of church affairs was combined with drinking tea, performing confession, reading biblical passages, and giving prophecies. Singing and prayer also took place. The main features of kerek were retained in the informal setting of a male discussion group. Women observed at a distance. It is interesting to speculate whether or not the overt absence of ritual would result in the increasing ritualization of everyday behavior.

During the discussion, the advisability of performing various rituals was questioned, considering the interdiction that existed. Elders (members 3 and 4), mature members (1 and 2), and junior members (5, 6, and 7) were present. There was no representation from the Committee of Twelve. Most of the young men were part of a subgroup of friends that worked and sang together.

Member 1: *Baba, kudi bonso banji kutendelela mu desele*— [Father, everyone has to pray out in the "desert"]
Member 2: —*mu nzubu bantu.* [people in the house]
Member 1: Hmmm.
Member 3: *Ku Kalonji kuya kutendelela nkayende, we munemus nkayebe.* [At Kalonji's he should pray by himself, you here by yourself]
Member 1: Aahh.
Member 2:   —Ah.
Member 3: *Bantu, groupe(s).* [People, group[(s)]
    (Gestures, two "groups")
Member 4: *Muntu yonso meme to.* [Everyone but me]
Member 5: *Kabena*— [They're not]
Member 6: —*mu ku tshisuku.* [out in the bush]
Member 7:   —*nansha, apa.* [no, here]
Member 5:   —*nansha, apa.* [no, here]

Member 3: *Apa nutshiikila bua malu.* [Here you're perched up (worried) on account of the problems]
Ah tisiku— [Cannot translate; becomes inaudible]
Member 7:   *—Ba mukanda—* [read the book]
Member 5:   *—ahm—*
Member 3: *—londa mu nansha malu aa, kulongamela bena eklesia. Kadi usomba nunku wa kutendelela. Tauya apa tshintu tshikuabo, tshi—* [tell these things or not, to get the church people ready. But sit like this to pray. A meeting here is another thing, a—]
[Break in transcription]
Member 4: *Tulalakuayi utuangana luala, nansha butuku, tubikila kudi muvanger utentekwa tshianza pa– pa–* [inaudible] [Let's sleep there, you come for us, even at night, we'll call an evangelist to lay hands on– on–]
Member 5: *–bu– bu– bu– bu– butuku abu muela Kwes– muela Kwese Kwese, ne Mwari Komborera.* [Tonight he (can) sing Kwes– sing Kwese Kwese, and Mwari Komborera]
Member 7: (sings) Kwese, Kwese—
(Laughter)

Levity helped smooth the tensions of attempting to worship without overt ceremony. Two members (1 and 5) suggested praying out in the bush. In many stories told by Apostles, praying in the bush was reputed to be one of the ways in which members were able to continue worship, in spite of attempts to curtail it. Member 4, the baptist who hosted the gathering, and Member 3, and elder baptist, favored remaining at the house, both to stay in contact with other Apostles in the neighborhood and because meeting in the yard was not technically public worship and was therefore permissible.

Format, in this case, was readily adaptable to ceremonial needs. Kerek-like activities such as Sabbath Bible reading were begun in the midst of palaver. When the recorded conversation occurred, members (who fluctuated from eight to ten persons during the afternoon) had been singing for several minutes. They had invoked a ceremonial order of reality but were reluctant to introduce the "Kwese, Kwese," since in their eyes it would qualify the setting as a full-blown kerek. When the elder baptist sang "Kwese, Kwese" in a high voice, the other members listened silently. Later in the afternoon, the group prayed in the manner used for masowe and read one biblical passage. As neighbors sauntered by with casual glances, prophecy and confession took place in the yard. This intermediary ceremonial innovation might well have represented the retreat of a church from public view, only to re-emerge in another form.

Rhetoric and Reasoning in Instruction Sessions

Ceremonial events are held together through the forms of reasoning that members use to interpret their activities in various contexts. The keti and preaching are also activities in which members apply biblical practices and doctrine directly to their lives. All aspects of everyday life are subjected to spiritual and doctrinal scrutiny.[11] Viewing ritual from a single perspective is, thus, often misleading. Without an awareness of elements of doctrine that members may consider obvious, the observer's desire for consistency denies the quality of events as they are actually experienced.[12] The consistency that members achieve provides them with a way of using biblical texts as moral

[11] Bittner (1963:933) stresses that members of radical movements apply "overriding principles" of action to all realms of daily life. This form of reasoning involves making some aspect of doctrine or ideology applicable to every activity as an instruction or an interpretation of events.

[12] Cf. James' (1965:70) concern with "simplifying" concepts, which he claims may radically modify the character of sense experience. These distortions are often the result of the scientist's or philosopher's desire to impose theoretical consistency on events. James states (p. 70): "The exaggerated dignity and value that philosophers have claimed for their solutions is thus greatly reduced. The only full virtue that their theoretic conception need have is simplicity, and a simple conception is equivalent for the world only insofar as the world is simple."

instructions. These instructions are in turn the basis for
further doctrinal principles. A format resembling that of
the palaver is used in this biblical instruction.

My notes contain a discussion involving Kananga Apostles at Christmas time, 1971. An agronomist who was an
interested outsider in the local community questioned
members on why they did not celebrate Christmas. In
quick response, the prophet Tshilumbu directed him to
Luke 1:26, reading: "In the sixth month the angel Gabriel
was sent from God to a city of Galilee named Nazareth,
to a virgin betrothed to a man whose name was Joseph."
When asked in what month Christmas fell, the agronomist
replied in December. The prophet then asked how it was
possible to celebrate the birth of a child six months after
it was conceived. When confronted with the fact that the
Hebrew calendar was different from our own, the Apostle
simply replied that Christmas was a pagan holiday in-
vented by the Romans and that it was not prescribed in the
Bible. The issue was then presented the following Saturday
in kerek, using a quotation from a Catholic scholar to demonstrate the questionable character of the traditional
Christmas celebration. Murphree (1969:145–146) reports a
similar incident among the Rhodesian Apostles.

Instructions compare biblical descriptions with aspects
of an Apostle's everyday life, showing them as typical and
required features of a member's environment. What is
often called a fundamentalist interpretation of the Bible
simply refers to clarifying the reading of biblical passages
as instructions that contrast with other actual alternatives.
Apostolic arguments against Christmas are not merely a
form of textual interpretation but are based on ritual practices that follow what are perceived as consciously expressed biblical precedents. These precedents are not considered complete. It is implicit that the text is interpreted
with respect to specific features of the situation in which
it is presented (cf. Garfinkel 1963:191, 1967:3). Apostles refer

to biblical descriptions of Passover feasts, of Christ's Last Supper, and of the New Jerusalem as a way of substantiating their Passover celebration. Musankano is sometimes compared with the Old Testament Feast of Booths.

In Apostolic preaching, competing forms of interpretation are presented as sinful, foolish, or illogical.[13] Such statements characterize the difference between the views of the member versus the nonmember. Often Apostles characterize their own beliefs as others would, stating that they are fools for Christ or are regarded as foolish by persons who have rejected God. The following excerpt uses this sort of reasoning and is directed to nonmembers:

Bapostolo, life to you. (Response.) We thus look like fools because we aggregate in the countryside. Jesus Christ was a fool because he sat with his disciples in the country discussing the kingdom of Heaven. Apostlehood is a dear thing before God. Do not fool yourselves. [Demba, 1969]

The speaker has turned the outside view of events into a definition of the world as seen by members. At the same time, he is presenting moral instructions to Apostles to meet in open fields for kerek as a way of following Christ's example, implying that those who do not are not true Apostles. These characterizations of membership were expanded on a number of occasions to define Apostles in relation to each other and to the church. Thus, some members who wished to build schools were defined as schismatic, because they had forgotten the manner of worship

[13] Rhetorical treatments of topics are often similar to jokes. Douglas (1968:361–376) points out that the joke may present a set of social obligations or a ritual pattern normally viewed as obligatory or "inescapable" as though it were "escapable." Nonmembers' accounts of Apostolic doctrine may resemble this joking pattern. Apostles also use outsiders' characterizations of their practices rhetorically in preaching to a mixed audience, for example, "You may think that we are fools for sitting here [but] do not fool yourselves."

of the first Apostles. In a broader context, meeting to discuss the kingdom of Heaven is presented as appearing foolish to outsiders but dear before God.

Reader: We shall read in Luke 12:49. The subject is: the news of
Jesus separates people.
Speaker: Bapostolo, life to you. (Response.) The news of Jesus
separates people. We all know in the world today almost everyone claims to be a Christian. We do not see when they are
separated. We have seen so many times so many people, grown-
ups and children alike, get baptized. You know the ceremonies
that follow. Have you heard or seen the Jesus news separating
them? We have experienced so many shameful events during
the ceremonies, the ceremonies which are supposed to initiate
the newly baptized to a holy life. These shameful happenings,
such as insulting each other, drinking and fighting, show us
what kind of spirit these people have got. Now, let us see how
the separation between those who know Jesus and those who
do not comes about.   [Demba, 1969]

Here, baptism, whose purpose is to initiate people to a
holy life and separate them from their former habits, is
contrasted with the non-Christian behavior that sometimes
occurs during or with relation to the ceremony. I became
aware of this resistance to baptism only after witnessing
several ceremonies, including a case of what members
termed "demon possession," in which the candidate
shouted and fainted before calmly refusing the baptism. In
this passage, it is not clear whether the speaker is referring
to Apostolic as well as other Christian baptisms or merely
to the latter, thus making the message suitable for both
members and outsiders. In any case, members use both
outside reactions to doctrine and the personal conflicts of
new initiates to reinforce their uniqueness.

Rhetorical strategies are used to reinforce moral lessons.
One strategy is the use of multiple sources in support of
a biblical interpretation:

Speaker: Now that I have told you that we won't get rid of you, let me share this secret with you. Believe me, today is the real seventh day of the week. Listen and understand how Saturday is defined in the French dictionary.

Reader: Saturday: seventh day of the week.
         Sunday: first day of the week.

Speaker: What should we believe? Your interpretation or Larousse's? Now you see that we are right, when we tell you that Saturday is the seventh day. Be attentive and listen to this. Acts 16:13. Somebody asked me about this. You will see why we sit here on Saturday and pray. Did the Apostles change anything when they were alone?   [Kananga, 1969]

In this sequence, Saturday is first introduced as a holy day or Sabbath with support from a secular source. Then a biblical passage is introduced to describe the day of worship. Like the original Apostles who prayed outdoors on the Sabbath, members are considered to use this form of worship while waiting for inspiration from the Holy Spirit. Prophetic testimonies provide another kind of validation for moral action. Though not directly taken from the Bible, these prophecies may serve as ways of interpreting a sacred text and as direct recommendations for behavior. The following testimony is intended to instruct members in precautions to be taken in a time of trouble for Christians:

Prophet: This is what will happen in the years '70's. There will be incessant wars all over the world, white man's country as well as black. This war will even spread to the countries bordering the Congo. The serpent symbolized the refusal of God to send destruction to the Congo. He does not agree that Congolese blood should be spilt once more. But famine will take over beginning the years '70's. . . . Do not become helpless. This is according to the Spirit of God.

Outsiders approach the church with certain expectations and questions about its beliefs, often based on a limited knowledge of Apostolic behavior. Apostles assume that these interpretations of doctrine and its purposes differ widely from anything that they intend. In order to engage in a discussion with Apostles, the nonmember is urged provisionally to accept the Scriptures as a point of departure. Even when he does not accept their doctrine, members encourage him to see Scripture as a point either of proof or of refutation. Joseph and Peter, two young neighbors, sat on a fence in baptist Luka's yard. Passersby turned to watch the end of the Apostles' palaver and to listen to their instruction of the two boys. Both of the boys wore long hair and were dressed in the latest style. They argued that they could never become Apostles and still be modern. Luka stressed that the Bible supported simplicity in dress and shaving the head. Personal desires in fashion, he argued, could not justify ignoring the advice of the Bible. If they were to continue their argument with Luka, the boys would have to use biblical passages as a basis of discussion, for Luka treated purely personal arguments as illegitimate.

The Bible is used by members as a handbook or road map for the spiritual way but not as the way itself. The mandates of the Bible provide inescapable verdicts on conduct and its correction. Murphree (1969:145–146) has pointed out that it is difficult for an Apostle to deny a biblical verdict on the application of a text of his life without also challenging his status as a member in good faith. This applies particularly to specific advice given in keti and accusations of witchcraft. When rules are broken, a member is thought to reject a text or commandment, a position that often results in defining him as "standing aside" (Chishona: akamira). The member is, therefore, considered to be temporarily "lost" to the community of the saved. He may attend kerek, but not in uniform, and may be temporarily ostracized or ridiculed by members until he repents. For members, the only closure which discussion of a sacred text may have lies in its treatment as a "blueprint" for Apostolic life and doctrine.

As an observing participant and member, I found that interpreting and living according to biblical rules became a daily concern. Carlos Castaneda discusses a similar phenomenon in the description of his apprenticeship to a Yaqui shaman, in which he stresses the necessity for frugality, discipline, and extraordinary effort to live within the bounds of his training.[14] He suggests that every participant's action can be regarded as a conscious decision to define the nonordinary domain of spiritual life and that such decisions determine how experiences are to be interpreted. Part of this process of conversion is the conscious learning of a new framework of interpretation, a separate order of reality. There is no way to reduce this learning to an outsider's frame of reference or to facts that would be accepted outside of a religious interpretation as a ground for "truth." [15] Evangelists and prophets, in particular, attempt to present the alternatives open to members through spiritual discipline. These decisions are not merely aesthetic preferences. Once the order of reality is "accepted," action within it has consequences for one's membership status.

Keti and Confession

After a long period in the Zaire, we returned to Zambia on our way to the 1972 Rhodesian Passover celebration.

[14] Castaneda's (1968:206) descriptions point to the importance of personal participation for preserving the intent and structure of a specialized body of knowledge.

[15] Castaneda (1971:34–38) indicates that a *mitote* (meeting of peyote gatherers) may be treated in terms of a system of cuing whereby members jointly acknowledge parts of the event's dramatic structure. To persons deeply involved in the mitote, the occurrence of cuing was not relevant to their conclusions about the setting. Attempts to reduce spiritual experiences to other forms of explanation may be noted in the interpretation of Jewish dietary laws in terms of principles of hygiene (cf. Douglas 1966: esp. 44–50).

Some Zambian members thought that we had returned to America in the interim. Those who knew that we had not were interested in the effects of our instruction in the Zairian congregations. Had we been able to become "real Apostles?" Had our faith been tested? It appeared that our status as members would again have to be scrutinized before we journeyed to Rhodesia. A change in our spiritual gifts had been predicted by several prophets. There was also the need to review our abilities to teach the "word" in a foreign land. Each keti that we experienced during this interlude in Zambia was especially significant. During the early days of my membership, I had reported keti as a form of "quality control," in which each member was examined in dress and deportment to determine candidacy for kerek. On my return to Zambia, this "quality control" became an increasingly personal experience. Members used every possible occasion to perfect my instruction, test my membership and assess my potential. Keti was no longer merely a preface to kerek, it was a preparation of events to come and an evaluation of my readiness for them.[16]

Peter was warned that a "bad influence" could turn him away from the church, and I was told to watch my temper and impatience. Each keti contained advice about illness prevention and about the discovery of transgressions for confession. My anger and frustration at certain circumstances caused me to be turned away from the main kerek and sent to confession several times. Like keti, confession was multilingual, and I attempted to remember the experi-

[16] Fitzgerald (1970:11–12) concludes his paper on Ga Spirit Mediumship with a brief presentation of the functions of mediumship as a form of social control. The medium instructs the candidate about appropriate religious and social attitudes by giving advice about the future. Although the perspectives from which persons use this information are not examined, Fitzgerald's conclusions could be applied with insight to Apostolic prophecies.

ences cued to me by prophets and convey them in a mixture of English, French and Tshiluba. While the prophet merely expected a "yes" or "no" answer to questions, the evangelist heard entire disputes and more extended case histories. This distinguishes prophecy from traditional divination, in which many inquiries may be addressed both to and by the diviner about the phenomena revealed. In Zambia, confessions were heard publicly, and this made each individual's predicament even more fully part of the collective welfare of the kerek.

The following excerpt records a keti performed shortly before our journey to Rhodesia. Prior to this examination, we had been told to seek instruction in new spiritual gifts, in particular those of prophecy and baptism. These gifts would be essential for establishing a new congregation in America. According to one prophet, special instruction from several church elders would be required, but the short journey to receive this instruction would have to be carefully timed so as not to overlap with the Sabbath day. An overview of this keti and of its background in daily life will illustrate the application of ceremony to social contexts.

The keti took place at Kabanana, on a section of the farm that had previously been cultivated. The return to Kabanana marked an end to one phase of our journey. It was the return to the very place where our decisions to join had begun to crystallize. On this occasion, about thirty persons, Peter among them, were examined by four prophets. High ridges from the year's ploughing covered the examination area. These ridges had become overgrown with small sharp plants and elephant grass. The two "gates" were approximately ten feet apart. Members stood on the ploughed ridges rather than in the furrows, and as each member approached the prophets for examination, he stepped down the ridge into a small depression in the ground. The officiating prophets presented Peter with two important prophecies in rapid succession. As he approached them, both prophets began the keti at once, speaking forcefully in tongues.

Glossolalia

Prophet 1: *Ye! Yezori be Satana tamba Jehovah tenzi okla—*
Prophet 2: *Jehovah ladi Satana nasper—*
Prophet 1: *—nachigarita akronga chikanza atashuwate esha mapro America, chuye profitater kam. Kumba waprasik wa gowa tili chaka shivarkapla matikai.*   [Keti, Kabanana, July 1972]

In an energetic manner, the beginnings of prophecies establish the prophet's spiritual communication. For Peter, the moment was one of anticipation for which he had prepared over a long period by close self-examination. Against the prophet's prior recommendation, he had embarked the day before on a journey to another congregation. The prophet knew this. Peter felt uneasy about the prophet's possible evaluation of his behavior but recognized that he would have to accept the verdict. If the prophet found him at fault, he would have to confess publicly before the evangelists. If not, he could be seated in kerek. Prophecy served in this context not only as a personal revelation but also as a form of social control introducing organizational standards for evaluating a candidate's behavior.[17]

As forms of social control, prophecies were respected both in keti and after preaching. If the member denied the validity of a prophecy, he was informed that he would have to take the spiritual consequences of his refusal, should he be proven wrong. The prophecy was treated as its own

[17] Murphree (1969:107–108) describes prophetic social control. See also Firth's (1973:202–203) explanation of symbols as forms of social control.

justification. Its truth was generally not affected by the candidate's verbal denial. Peter recognized that candidates called to a full public confession had to justify their actions to the entire congregation and that a denial would constitute a test of the candidate's membership and the prophet's competence. The forcefulness of the prophet's prayer, which Peter felt as a physical sensation in his chest, convinced him that a message of extraordinary seriousness was about to be delivered.

Through the glossolalia, each prophet stressed that his communications came from God and were not of his own creation. Yet the prophet Emmanuel (Prophet 1), like others, used personal information, even if indirectly, to elicit further responses that referred to the candidate's past and his attitudes. The prophetic communications were distinguished from Emmanuel's knowledge of Peter's ill-advised journey of the previous day and comments that he made about it when he was not under spiritual influence.

Members emphasized that each prophecy must be dedicated to God or Christ. When Apostles made ordinary evaluative statements about members, they were always careful to preface them by qualifications such as "this is my opinion" or "this remark comes from me and not from God." By restricting themselves to esoteric interpretations in ceremony, Apostles tested the truth of prophecies. When a prophet did not receive a vision or special communication concerning a candidate, he immediately allowed him to pass through the gate. In this way, members were reassured that only messages coming from God were put into effect. The two prophets at Kabanana continued to present a spiritual reading for Peter.

Prophet Emmanuel: *Aah Jehovah tenzi ukrasuwa numa—Eh, je vois, j'ai appris la parole de l'Esprit de Dieu, camuc. L'Esprit de Dieu m'a dit, qu'il attache ses pieds, et ça n'est pas bon, partout, partout ici,*

partout là-bas, partout ici, partout là-bas. Vous entendez? Attachez
vos pieds et ne pas se promener, partout, partout, partout. Wup ! Jeso.
A cette raison vous pouvez avoir des difficultés, même si cette difficulté-
là est loin, qui venait vous attraper et vous ne voulez pas attacher vos
pieds.
[I see, I have heard the word of the Spirit of God, *camuc.* The
Spirit of God said to me, let him arrest his feet, and this is no
good, everywhere, everywhere here, everywhere there, everywhere here, everywhere there. Do you hear? Arrest your feet
and do not go about, everywhere, everywhere, everywhere.
Wup! Jesus. For this reason you could have difficulties, even
if that difficulty is far off, which came to trap you and you don't
want to arrest your feet.]

No matter when problems arise, no matter how far off
they are, they can be traced to a prophecy. Each prophetic
revelation was preceded by speaking in tongues, which
stressed its authenticity. Emmanuel preceded his revelation by these expressions: "Aah Jehovah tenzi—je vois; camuc—L'Esprit de Dieu; Wup! Jeso—à cette raison." The
expressions pointed to an order of reality that he attained
through spiritual communication and that could be shared
with the candidate through the prophecy itself. As the
communication continued, Peter's situation was treated in
increasing detail. His past and future actions were compared, and his life as an Apostle was characterized morally.
The comparison revealed ways in which the candidate's
behaviors were normal and acceptable.

Peter asked the prophet about the sense of his statements,
thinking that the prophecy applied literally to events then
taking place. But the prophet was careful to suggest that
the time frame on the events discussed was not fixed. As
a consequence, Peter told me that he then reinterpreted the
prophecy as applying to each of his attempts to move or
journey from one place to another for the next few months.
Emmanuel answered his immediate questions about the

range of events for which the reading was intended by further prayer and consultation.

Prophet Emmanuel: . . . *vous serez comme un enfant, un égaré qui n'a pas un conducteur.* [You will be like a child, a lost one who has no guide]

Peter: *Mais le prophète la semaine passée m'a dit de passer chez William à Nyangwena. Est-ce que Dieu défend ça maintenant aussi?* [But the prophet last week told me to visit William at Nyangwena. Does God forbid that now too?]

Prophet Emmanuel: *Eh, c'est la question? Que je, je sonde à l'– à l'Et– à l'Eternel?* [Eh, is that the question? That I, I pose to th– to the Et– to the Eternal?]

Replari plorbo vladi form bladi bensom ladi hosanna ditrobeit.

Peter: —ah.

Prophet Emmanuel: *Led, led ladava, prie. Jehovah, Jesu* [. . . pray. Jehovah, Jesus]

remerce, je vais là. Il est bon que vous partirez à Nyangwena. Alors, l'Esprit de Dieu me dit, lors que vous arrivez dans une village, restez à la– à la– à une même maison. Ce que l'Esprit me dit: que cherchait-lui? [thank, I'm going there. It is good that you should go to Nyangwena. Then, the Spirit of God tells me, when you arrive in a village, stay at the– at the– at the same house. What the Spirit tells me: what was he looking for?]

The candidate introduced the previous day's journey as the literal point of reference for the prophecy. The prophet had not introduced this material and did not address it directly. Nonetheless, Peter's immediate and future behaviors were considered crucial to his spiritual welfare. When Peter asked the prophet to qualify his answer, he rephrased this response as a request for further spiritual information: "Eh, c'est la question? Que je, je sonde à l– à l'Et– à l'Eternel?" At this point Peter signaled the prophet to proceed (Ah), but he had already begun to speak in tongues. He then gave an answer that reformulated the candidate's view of

his own actions, presenting the consequences of his conduct as a battle between God and Satan.

Prophet Emmanuel: . . . *Choisissez ce que vous? Vous voulez. En tant
que la vie, et la mort. Par l't– par l'Eternel.* [Choose what you? You
want. Insofar as life and death are concerned. By th't– by the
Eternal]

This statement of the choice between God and Satan, life
and death, terminated the first prophecy, and the second
prophet picked up the interchange:

Prophet Eli: *Oui.* [Yes]
Peter: Yeah.
Prophet Eli: *Empare, empare–m–ah. Premièrement je vois derrière vous.*
[. . . First I see behind you]
Prophet Emmanuel: Ep! Yes!
Peter: *Derrière moi*—[Behind me]
Prophet Eli: *Un homme qui vient pour vous attraper, pour qu– ps– et
pour vous faire tomber dans les puits. Mais donc, quand Dieu me dise
que, le voilà, je le dis toute ouverte, il ne faut pas prendre la parole
de gens.* [A man who comes to trap you, so the– ps– and to make
you fail. But then, when God tells me that, there he is, I tell
him right out, don't take people's word]
Peter: Aah.
Prophet Eli: *Il faut prendre seulement la? La parole de Dieu.* [You
must take only the? The word of God]

Peter was told by both prophets that he would ultimately
succeed, if he followed the word of God instead of the ways
of men. Their agreement seemed to be a validation of the
prophecy. The interesting interactions between the two
prophets were evidently spontaneous. The second prophet
attracted Peter's attention with "oui." Just as Eli began to
prophesy, Emmanuel had further revelations that corroborated his statements. Peter attempted to make sense
out of the emerging prophecy by comparing the new ad-

vice with Emmanuel's description. By virtue of comparison, a special consensus was established among all three
participants, thereby validating for them the relationship
of spiritual communication to everyday events.[18] The
prophecy closed by urging Peter to use his own judgment
and return to his perception of the word of God as an
ultimate validation.

In advising him to limit his travels, Peter felt that the
prophet corroborated past warnings. He could interpret
this particular ceremony as influencing a broad spectrum
of everyday events. It emerged, however, in the context of
past prophecies. The previous week, Peter had been advised by other prophets to visit the baptist William at
Nyangwena, about sixty miles from Lusaka. While attempting this trip, Peter, another evangelist, and I had a
number of mishaps that prevented us from reaching
Nyangwena. We were to meet the wife of baptist William
near the Lusaka market and accompany her to the farm.
There Peter was to receive new ritual instructions for the
gift of baptist that the prophets predicted would be confirmed in Rhodesia.

On Friday afternoon, the prophet Emmanuel and three
friends came from their nearby farm to visit Peter for the
Sabbath and were disappointed and a little insulted to find
that we were preparing to leave. We left for Nyangwena,
despite Emmanuel's request that we remain. The trip
started in an overloaded taxi with faulty brakes. In addition
to the group of four Apostles, there were three other passengers, and the driver stopped to pick up another as we
pulled away from the market place. Very shortly the
Lusaka road police stopped and impounded the taxi. During the resulting confusion, the baptist's wife quietly

---

[18] Castaneda (1968:249–250) discusses the importance and uses of a special consensus between himself and his teacher in establishing the reality
of nonordinary experience and its features.

Plate 11. Prophetic examination. Zambian Apostles stand in line to be examined by prophets before kerek. (Kerek, Lusaka, Zambia, 1971)

slipped out of the car and embarked on the Great East Road to avoid the police station. Her groceries were still in the taxi. We left the impounded taxi some seven miles from Lusaka and attempted to continue on foot with the groceries, until the police sent an envoy to tell us that the baptist's wife had also left a large can of diesel fuel in the taxi. We tried to walk with the fuel but could not. Night fell. No transportation was available to Nyangwena, and we finally managed to secure a ride back to town. When we returned, those who had remained remarked, with little sympathy, that we never should have left in the first place.

The next day, the prophet Emmanuel, knowing our problems, had already interpreted the adventure as a spiritual decision for the group. We had been too impatient to wait for the right time to depart. Peter felt that this

Plate 12. The prophets form a gate. They pray over each member in turn. (Kerek, Lusaka, Zambia, 1971)

information influenced the Sabbath prophetic examination that is excerpted above. Although the prophet never mentioned the incident directly and expressed some surprise when Peter did, the substance of the prophecy seemed to point to the aborted trip. Emmanuel insisted privately that the mishap had little bearing on the likelihood of another trip to Nyangwena. In fact, he later stated that he would take Peter when the time was right. Meanwhile, Emmanuel repeated informally that Peter had made a poor spiritual choice in deciding to leave his friends. In this case, the esoteric explanation had relied on knowledge of the candidate's experience, in addition to a spiritual and doctrinal interpretation of surrounding events. The events that Peter used to interpret the prophecies were part of the construction of a total context by the participants involved.

Each part of the ceremony represented a member's symbolic preparation for a spiritual life. In this way, Apostolic ritual is itself a form of "living theology" in which elements of doctrine and rhetorical reasoning are displayed.[19]

Thus it is through their performance that ritual forms emerge and through their substance or specific purpose that each becomes identified with the spiritual works of specialized performers. Each setting differs somewhat in its style of performance, and a specific style can result in the ceremonializing of a single setting, for example the palaver or the curing rituals, so that they can at any moment be expanded to major ritual events. A similar fluidity is inherent in specialties and statuses of members, making the relationship of ceremonial leadership to the daily activities of members a matter of performance as well. Through each ritual setting, members construct a religious world that is available in various ways to all.

[19] In describing the early Christian church at Antioch, Siman (1971:18) stresses the importance of liturgy as a reflection of the church's doctrine and message. He states that liturgy is a form of living theology.

PART THREE

A VISION OF CHANGE

CHAPTER 6

The Living Ritual

I was given the order to go all over the world preaching, and whoever repented was to be baptized and they were going to be saved. The converts were to be baptized, and as soon as they repented they could also carry a new name, the Apostles. The whole congregation was then called the Apostolic Church.

John Maranke

In my travels to various congregations, I was surprised at the similarities in Apostolic worship and doctrine. Apostles created changes in traditional customs both through unique visionary experiences and through modifications in ritual. While some of their practices move away from customary ritual, it is difficult to view Apostolic liturgy as a general decline of or a reaction to the proliferation of ceremony.[1] Nor is it a simple matter to locate an Apostolic cosmology and a pattern of beliefs as consistent reinterpretations of the local traditional religions. Instead, the vision of change that Apostles propose applies general standards of action to concrete situations. Universal symbolic forms are used within the context of highly specific ritual performances.

Types of Orientations to Custom

The Apostles' reliance on this conscious reformulation of concepts is a source of their appeal to members and is critical to the recruitment of new converts.[2] The combined imagery of the old and the new, the concrete and the uni-

[1] Weber (1958:71ff) asserts that the basic Protestant beliefs in work and salvation gradually lose their religious connections and are replaced by a secular discipline. Cf. also Douglas 1970:3–8.

[2] Wilson (1970:2f) stresses the importance of recruitment in sects as a "deliberate and conscious" process.

versal, provides new points of access to social relationships and the spiritual world. Membership involves learning a set of instructions and rules relative to traditional customs. This learning is not peculiar to the Apostles. Those groups characterized as nativistic and those labeled as acculturative also present alternative reactions to custom. As examples of "nativistic" groups, we have the Lukusu among the Bashilele and the Eglise des Ancêtres, an urban church in the Kasai that perpetuates traditional practices of ancestor worship (Lanternari 1958:5). These groups maintain traditional ways of seeing the world while external conditions have altered other aspects of their social lives.

In such formulations, new institutions are interpreted by anthropologists as a return to and revitalization of custom or social life as it has always been. This approach to revitalistic and cult movements has been widely employed.[3] Nativism proposes a disjuncture between religious symbols and the quality of a member's life. It has been stated:

Sacred symbols function to synthesize a people's ethos—the tone, character and quality of their life, its moral and aesthetic style and mood—and their world view—the picture they have of the way things in sheer actuality are, their most comprehensive ideas of order.   [Geertz 1965:205]

According to this principle, a nativistic movement: (a) attempts to preserve a unified ethos and quality of life despite changing external conditions, and (b) defines its adherents as slighted with respect to traditional beliefs and practices. These movements represent only one form of cultural adaptation and are generally contrasted with ac-

[3] The assumptions underlying these studies are presented in a number of anthropological works including Linton 1953:230–240; Wallace 1957: 23–27; 1966:157–166. Wallace's (1957) argument suggests that the breakdown of previously adequate cognitive systems (i.e., of traditional thought) contributes to the innovative potential of nativistic and syncretistic movements offering new forms of thought.

culturative groups that strive to abandon custom and adopt Western or completely altered themes and goals (Fernandez 1964:531–549). The distinction between nativistic and acculturative groups is upheld not so much in terms of the amount of ritual in these groups as of its avowed orientations. Since it is possible for a group to redefine one set of symbols—for example, those related to familial morality —in an acculturative way while clinging to other traditional religious or political symbols, the distinction among types is often muted.[4] In addition, a given religious movement may go through several phases, moving from a more nativistic to a completely innovative variation.

I have spoken of the vocabulary acquired through Apostolic membership with regard to the conversion experience. It also includes ways of translating and dealing with traditional practices that are neither fully nativistic nor acculturative. Rather than isolating traditional elements as disembodied categories, I prefer to examine classifications of the natural and social world in Apostolic practice, pointing to parallels as they arise, for, in fact, during field research most of my contact with traditional practices was seen in Apostolic terms. How much influence the symbolism and ideals of independency in general and the Apostolic group in particular have on a society at large is difficult to ascertain. The Apostles do, however, present one combination of old and new thought forms and approaches to secular life that presumably is capable of spreading to social groups not explicitly involved with the church. Although it can be documented only in a piecemeal fashion,

[4] De Craemer et al. (1963:156–158) indicate that the Jamaa movement developed redefinitions of traditional religious and cultural concerns but never became overtly concerned with political symbolism. The Jamaa or Family movement is an indigenous grouping within the Zairian Catholic church and has spread chiefly in the Shaba and Kasai provinces.

even from the point of view of practitioners, it is this process of cultural combination and borrowing that is of interest here.[5]

A Man's Church

The appeal of independent churches, including the Maranke Apostles, has been described by several observers in
terms of the range of alternative life styles that they offer
(Murphree 1971:178; Oosthuizen 1968:178–180). In particular,
the freedom to maintain polygamy has been used to explain
the appeal of the Apostles and similar churches to large
numbers of men dissatisfied with mission Christianity. Isolating polygamy in this manner is an example of the causal
use of aspects of traditional culture to predict the content
and direction of change. For example, Barrett cites several
"causal" factors found across cultures: tribal size, the resil-
iency of traditional religious, familial, and political systems
maintained under colonial governments, and the history of
mission religion (Barrett 1968:101–108). Like the assertion
that the Apostles form a man's church (Murphree 1969:
97–98), these factors tend to divert attention from the com-
plexity of ceremonial relations in the groups studied and
the importance of these interactions in the daily lives of
members. The causal factor freezes the view of traditional
culture and its diversity and assumes that the member-valid
reasons may either be reduced to a set of primary variables
or ignored.

The process of symbolic combination that takes place in
Apostolic reasoning and ritual is far more complex. While
men and women perform separately, as in many traditional
ceremonies, their participation is based on an element of

---

[5] Cf. Schutz' (1964a:14–15) notion of the social distribution of knowledge in terms of the extent, uses, and sources of access to the categories
of common-sense understandings of a group or society.

equality of status, their equality before God and the notion of salvation. The kerek has been compared with Shona patterns of ancestor worship (Daneel 1971:333). Certainly, a spiritual invocation does take place whether or not members recognize an explicit parallel. The difficulty arises when an attempt is made to pinpoint exactly what is similar between traditional and Apostolic rites and what is different. The reactions of members are ambivalent, and they will claim little noticeable similarity among the performances. Yet they will just as readily state that new rituals substitute for or surpass the old and that new customs uphold the spirit of the old. The claims relative to tradition are specific to the social and ritual contexts to which they are applied. It is not sufficient to say that Apostolic ceremonies represent an expressive combination with Western thought forms (that is, Christianity) rather than one with a more direct and instrumental effect on present conditions. Seen from one perspective, perhaps the ceremonies propose little change from traditional thought about the cosmos and ritual action. From another perspective, the very expressive acts of song and sermon may be seen as introducing new themes, such as the Christian doctrine of salvation and the altered ceremonial and social ways of achieving it that extend throughout a member's life.[6]

A category is not simply a fixed way of conceiving of the world but also a way of expressing an individual's or a group's changing relationship to it. The new categories are basic to the process of cultural adaptation through redefining religious practice, community, social relationships, marriage, and treatment of the body. Even more impor-

---

[6] Peacock (1968:239–246) describes Javanese ludruk theatre as a folk drama form that instructs participants in modern values, not through active ceremonial participation but through the empathy that ludruk viewers experience for the performance and the dramatic life stories portrayed.

tant, independency is based on applications of Christian doctrine to local cultural practices. Leo Kuper (1962:20) summarizes the Zulu chief Albert Luthuli's statement on the effects of conversion on his group:

Conversion meant an entirely new outlook, a new set of beliefs—the creation, almost, of a new kind of people. They were still Zulus to the backbone—that remained unchanged except for a few irrelevant externals. But they were Christian Zulus and not heathen Zulus, and conversion affected their lives to the core.

Somehow, the converts have used Christianity to alter subtly their way of life and recast it spiritually. In studying the Apostolic church, there are indications that Christianity has offered members a special form of discipline to deal with mundane social practices and the nonmundane world of traditional spirit cosmologies. For Apostles, traditional religion is referred to in a selective manner to define an illness or a familiar situation. Yet, these situations are handled in terms of the doctrine and mandates of a Christian belief.

The Apostles' Ambivalence to Tradition

Members accept that the most basic doctrine and rituals in the church originated with John Maranke and are therefore somewhat rooted in Shona tradition. With an echo of his own shock, a member once described to me a group of Warega Apostles who allowed women to wear the mutambo (man's skirt), carry the long staffs reserved for men, and mix with men freely during musankano. This was not the Shona way accepted in the rest of the church and marked definite limits for ritual innovation. Cultural diffusion did not give license to mix the sacred and profane as implied by ignoring the distinctness of the sexes maintained in both traditional Shona and Apostolic worship. While Apostles reject the use of a traditional spirit cosmology as a way of defining ceremonial and everyday occasions, they do not deny the existence of ancestral and alien spirits and their potential influence, particularly on the wayward convert. The Shona spirit cosmology is hierarchical, with no single word for "spirit" but at least three major forms of spirit entities that directly interact with persons in a waking state: the *vadzimu* (clan or family spirits), the *mashave* (alien spirits), often conceived of by both traditional religionists and Apostles as among the major causes of illness and possession, and the *varoyi* (evil spirits), associated with the harmful practices of hereditary witchcraft.[7] Apostles recognize that possession by these spirits is possible but equate it with the works of demons as depicted in the Bible. Through Christ and the Holy Spirit, Apostolic healers and prophets are considered capable of recognizing and casting out these demons. Thus they return to an animistic cosmos, not with skepticism but with the goals of allaying its effects.

Like the Shona, the Kasai tribes have no single term to designate spirits, although they too have a single high God (Mwari among the Shona; *Nzambi, Mvidye Mukulu Maweja Nangila* or *Kabezya Mpungu* among the Kasai tribes) (Van Caeneghem 1956:41–42 ff). The traditional Shona spiritual hierarchy was portrayed by Apostles as more complex than that of the Bena Lulua. While village, clan, and family spirits can be specified in Lulua tradition, members lumped them all together as *bakishi* (ancestral spirits). In Apostolic practice, all of these spirits were referred to as demons, which certain types of church prophets *(baprophet mapipi)* are particularly adept at discovering. There are more difficult demons and less troublesome ones, recognized through the illnesses and complications that they produce.

[7] For comparative perspectives on Shona religion and a sketch of the Mwari cult in Rhodesia, see Gelfand 1967; Daneel 1970.

The following case of exorcism is extracted from John Maranke's description of the early days of the church and illustrates the combination of traditional and Christian categories:

We went to a certain village and came to a stream where there was a synagogue of the Seventh Day Adventists. We preached there, and the Lord Jesus performed many miracles. The demons were casted, the sick healed, and 77 members of that synagogue were converted. We baptized them including their minister.

That Saturday, we held our Sabbath service in this synagogue. The following day a girl of that synagogue who had a Chikwambo demon came, and many people wondered when the evil spirit was cast out of her. The name of the girl was Chikware. The Holy Spirit took over the place of the demon, and the Voice told me that I was going to see more and greater miracles than that. [1953:25–26).

The traditional Chikwambo spirit became a demon causing recognizable symptoms of illness. Although the illness is not deemed to result from physiological causes, the term demon has connotations within a Christian system of thought. Faith healing through the Holy Spirit supplants traditional divination. In this case, the "syncretism" is not random but results from a partial and calculated suspension of traditional definitions of spiritual and social reality. When I asked Tshiaba about the spirits that Apostles invoke, he had replied that they were all angels. Michael leads the forces of good against the forces of Satan. Melchisedek heals, and his healing power was directly transmitted to John Maranke and his brothers. Gabriel watches over the Apostles. Thus, for many of the spirits in the traditional hierarchy, Tshiaba indicated that there was a corresponding angel. The "Kwese, Kwese" ushers an army of angels into the place of prayer. Apostles rarely speak openly, however, of the different angels and their skills.

Apostles consider the use of alien spirits to inflict illness and misfortune as witchcraft *(varoyi wedzima)*. This is considered a sin, punished, depending on circumstances, by temporary suspension from the group. Witchcraft must be proven through prophecy and tried in an open court. Like witchcraft, the use of traditional medicines and divination is sinful. Murphree records the case of an Apostolic leader who temporarily left the congregation to seek a diviner's assistance. During this period, he was presumably not subject to Apostolic law but confessed, once he returned.

Since 1895 a Rhodesian regulation, subsequently converted into the Witchcraft Ordinance of 1899, has officially prohibited the use or accusation of witchcraft (Gelfand 1967:4). Similar ordinances were passed by the colonial governments of British Central and East Africa to diminish local disturbances and curtail traditional religious practices. Despite the ordinance, Apostolic accusations of witchcraft have continued independently, largely without government intervention (Murphree 1969:56, 106). Members claim that the government's lack of interference is due to the recognition that they are indeed the "people of God." Murphree, however, suggests that the government is reluctant to intervene in the internal affairs of a religious movement as long as outsiders are not involved. In terms of cultural adaptation, members uncover and morally evaluate witchcraft independently of either traditional or administrative legal systems but in awareness of both.

To some, the Apostolic approach may appear inadequate. Heimer states:

The Bapostolo, like the Zionists mentioned in Sundkler, have been reluctant to deal with difficult situations in direct ways. Instead of readjustment to face the new situation, the frustrations result in visionary and supernatural experiences in which a strong emotional tone develops. . . . It is thus that the Bapostolo, in a kind of passive resignation, receive other compensations in the form of ritual, song, dress, and visions without relating themselves to the outside world.   [1971:357]

Heimer's statement does not account for the social life of members, but does point to the importance that visionary experience has for them. Nyalongo indicated this when he explained that though initially reluctant to shave his head and abandon a tie, the tremendous healing powers that he had received validated these ritual constraints. A prophet expressed a similar orientation, stating that the commandments are complied with not through personal effort but through the Holy Spirit. Members evaluate the use and proliferation of ritual and law with regard to its spiritual benefits. Ritual is regarded as an instrumental means toward the attainment of spiritual goals rather than as empty ceremony.[8] It is pragmatic. Without keti, for example, as a ritual preparation, songs and preaching in kerek would not be possible. The rhetorical reasoning used in ceremony is also considered pragmatic. It points to the member-recognized causes of illness and misfortune that are resolved through ritual.

Ritual performances are the training grounds for forms of thought and expression that may be translated directly from religious experience to daily life. They provide the interface between old and new thought forms. In many cases, social and ritual action are complementary. Ritual provides satisfying personal and public alternatives for interpreting events and resolving conflicts of interpretation.[9] While a member can fail to comprehend esoteric reasoning,

[8] Cf. Needleman's (1972:16–17) discussion of non-Western religions and their pragmatic elements.

[9] Leach (1967:102) stresses the importance of recognizing how the public and private aspects of ritual symbols complement each other and provide special personal meaning for collectively observed ritual and ceremonial acts.

he cannot fault the legitimacy of the reasoning process sustained by the group's doctrine. Using esoteric reasoning in secular situations is not just a matter of applying rules to events. In many cases, there is no rule other than a member's own assertion of visionary guidance.

For personal decisions, members may even claim that visionary discernment is necessary to determine the right alternative. From the decision to eat a meal with friends or strangers to the images and aims of childrearing, Apostles apply esoteric interpretations to a broad range of events. The spiritual inspiration that they await is distinct from other Christian and traditional moralities. Whether or not to comply with external medical regulations, how and when to participate in political affairs, where and how to live in an urban environment are all examples of practical questions for which Apostles consult God. In this sense, members describe every motivation to action as understandable, insofar as it has a spiritual source. Membership and the learning that it involves instruct Apostles in making inferences from doctrine to action and in developing accounts of their motivations as products of inspired doctrine.[10]

Polygamy, Monogamy, and Restraint

At the Rhodesian Passover, the young daughter of a head evangelist was assigned to serve Peter his meals. She dutifully brought them to the men's encampment but was embarrassed. Her acts, she informed me with some trepidation, could be interpreted as preliminary to betrothal. Apostles encourage voluntary polygamy and, therefore, in-

[10] Blum and McHugh (1971:98–109) emphasize that a motive can be treated as a member's practical account of conduct. A motive is thus an interpretation based on ways of assigning sense to observed behaviors. Motives or motive accounts are based on common-sense knowledge and ways of reasoning or making imputations about persons or events.

corporate some aspects of traditional marriage customs with their own. The term "tradition," however, is enormously ambiguous, even with reference to the cultures associated with the church. Depending on the group, the principle of exogamy within clans is combined with village and tribal patterns of intergroup marriage. Among the Bena Lula, members of a single *diku* ("family of the hearth," containing children, mother, father, grandparents, parental siblings, and, often, "cousins") and of a *tshiota* (clan of about nine men and their blood relatives within a patrilineage) cannot intermarry.[11] Preferential marriage takes place among clans in the same *ditunga*, or village. A dowry is required. An Apostle stated that the dowry, paid to the bride's parents in compensation for the loss of her services, is lower among the people of the Kasai than among the Shona and is very low among matrilineal groups such as the Bemba of Zambia. Among the Shona tribes, certain degrees of relationship between patrilineages exclude marriage, either because they are too close and are considered incestuous, or because they cause status contradictions in the treatment of the spouses by members of the lineage. Among lineages that have no previous relations by marriage, choice of spouse is much less restricted (Holleman 1969:30–59).

Tshiaba Daniel, who had visited Rhodesia several times, expressed personal dismay at the lack of continuity between Zairian and Rhodesian rules of marriage and other principles within the church. With the assistance of Zivuku Gibson, a Rhodesian evangelist on *matimana* (a teaching journey), Tshiaba attempted to codify a set of Apostolic

[11] Heimer (1971:88) and Vansina (1965:165–167) provide brief descriptions of Luba family and clan structure. Analyses of family and clan among the Luba Kasai and the Luba Shaba respectively may be found in Mukange 1968; Yezi 1970:3–92.

instructions *(mikenji ya tshipostolo)*.[12] He retained the clan-based rules of exogamy defining incestuous relations *(tshibindi)* among the Bena Lulua.[13] Six explicit principles of marriage and mate selection were then outlined with a seventh, autonomous choice of a mate for both sexes, implicitly present. The marriage rules provide an excellent example of the type of transformations that Apostolic thought places on custom. While residues of the old are present, these rules are universalized. They become more general and less dependent on locally recognized ascriptive criteria.

Based on village endogamy, the first principle of marriage is translated into Apostolic law as follows: An Apostle must not marry a pagan or marry his daughter to a pagan (literally from Tshiluba *muena diabolo*, or person of the devil). The ditunga, with its intermarrying clans, is replaced by eligible Apostles of different clans. The marriageable group expands beyond the tribe, including members of various tribes and nations who derive their eligibility not ascriptively but through being Apostles. Nonetheless, it is possible to view this endogamy as a form of incapsulation (cf. Mayer 1961:90–95), whereby Apostles ensure that their major associations remain within the group even in a varied environment.

According to the second principle, no dowry is required for marriage. This rule has various applications in practice.

[12] The mikenji of the Kananga kerek were first presented in written form by head evangelist Tshiaba Daniel, who compiled them through questioning the evangelist Zivuku Gibson concerning doctrine as interpreted at the Rhodesian center (Tshiaba 1970).

[13] Heimer (1971:86–87) describes clan relationships in general terms. He does not present in detail taboos observed by tshiota members or describe changes, if any, in these relationships in urban areas. Evidence indicates that the diku, much more than the entire clan, was the seat of traditional Lulua-Luba religious practices.

Generally, only a small dowry is required, but it is still considered an important gesture to seal the marriage contract. Apostles have expressed discontent with traditional treatments of the dowry. The Zambians stated that the Bemba had difficulty living as Apostles, because their dowry was usually too low ($.50), showing that they did not value a woman's labor enough. Members explain that to display respect for the wife's skills and the husband's authority, the exchange of dowries is still used among Apostles and often takes the place of a marriage ceremony. Apostles do not hold an elaborate marriage ceremony of either the traditional or the Western type, although a light meal or visiting day may be in order. An interesting case developed relative to the dowry in which Kananga evangelists labeled a marriage illegal cohabitation, since only a small dowry of Z1,40 ($2.80) had been paid without prior consultation with the bride's parents.

The ambivalence toward tradition is shown in choosing a mate. Relative de-emphasis of the dowry reinforces the principle of free marital choice within a group of eligibles. All girls who pass a ceremonial virginity examination (Chishona: *mushecho*) administered by the female elders are allowed their marriage preferences. This examination is conducted during both the regional musankano and the musankano of Passover, held a few days before the sacrament is eaten (Murphree 1969:103). The virgin is rewarded by the status of head wife in the marriage of her choice. Nonvirgins are generally placed in polygamous marriages to older men in the church. Persons married prior to membership are not affected: it is merely emphasized that when the husband joins, the wife ideally should follow suit.

The following two principles relate to the status of married women: An Apostle is, in theory, not to marry another's wife (except in the case of widowhood) or a divorced woman, once he has joined the church (Tshiluba: *mukaji wa bende nansha mukaji wakadi ku dibaka dikuabo*). This rule is an application of Christian doctrine following Matthew 19:3–9 rather than traditional law. Divorce is allowed, though rare in most patrilineal African societies (cf. Mbiti 1969:146–147). The failure to bear children is one of the few acceptable reasons for divorce under the traditional Lulua system. A related custom claimed by the Bena Lulua is the existence of leviratic marriage once a brother has died. While Lulua Apostles do not allow sororal polygamy as do the Shona members, arguing that their customs are exactly those of the Jews, they also invoke biblical and traditional cases to support the levirate. These types of marriage are voluntary in the Apostolic church. There is some dispute over which congregation's interpretations are most valid and whether a single interpretation should be sought throughout the church.

A fourth principle governs an extramarital relationship, should it arise. If an Apostle deflowers a virgin, he must marry her. Although this rule might simply be treated as a warning against sexual incontinence and therefore specific to Christian obligations, its historical status is ambiguous in both tribal and biblical traditions. Cases of adultery are judged on an individual basis and settled according to circumstance. One incident, taking place during a Passover ceremony, resulted in the removal of a Lieb-Umah's rank.

Two final prescriptions relate to in-laws. On divorce, an Apostle cannot reclaim his dowry as he would under traditional law, a rule that again de-emphasizes the importance of the dowry. On marriage to an outsider, who must be converted, the member should also attempt to convert his in-laws. This practice has encountered difficulties. If immediate conversion of the spouse or the spouse's family fails, the only legitimate reason for divorce is adultery, for barrenness may be resolved for Apostles by polygamy. Since marriage is viewed from a Christian perspective as

a holy union and also as an arena for conversion, its regulation is a personal and public concern both for the member's
spiritual state and for the growth of the church.

I asked Mama Esthere what would happen to the three
women who had deserted their husband, Joseph. They had
claimed that their husband mistreated them severely, and
they could no longer live with him. En masse, all three had
left, leaving only the head wife behind. Joseph quickly
married two younger wives. Esthere answered vaguely. We
were not to shake their hands openly in the market place,
for they were fallen women. The only hope for the "fallen
women" within the church, she had speculated, was to
leave the Kasai and join another congregation elsewhere.
There, they would be "on trial" for several years, until
their good faith as members had been re-established.

The Apostolic statements about marriage illustrate an
effort to make traditional conceptions of the relationship
relevant in a changing social context. But a complete return to tradition would not be desirable. If members failed
to convert their families, marriage regulations would have
to leave them freedom from parental control in a choice of
mate. Thus, parental consent for marriage could no longer
be required.[14] Even in cases where Apostolic families arrange the marriage of their daughters, eligible (that is, virgin) girls can freely reject their suitors. The relationship
between custom and change is not always correlative.
Lulua Apostles claimed, for example, that polygamy had
been rare for them as a traditional custom and increased
once local men joined the group. All in all, the marriage
regulation provides Apostles with the best of several

[14] Lanzas and Bernard (1966:199–200) remark that the dowry and familial consent are no longer necessary conditions for Apostolic marriage
although they may be sought in individual cases. Free choice of a spouse
for the virginal girl is a key innovation of Apostolic practice in contrast
to many traditional customs.

worlds, allowing them flexibly to manipulate standards in conjunction with tradition and a changing environment. Even Tshiaba's mikenji, of which flexibility is a key feature, are merely attempts to standardize instructions that are, in fact, highly negotiable for individual cases.

The Reclassification of Natural and Social Categories

The natural and social world as perceived through Apostolic belief are comprehended as though unmediated by reflection.[15] As a member, I thus learned to perceive pork as impure, as though this impurity, produced by doctrine and symbolic classification, were an inherent natural quality of the pig. Apostles not only classify the pig as impure, they sensorily experience it as such [16] and feel a sense of urgency whenever they come into contact with a taboo food or object. This experience of the impure is particularly evident in its combination with Hebraic dietary law. Animals that are considered unusual or are prohibited in aspects of Shona and Lulua custom are also integrated into this framework. Explaining the logic of the reclassified animal taboos other than arbitrarily is difficult.

When I asked Tshiaba why the duck, which was not listed in Leviticus as inedible, was impure to Apostles, he replied that its webbed feet and indiscriminate appetite were the cause. As he spoke, he threw pebbles at a flock of geese surrounding a nearby sewer. "These birds eat food that is spoiled and therefore are not good for us to eat." When I stated that this was a strange reading of the Bible,

[15] Merleau-Ponty (1962:xvi) asserts that we experience the world in terms of images or precognition perceptions. He terms these perceptions "our primordial knowledge of the 'real.' " Yet many perceptions, including sensory ones, are influenced by learning and, especially once verbalized, have been mediated by cultural categories.
[16] Turner (1967:28–29) discusses the ideological and sensory components of a ritual symbol.

Tshiaba questioned my sincerity. Several days later, observing two turkeys pecking in the evangelist Kabeya's yard, I suggested that they might be good to eat. He responded in horror that the turkey is forbidden to all Apostles. The turkey, like the duck, was not proscribed in the Torah, but its wattle and its unusual appearance, distantly resembling a vulture, were given as reasons for its impurity. Thus, Apostles state that ducks, turkeys, and peacocks, despite their exclusion from biblical prohibitions, cannot be touched as carcasses or eaten. Touching the live animal is permissible but avoided.

The logic of the Hebraic laws was already complex, involving its own order of syncretism. One interpretation of the distinction between pure and impure birds is predation. Citing the Mishnah, the first section of the Talmud, Mary Douglas states that unclean birds are predators and eaters of blood (1972:61–81; 1966:55–56). Since blood must be drained when sacrificing an animal, any animal eating flesh and blood would be impure. Leviticus II seems to suggest carrion-eating as one principle of impurity. This evidence, however, is obviously open to diverse interpretations.

And these you shall have in abomination among the birds, they shall not be eaten, they are an abomination: the eagle, the ossifrage, the osprey: the kite, the falcon according to its kind; every raven after its kind; the ostrich, the night hawk, the sea gull, the hawk according to its kind, the owl, the cormorant, the ibis; the waterhen, the pelican, the vulture; the stork, the heron according to its kind; the hoopoe and the bat.   [Lev. II:13–19]

While birds of prey form the largest category, there are also several subgroups: waterbirds with webbed feet, a land bird with three toes (the ostrich), and two night creatures, one a bird and one a mammal. These flying creatures seemed to be classed along with the impure birds by virtue of their peculiar traits. The bat is not only a predator, it is an anomolous creature, neither bird nor animal. Even more than predation, peculiarity seems to underlie the bird classifications (cf. Douglas 1966:41–57; 1967:231–247). Apostles state that in addition to their presumed habits or symbolic associations with foolishness and pride, it is the duck's webbed foot, the peacock's extraordinary plumage and the turkey's odd appearance that make them impure. These are incongruities, some of which were already forecast in custom.

Among the Bena Lulua, creatures possessing peculiar traits must be avoided by certain classes of people. Pregnant women do not touch or eat duck because of its dual association with the water, somehow linked to conception, and with rotten food. Certain kinds of fish are similarly forbidden to Lulua women during pregnancy and are considered to upset the fetus and cause vomiting. Apostles also avoid these fish on the grounds that the fish do not have scales. Whether consciously or not, Apostles have articulated traditional lore with their own and often refer to these connections. The taboos classify both nature and culture. They set the Apostles apart from both their Christian and traditional neighbors.

When pressed about the inconsistencies of their explanations with biblical ones, members see no difficulty in returning to tradition for support. But where tradition blatantly contradicts the Hebraic laws, it is abandoned as unenlightened. These interpretations are bolstered by literal readings of vernacular Bibles and appeals to the history of biblical traditions. In this respect, it is interesting to review Robertson Smith's (1899:125) argument that original Hebrew clan and tribal names were actually totemic names bound to a system of sacred objects and taboos. Thus, clan and tribal names identified groups and associated them with natural categories: the clan name Simeon means "lion"; Caleb, "dog"; Deborah, "bee"; and

Rachel, "owl." (Oesterly and Robinson 1961:66). According to this argument, the dietary laws themselves may have partially stemmed from totemic interdictions.

To explain the classification of the duck, Tshiaba had returned to the Tshiluba Bible. Its rendition of the listing for carrion vulture was ambiguous to me. It is translated: *nyunyu mutoke udi wadia bintu bibole* (white bird that eats carrion or spoiled matter). The description of the bird and its diet could also be applied to the duck. Tshiaba also stated that the duck was closely related to the swan, directly listed as impure. He then read the list again in the French Bible to validate his claim, ignoring the difference in wording between the two versions. The literal reading was also supported by animistic characterizations of birds and animals, emphasized at will when they could be made to coincide with the Bible. Tshiaba described the owl as a witch's familiar whose cry signals the imminent death of someone near it. No wonder, he asserted, that it too is listed as impure in the Bible. In this case, however, he made no reference to the owl's nocturnal habits, predation, or unusual appearance. The forcefulness of tradition seemed more important.

Four-legged creatures have similar animistic qualities. The Shona consider pawed animals, such as the lion, the leopard, and, especially, the hyena, to be the special vehicles of the alien spirits of witchcraft. Though the Bible prohibits these creatures only as food, Apostles are not allowed to possess pawed creatures, such as the common dog or cat, as pets. When walking with Apostles in town, I was warned to avoid the owners of such animals. The pig is similarly considered to be an abode for demonic spirits and a sorcerer's familiar. In this case, the biblical account of the exorcism of Legion, by which demons were said to enter pigs, was cited. The addition of animistic explanations made it clear that a single animal or object could be described as impure on several counts. Depending on the context of discussion and the member asked, different explanations were provided. While Apostles would always begin with the Bible, layers of alternative explanations could be produced for a single case.

The layers of explanations were initially confusing to me until I learned to expect that the rhetorical strength of a single interpretation was more important than a consistency operating across explanations.[17] If one order of explanation contradicted another, this was less relevant than the style and convincing character of a single explanation. The hierarchy of alternative explanations can be depicted as follows:

biblical

customary animistic interpretation   Christian lore

The simultaneous use of all three levels of explanation was considered particularly effective. To learn to talk effectively as a member, I was required to alter my standards of coherence and the criteria that I might otherwise have accepted as logical argument. In the last analysis, it was most important to accept the experienced meaning of a category and its ritual consequences.

The qualities considered inherent in natural objects were extended to individuals and social groups (cf. Lévi-Strauss 1966:9). The Apostolic taboos and the reasoning used to sustain them were employed to set the Apostles off from outsiders. Tshiaba remarked that many people did not join the group because they felt that its regulations on alcohol and food were too harsh. The rules served as a preliminary way of designating a community of the saved.

[17] Albert (1966:35–54) emphasizes a similar importance placed on rhetoric and formal oratory at the expense of a particular level of explanation.

Transgressing the law could result in illness, misfortune, and demon possession. Yet some transgression was inevitable. Hence, an Apostle in Kananga recommended that we keep an evangelist at our side at all times. If a sin was left unconfessed, our spiritual powers would diminish. This would not be a fall from grace so much as a state of vulnerability. While inspired by Christian tradition, the constant vigilance that members encouraged also resembled the confession and sacrifice of traditional religion.

The Body

In both Shona and Lulua traditional religion, the state of an initiate's body communicates a great deal. For Apostles, bodily signs are also manipulated as aspects of membership. The Pauline principle that the body is "God's Temple" is taken literally. It thus receives special ritual treatment. Members include in this treatment the prohibition of incisions; the rejection of medicines, alcoholic beverages, and cigarettes, which are considered to defile the body; the restriction of bodily ornamentation; and the abstention from sex on holy days. A reaction to tradition is implicit in the abandonment of herbal medicines, body ornamentation and incisions. A reaction to Western influence occurs with the refusal of patent medicines and modern styles. In this case, the Apostolic approach contains ambivalence to both systems of thought.

Head shaving, not unusual as an expression of religious commitment, is one of the major forms of Apostolic bodily communication. Upon baptism, members explain that each male Apostle's head is shaved as a vow to God. The beard is allowed to grow as "the glory of God." Women maintain their hair "in praise of God," except in cases of penance, during which time they too are required to shave their heads. For women, the shaved head is a mark of shame or of sacrifice; for men it is considered a sign of pride and strength. Pauline advice is cited regarding this. Like the dietary laws, hair cutting insulates members from outsiders by providing a visible symbol of separation. Leach also suggests that hair shaving generally represents discipline, self-control, and the repression of desires (1967:77 ff). This interpretation is interesting in the light of the other ritual restrictions imposed by Apostles.

The Apostles have reacted to traditional treatments of the body much as they have to animal taboos. They have provided substitutes for abandoned rules and have modified rather than decreased ceremony. Nonetheless, these modifications have relied on the notion of spiritual inspiration. A description of the Kenyan Mumbo or "Speaking Serpent" cult makes this process even clearer. In contrast to the cleanly shaved surrounding tribesmen and women, the Mumboists, appearing near Lake Victoria in 1908, refused to wash or cut their hair. They were noted chiefly for their dedication to Mumbo, a serpent god reputed to have his abode in Lake Tanganyika. Although the cult had a few marginally Christian elements, the followers of Mumbo attempted to identify themselves thoroughly with the wilderness, refusing to cultivate their fields and killing all their cattle in sacrifice. They were accused of engaging in incestuous sexual practices, hemp smoking, and other activities that challenged traditional Luo life (Perrin Jassy 1970:73–74). Mumboism was one of the earliest contemporary syncretist movements. As such, it combined a reaction against tradition with direct protest against European rule, while piecing together both traditional and Western ideological elements.

Within the traditional societies in which Mumboism arose, marginal or special status was conveyed by the treatment of physical appearance. Diviners often grew longer hair, either plaiting it or allowing it to become matted. Virginal girls and children in some tribes would shave their heads, while married women allowed their hair to grow, coiffing it specially to convey a change in status. The hair as well as the body was felt to possess magical potency. Apostles also believe that demons lodge in the hair on top of the head, which is rubbed by male members to remove evil forces during exorcism and before baptism. The beard, however, is associated with the moral authority of the patriarchs. In a vision of heaven, John Maranke reported that he saw "elders whose beards were as long as an arm from the elbow to the tip of the middle finger" (1953:5). Their state of grace was represented by their appearance.

Social anthropologists have claimed that the treatment of the physical body is influenced by and reflects conceptions that groups hold about the social body. Bodily mutilations and ornamentations separate one group from another or mark changes in status through life. It has also been suggested that the social structure of a group influences the abandon tolerated in bodily behavior (Douglas 1970:73–75). Groups that are less hierarchical and less highly structured, like the Mumbo, would tend to be more favorable to visionary and ecstatic states. Groups more careful to enforce compliance to their standards would be less tolerant of such abandon. Applying this assumption to sect groups and religious movements is difficult, in that many of these groups are highly insulated and have elaborate leadership hierarchies regardless of the treatment of the body. Following this theory, the proliferation of rules and ritual among the Apostles would tend to place them in the category of groups that do not tolerate abandon. Indeed, if an Apostle fell unconscious in kerek, this act would be attributed to demon possession and would cause some alarm.

There is, however, a more crucial flaw in the body correspondence assumption. It does not account for the possibility that ritual action is an intentional performance. While the Mumboists conceived of themselves as purposively breaking traditional taboos in reaching ecstatic states through rituals, the Apostles do not. They use these rules as a resource for ritual and, more importantly, are concerned with the creation of a specific type of ecstatic state, a heaven on earth during worship. The emphasis on vision and ecstasy is implemented rather than diminished through the presence of a social organization that includes elements of hierarchy. Though important for reaching an ecstatic state in ritual, the aggressive exercise of hierarchical leadership is de-emphasized. All rules concerning the social and physical body are subordinated to the attainment of ecstatic states in ritual and their exercise as spiritual gifts.

The Apostles' Ambivalence to the World and Its Temptations

To argue that the traditional forms of thought begin to change with the development of new religions presumes an internal comparability among the old and new cultural forms. Demonstrating this comparability, however, is quite difficult. Sometimes new symbolic patterns such as Apostolic taboos and prescriptions derive an obvious appeal from mirroring established mores. In other cases, despite the potential for this appeal, the new cultural and social forms are rejected, even by groups neighboring those who find a sect appealing (Biebuyck 1957:7–40). Barrett explains that receptivity to independency is created by an "unconscious" communication with adjacent tribes by the "unwitting" agents of change, such as migrant and itinerant laborers passing from one group to another (Barrett 1968:276). Rather than the specific doctrinal and ritual forms of independency, the idea of religious separation and change is transmitted. This theory does not explain the expansion of the Apostolic and similar groups with respect to deliberate acts of conversion.

Ascetism, frugality and sacrifice separate the Apostles symbolically from the outside world. So great is the commitment to this separation that members emphasize that the truly righteous man can expect to die a violent death, martyred at the hands of those who are spiritually lost.[18] This interpretation of the world is continually reinforced by faith in the propositions of that world view, a faith that becomes the basis of action and the affirmation of its own logic. When every act is one of faith, it becomes clear why economic and other social relations are subject to strict scrutiny. In economic relations, the Apostle comes in contact with the world and its "temptations." Although lightly criticized by other members, one member even refused to touch money directly, summoning others to handle it for him in stores or holding it in a handkerchief. Direct contact with money, he claimed, was a sin, for it demonstrated attachment to this amassing of wealth and to the economic situation perpetuating it. For other members, economic activities such as farming and commerce are communally performed and relegated to certain months of the year, leaving the rest of the year exclusively for worship.

Their strict categorization of spiritual and work activities causes Apostles in many African communities to be regarded as men and women who "seek heaven" (*watendi kudenga*—holy believers or holy men). The differences perceived by outsiders influence their stereotyping of members: as generous only to other members of their own community; as reliable only because they seek heaven; or as unreliable because they refuse to work at certain times, setting a poor example for the community. Regardless of what the image is, almost every African community in

[18] Aquina (1967:208) records a sermon in which an Apostle stresses the joys of a life to come and the anticipation of a violent death. Members also informed me that every good Apostle hopes for a martyr's death.

which the Apostles live is impressed by their presence. As white-robed Apostles wend their way through the streets to a place of prayer, comments from onlookers attest to the uniqueness of their response to urban life. When the prophet Emmanuel warned Peter not to submit to the ways of the world, he was suggesting that too much attention to outsiders' priorities would weaken his commitment. On the other hand, members stress the importance of living under everyday, rather than monastic, conditions in order to spread the message to their families and the surrounding community.

Religion and Cultural Innovation

Membership as an Apostle involves learning a vocabulary that transmutes tradition into new practices. Tradition consists both of local customs or religious practices and of Shona tradition that Apostles regard as intimately tied to the origin of the church. Exactly how the content of traditional categories is applied in Apostolic practice is often difficult to discern. I learned about local traditions chiefly through Apostles as part of their description and justification of religious rules. Where necessary, the validation of tradition was used rhetorically, especially in conversations with outsiders, to explain and expand upon Apostolic practices. Members, however, were careful not to let the similarities go too far. In my conversations with elders, it was often forgotten or ignored that I had little knowledge of the customs that they shared. Extended talk about them generally took the form of banter or comparison, when aspects of custom were not specifically integrated with Apostolic practice. Even after I joined the group, I felt that members complicated points of doctrine by shifting their frame of reference from one order of reality to another, all the while expanding on a single biblical verse.

Ezekiel and another young evangelist argued whether

Americans could ever become good Apostles. One stated that their traditions and attachment to the material world would make it impossible for them to become true converts, while the other retorted that the Holy Spirit could teach the hearts of all men. "Why then," complained the evangelist, "has the message of Christ fallen on deaf ears in Europe?" "This is difficult to know," Ezekiel replied. The baptist William intervened to support Ezekiel's position. "All people can learn. It's just a matter of patience and discipline." The evangelist's concern, however, was legitimate.

Apostolic rules and ritual are based on placing a universal content upon specific applications. When important to the group's survival, the old is left behind but never without a substitute. This innovation is either simpler than or equally as explicit as traditional rules. Holy water substitutes for herbal medicines, and biblical taboos for many clanic prohibitions. The overlay of substitution is not complete. The Apostle avoids his mother-in-law, addresses elders with respect, and shies away from animals customarily considered taboo. It is often difficult to pull apart the customary and the new as both become woven into daily expectations. But as Apostles travel from one congregation to another, they are faced with doing just that. Diverse languages and customs blend in ritual and lore. Through contact, each group enriches the others, but not without a subtle balancing of the relationship between custom and a vision of change. As I prepared to return, members speculated about whether this delicate balance could be conveyed outside of Africa.

CHAPTER 7

The Apostles' Journey

In a vision I was traveling to many countries and a lot of people followed me. I led them with a staff in my hand. As I flew, my followers walked behind. I came through a flame of fire, and as I rose up my scepter, nobody got burnt. I led them on, and thousands of people were converted. They were becoming so many that I could not count them. Amen.

John Maranke

The Apostles' journey has taken place across time and space, and both dimensions must be examined to understand the church. Many of the answers to questions about its future in Africa and America can be found by looking at its past. Like any organization, the Apostolic church viewed over a period of time is a phenomenon in flux, continually being recast by members and people who approach the group from without. Their history is found in living lore, in documents of experiences and visions that Apostles themselves have preserved, and in the traces of their contact with other groups.

The Early History

The early years of Muchabaya Momberume (John Maranke) and his visionary experiences have been written as revelations to the Apostles (Maranke 1953; Daneel 1971:329). These revelations constitute a historical document, a theological point of reference, and a model on which other Apostles base their accounts of spiritual experiences. When John was five years old, he began to hear strange voices and see visions. After a year of Methodist primary school, he left, claiming that he had been visited by the Holy Spirit at the age of six. He prayed continuously and stood on top of anthills (in Rhodesia they are up to twenty feet high), preaching to the trees. During this time, John was plagued by a mysterious illness that traditional and mission doctors could not diagnose.

Finally, he recounted, a Methodist clergyman affirmed that the Holy Spirit was in him and that he was destined to heal the sick. For a short period he lived alone in the surrounding mountains and was actually thought by his relatives and friends to be dead. When he emerged, he again felt the confirmation of the Holy Spirit, this time to preach, heal, and prophesy. In a vision, he was given the basic commandments for establishing the church. This experience seems patterned on that of Moses and John the Baptist and resembles the accounts of other Shona prophets.[1]

Most of the early conversions and miraculous healings recorded in "The New Witness of the Apostles" took place between 1932 and 1934, when John's church grew rapidly among his relatives, the first to be converted and to receive leadership positions (Daneel 1971:321–325; Barrett 1968:124). Each post was administered through John's direct spiritual confirmation. John himself was baptized by another member, Ruka (Luke) Mataruka, his brother-in-law, who later left the church. After John's death in 1963, a schism divided the Rhodesian church when his cousin, Simon Mushati, broke away, but did not ultimately affect the allegiance of most members to John's message as represented by his elder sons. A more detailed discussion of the major and minor schisms in the church is presented in Marthinus Daneel's (1971:331–339) history of the Rhodesian branch.

Some of my first impressions came not from the Rhodesian histories but from a file of reports and letters compiled by the Congolese AIMO (Affaires Indigènes et Main-

---

[1] The visionary callings of Mai Chaza and John Masowe, both of whom established churches in Rhodesia, resemble John Maranke's experience. See Martin 1970:110–112; Sundkler 1961:323–325.

d'Oeuvres), the labor and indigenous affairs department of the Belgian colonial administration. These documents were kept as part of the administration's surveillance and record-keeping on a number of religious and social movements in the Kasai. The documents contained letters and statements by Apostles and were turned over to them after independence. I naively treated the documents as representative of the present, although they covered only the years from 1956 to 1959.

In piecemeal fashion, these documents traced the Apostles' journey northward from the Rhodesias to the Belgian Congo, their entry into the southeastern part of Katanga province in 1952, and their move northwest to the Kasai over the following four years. Although some of the documents were detailed, they contained little information about the Rhodesian branch and seemed uncertain about its location.[2] In my early conversations with missionaries and researchers, I had heard that Luluabourg was the center of the church and that the Kasai-Katanga railroad was one source of its growth. The railroad linked the Kasai mining towns to the Katanga province and thence to Northern and Southern Rhodesia. Nawezi's migration to Rhodesia had introduced the church to Lubumbashi (then Elisabethville), and he was followed by a number of Kasaians who came in contact with the Apostles through work in the Copperbelt towns of Northern Rhodesia—Lusaka, Broken Hill, Kitwe, and Ndola (see Map 1).[3]

[2] Lanzas and Bernard (1966:189), who probably had access to these documents, listed the seat of the Maranke church as Lusaka, Zambia. It is possible that they also confused the Maranke and Masowe Apostles.

[3] Once a church achieves local appeal, it often has a base to spread locally and transethnically (see Barrett 1968:230–232). Examples of other churches achieving such diffusion are: (1) The African Israel church, begun among Kenya's Luo (Welbourn and Ogot 1966); (2) The Watchtower (Kitawala) or Jehovah's Witnesses movement that spread northwest from Nyasaland beginning in 1908 (Young 1965:287–288; Biebuyck

Although the documents vividly depicted the Apostles'
manner of dress and worship, they were also ambiguous.
The church organization, as reported by colonial administrators, seemed to be a hierarchy, but how the positions
were selected or what they were was not clear. The
church's founder, "John Malangu," was portrayed as a
mysterious and elusive figure. It was suggested that he was
hungry for power and had deluded many people into following him. These early records also presented an over-
whelming image of the church's complicated relations with
the government and of its secret ceremonies, described as
native orgies, trances, and hysteria. It was this exaggeration
of the Apostles' "mysterious rites" that had initially made
me both curious about and fearful of the all night masowe
and musankano gatherings.

Introduction of the Church to the Kasai, 1956–1959

There is little written about the growth of the Maranke
church between its formal inception in 1932 and its spread
outside of the Rhodesias in the early 1950's. Church leaders
in the Congo, however, kept personal records that, in combination with the AIMO files, represent a brief portrait of
the following years. The Congolese church emerged in the
1950's in the midst of a number of social and protopolitical
movements, including the first political parties in the
Kasai. For this reason, the colonial régime regarded it with
the same suspicion as it did the political organizations.
According to the AIMO records, the church first became
known to the provincial administration of the Kasai in
August, 1956, when two Congolese, one wearing a white
robe and one carrying a Bible printed in Tshiluba, were
arrested near a village in the interior. They were released

1957:7–40; Shepperson 1962:144–159); (3) The Apostles of John Masowe
(Sundkler 1961:323–325; Kileff 1973:1–73).

after questioning established that they were the only "adepts" of the religion in the region and that the head of the church lived in Rhodesia. In his report to central headquarters in Léopoldville, the chief of police for the Kasai requested a total investigation of the religion and its leaders (Royers 1956).

Although a woman, whose name remains obscure, is said to be responsible for introducing the church into the West Kasai, much of the early proselytizing was done by Mujanaie Marcel. He first came into contact with Shona members in Northern Rhodesia (now Zambia), where he claimed to have met John Maranke. In 1957 and 1958, Kadima Alphonse, a Kasaian living in Katanga, and Kasanda Vincent, a self-styled religious prophet before becoming an Apostle, continued the work of evangelization throughout the Kasai. Outspoken and assertive, Kasanda was quickly investigated by the colonial authorities.

The church had already been introduced to Katanga province in 1953 by Nawezi Petro, then a local merchant, who converted when Shona Apostles healed his wife of tuberculosis, after a series of European doctors had failed to do so. He has recorded an account of this conversion as part of his congregation's history (Tshibangu 1970:1–8). In 1958, Nawezi tried to register his group with the colonial government in Elisabethville as the Eglise Apostolique Africaine. I have already alluded to the series of troubles that Nawezi encountered with the colonial régime. The government refused him this time, citing administrative regulations dating from 1888, before the Congo had even become an official Belgian colony (Heynen 1958).

In November 1956, the church was formally dissolved in Katanga by the application of a law from 1926 forbidding "indigenous associations whose existence could counteract the civilization of the natives or constitute a menace to tranquility and public order" (Moriame 1956; Rutten 1926).

An article in the Katanga press gave some indication of current colonial opinion on religious movements in Elisabethville. The article, favoring the interdiction, compared the church with the Kimbanguist and Kitawala movements, which it described as regressive politico-religious sects led by false prophets who "promised the moon" to their followers. It further stated that the movement, probably subversive, played upon people's credulity and "undermined the evolution of the population" (*Essor* 1956).

The notion of independent churches as anticolonialist, politically subversive bodies had developed during the 1920's, when Kimbangu's church had preached faith-healing, the descent of the Holy Spirit, and belief in Simon Kimbangu as the new black savior and messenger of God to the Africans. The colonial administration claimed that Kimbangu incited the people to avoid paying taxes and cultivating the land. This he and his followers denied. Nonetheless, Kimbangu was tried and imprisoned in 1921 and was subsequently shipped to Elisabethville, where he died in prison in 1953. Administrative decrees, including the law of 1926, dissolved the movement as a threat to public order.[4] A relocation of many followers ensued. Religious groups that allegedly held political doctrines were suppressed in similar fashion during the 1930's and 1940's. Local authorities were authorized to outlaw any indigenous movement having a hierarchical leadership structure. All independent sects and cults were routinely held under surveillance.

European conceptions of independent churches as politically oriented were thus definitely influenced by the Kimbanguist church, many of whose members returned from their rural exile to become organizers in the ABAKO political party in the late 1950's. The news article did not

[4] For a description of the life of Simon Kimbangu, see Chomé 1959.

charge the Apostolic church with political activity or compare it with the Kimbanguist movement. Instead, it
pointed to the state of trance entered by members, to the
refusal to take medicines, and to the claims of prophets,
described as misleading and extravagant, as evidence of the
sect's "regressive" nature. The colonial officials in the
Kasai, who, like those in the Katanga, were watching independent churches as a source of political protest, initially
treated these practices as the most sensitive areas of Apostolic ritual. Administrators in Elisabethville continued to
make direct comparisons between Kimbanguism and the
churches that followed it.

The Belgian program of gradual "evolution" for the
Congolese was interpreted differently in the Kasai. This
colonial policy was intended, in time, to produce a broad
middle class of Congolese, who, according to a European
settlers' organization:

. . . will declare their acceptance of the ideals and principles of
our Western civilization and who will be, if on an equal standing,
our equal in rights and duties, less numerous than the native mass,
but powerful and influential, they will be the allies it is so indis-
pensable for us to find in the native communities.[5]

This gradualist approach was carried out in a policy of
paternalistic control in which housing, public health and
hygiene, labor relations, justice, agriculture, and traditional political structures were maintained under strict
supervision (Young 1965:59–65). Under this system of pater-
nalism, the colonizers saw as their task the instruction of
the Congolese in every area of life, from romantic love in
monogamous marriage to standards of Western dress and
hygiene. A vaccination program was initiated, and the
Kasai authorities took the Apostles' rejection of injections

[5] Here Young (1965:44) quotes a note from the European settler organization Fedacol to the Colonial Minister Buisseret, 1955.

or blood tests as evidence that the church seemed to be "counteracting civilization."

Kasanda and Mujanaie were questioned when a medical officer informed the government that an Apostle had refused to take the blood test. The provincial governor warned the members that the sect would escape dissolution only as long as it confined its activity to religious questions (Lemborelle 1958). This did not include assessing modern medical treatment. The Apostles responded that they would submit to the medical censuses but that each member would be free to act according to his own conscience regarding the blood test. The issue of bloodtaking had already appeared in the Kasai in another context. In 1944, the Luluabourg garrison had revolted, apparently in the belief that blood tests were an attempt to poison them (Fetter 1969:269–277). The administration was prepared to interpret the refusal to give blood as a challenge to its authority. The Apostles, on the other hand, were bound by religious restrictions to obey the laws of the government, to refrain from explicit political activity, and, especially, to abstain from medication. Members thus had to resolve apparent contradictions in their own beliefs. (In later years, Apostolic leadership conceded to government medical regulations.)

Apostolic leaders, including Mujanaie and Kasanda, were called to the offices of several territorial administrators and warned of the serious consequences of refusing to submit to the medical authorities. Kasanda replied with a number of biblical citations showing that healing was done by God rather than by medicine. Several such interviews took place and were manipulated by the authorities to bring about conflicts of leadership within the church (Hentgen 1958). Mujanaie and Kasanda both promised to consult with John Maranke about the matter. Upon returning from Rhodesia, Kasanda reiterated his position, so the affair was dropped (Goffard 1958). The medical issue was finally categorized as a matter of religious conviction by the authorities, since no new incidents were created (Hentgen 1959). The administration, which was growing uneasy at the presence of ethnic political associations in the area, was reluctant to create disputes over theological issues as long as a minimum of compliance could be extracted from the group. When I crossed the Malawian border with several Apostles in 1971, those without health cards were required to have vaccinations immediately. After being injected, they reversed the ill effects of the medicines by the laying on of hands.

The Kasaian government allowed the church to continue, since its activities seemed to be contained within the religious domain. It was felt that outlawing the church would increase its appeal and its opposition to the colonial regime. As before, the government still examined the church in political terms. One report claimed that the church was only of transient impact, unlike some other sectarian groups which it termed subversive (Arnols 1958).

From the members' point of view, there was no possibility of political activity for the church, whether outlawed or not, since direct involvement with external political institutions was expressly forbidden. This separation of religious and political commitments was recognized from the outside to a greater extent in the Kasai than in the Katanga, where the church was outlawed a second time in 1959, despite a letter from the central government urging the Katangan authorities to adopt the Kasai's more lenient policy toward sectarian organizations (Thilmany 1959; Belgian Congo, Gov. Gen. 1957). An interdiction had been drafted in the Kasai but never promulgated (Lemborelle 1957).

Apostolic forms of prayer confounded officials, who described them as nervous trembling, dervishism, hysteria, and epileptic crisis. Personal expressiveness was no longer considered an active threat, however, and several administrators urged a policy of tolerance and cooperation with the church, presenting more sympathetic accounts of various aspects of Apostolic practice. A report written by an enlightened administrator, R. J. A. Desmedt, in June 1958, provided the most detailed study of the Congolese branch during the colonial period. Desmedt denied that the church was xenophobic or that its doctrines were held in bad faith. He did, however, warn that if there was a danger to the colonial power, it was in the church's susceptibility to a takeover by outside political agitators who might attempt to gather it into a union of politico-religious movements (Desmedt 1958a; 1958b). Desmedt's views were well known among the Kasaian Apostles to whom I talked in 1971. They affirmed that after having written the report, he journeyed to Rhodesia where he met the "mysterious" John Maranke.

The activities of new political organizations, both in the Kasai and in other provinces, contributed to a benign indifference to the church. The Lulua Frères, an ethnic association of the Bena Lulua, the tribe most strongly represented in the West Kasai, took part in the general elections of 1958. Lumumba's MNC party also began political activity in the Kasai soon thereafter, in November 1958 (Young 1965: 294, 297). When I showed an Apostle the AIMO documents that suggested some governmental apprehensions about the connections of members with political activities, he remarked that during the time that the "militants of Lumumba" had been meeting regularly in the Kasai, no Apostle had gone to their gatherings. His apparent defensiveness reflected the administration's concern with secret political movements. Apostles' nightly masowes were often interrupted when officials tried to stop the prayer meetings. The informant stressed that a cross-fertilization of the Apostles with political movements had not occurred.

The Passover's Ceremonial Importance

There was a new development in August of 1959, when Kasanda Vincent, then an Apostolic prophet in Luluabourg, wrote letters to the administration requesting permission to hold a Passover celebration in the Kasai (Kasanda 1959). The request was refused on a technicality of application procedure. Every year from 1959 until 1963 Kasanda repeated the request, until the ceremony was finally authorized by the newly independent Congolese government. John Maranke traveled to the Kasai to administer the Passover and confirm spiritual gifts for the first and only time in 1963, a few months before his death. The prophet's arrival constituted an official recognition by the Rhodesian leadership of all of the Apostolic congregations in the Congo. It marked a full acceptance of the Congolese branches, of their officers, and of their ceremonial innovations.

The importance of the Passover as an integral feature of the Apostles' growth and social organization is hinted at in Desmedt's report, but none of the AIMO documents convey an understanding of why members considered it necessary for the Passover to come to the Congo. The major reason for the ceremony, John Maranke's goal of direct control over outlying congregations, is not discussed. Speaking in tongues and "trance," those same aspects of Apostolic practice that had always been referred to as examples of "uncontrolled" behavior, were again invoked in 1959, when there was a question of authorizing a large public Passover gathering in the country (Van Holsbeke 1959).

Up to the present, only two Passover ceremonies have been held in the Kasai (1963 and 1964). Subsequent ceremonies held by Abel in Lubumbashi have been curtailed by border restrictions placed on Rhodesian church leaders. As a result, positions vacated by schism, departure, and death are still open in many Kasaian and Katangan (Shaba) congregations, since without confirmation from the Rhodesian hierarchy, they cannot be filled. Even once the Passover arrives, the schism among various subgroupings continues to reinforce the leadership struggle.

During the 1960's the church grew rapidly. In the Kasai, the arrival of John Maranke in 1963 and his son, Abel, in 1964 to give the Passover were special ceremonial incentives to conversion that brought many new members into the church. The number of paschal sites in the Kasai grew from one in 1963 to six in 1964. Throughout this period, the church received tolerance and cooperation from succeeding Congolese régimes, for which the Apostles and the other independent churches became a regular feature of the local religious communities.[6]

The Passover Pilgrimage and Church Expansion in the 1960's

The Passover celebration is the most direct point of international contact for most Apostles. The question, "When will the Passover arrive?" was a continual echo throughout both of my stays in Zaire. Tshiaba speculated that Abel would not be able to travel as far north as the Zaire for three more years, while others said that he would arrive in a matter of months or was, in fact, already on his way. If a pilgrimage was not being made to the Passover, the members' constant concern was participating in arrangements for the Passover to arrive.

For the first two years of its growth, the Maranke church had no Passover. Spiritual gifts abounded, with each new

[6] Another such church that has been studied in both the Kasai and Shaba Provinces is the Eglise des Dignes (Church of the Worthy), founded by the prophet Emmanuel Vanda in the Kasai in the 1920's and incorporated in Kananga in 1962 (Anyenyola 1972:57–88).

member becoming a congregational leader. To participate in the sacrament, organize matters of leadership, and strengthen the congregations spiritually, John held the first Passover ceremony on August 24, 1934, on the Maranke reserve (Daneel 1971:329; Maranke 1953:21). The Holy Spirit, he said, had informed him that all members in good standing must eat the Passover annually, whenever possible.

The Passover contains more than the symbolism of the sacrament for each member. It is symbolic and real journey to the Apostles' "New Jerusalem," a heavenly city into which only those purified of their sins may enter. After John's death, the date of the Rhodesian church's main Passover ceremony was shifted to July 17, in honor of the day on which he received the spiritual message to found the church. As the church grew, the main ceremony at Bocha no longer sufficed. New paschal sites were introduced, to which John, with a baptist and prophet, traveled to deliver the communion. Many pilgrimages took place—those of the priest and those of members of various congregations to the designated paschal centers—from May to October each year. By the late 1950's, visiting paschal sites not only necessitated several months a year, it called for more than one team of "priests." John gave the burden of the outlying congregations to his eldest sons Abel and Makebi who in turn selected a team of two assistants each (Daneel 1971:331). Now the two sons divide the work, with Makebi traveling east to Mozambique and Malawi, and Abel covering the northwest including Zambia and Zaire.

A total of one hundred and fifty paschal locations has been cited in Rhodesia, and this number is still growing (Barrett 1968:296). I was told by Rhodesian Apostles that there is one paschal site for each chiefdom in the country. The number of regional paschal sites is considerably reduced outside of Rhodesia. Each site is a political ward as well and marks a region for which one or several groups

Plate 13. John Maranke, Kangwa William, and associates. John Maranke *(center),* along with his associate Robert *(second from right),* the baptist Kangwa William *(right),* and other Apostles, administers the Passover in Zambia. Annually the founder and later his two oldest sons traveled with a team of members as far north as the Zaire to deliver the sacrament. (Passover, Lusaka, Zambia, 1958)

of high leaders may be appointed. If schisms or competing claims are present, a single region may contain more than one paschal site. During the paschal period each year, at least 116 celebrations are given by Abel, with a comparable number by Makebi. For nine years, between October of 1964 and 1973, no Passover was given in the Zaire. Many members who were not able to make the journey to a paschal site regarded themselves as spiritually isolated. The church anxiously awaited the arrival of the Passover to arbitrate major leadership disputes and points of doctrine. When it was finally celebrated in 1973, schism prevented some members from participating, and conflict continued.

Map 1. Apostolic communities

Although Zairian members have traveled widely, in part to secure closer contact with the church's center, their pilgrimages have often been thwarted. Even during the colonial period, when passports were not necessary and travel from one country to another was relatively simple, only a few made the journey as far as the Maranke reserve. The present regulations make such journeys possible only for those with passports and the financial means for long trips. From September through October 1971, Tshiaba and Kasanda tried to enter Rhodesia several times and finally succeeded at the end of October. They arrived too late to join the Passover at the Maranke reserve and had to travel west to Wankie, following Makebi's group. The following July, when they tried again, they were unable to enter Rhodesia at all. Others, without the congregational support that these leaders were able to gather for their journeys, were simply not able to travel.

The void left by sporadic Passovers outside of Rhodesia remains. Many have not experienced the spiritual purification, fervor, and cross-cultural sharing that it brings. The retreat, musankano, and masowe provide a regional substitute, but they lack the spiritual intensity and inclusiveness of the Passover setting. Despite the periodic closing of the Rhodesian borders with Zambia, however, Abel says that he is confident that God will show him the appropriate time to cross the border and thereby fulfill the church's promise unhindered. It is through the Passover that the church becomes international, while remaining cohesive enough to permit each member's direct contact with the Rhodesian center.

The Background of Geographic Mobility

There are three major types of mobility within the church: international growth and migration, interregional movement, and intraregional mobility between villages

and urban centers. Each type of movement implies a con-
comitant form of cultural adjustment that may be compared with rites of passage, those elements of ceremony
and social context that allow members to make adjustments
from one environment to another (Van Gennep 1909:13–17).
These changes may involve actual physical mobility across
regions or from village to city; they also include changes
within the church itself that affect local members.

A broad range of interviewing in the Kasai made me
aware of some of these alterations. A sample was taken
from the Kananga central kerek between the months of
January and April of 1972. Baptist Luka assisted me in locating many of the members and encouraged them to submit
to formal interviews. For two reasons, the period was one
of tension. Members were still waiting for that year's Passover, and many believed that it would take place "any day."
Meanwhile, outside surveillance of the church had increased, for official policy toward independent churches
had shifted. Nonetheless, I was able to contact 115 members,
approximately a third of the regular attendants in the
Kananga kerek at this time. The number of regular kerek
attendants fluctuated from 300 to 600, or an average of .1
per cent of Kananga's total population (De Saint Moulin
1970:377 ff). Their profiles can be reconstructed to provide
a history of the church's growth in Kananga during the
1960's. The conditions under which they were interviewed
also provided a useful guide to the composition of local
community subkereks and internal groupings. Some of
these groupings are based on village and family ties and
others on new neighborhood associations. In many cases,
village and neighborhood ties overlapped, making the overall picture of the church's growth an elaborate interweav-
ing of personal contacts.

Of the family groupings that emerged, those of the head
baptist and of some of the subkerek baptists seemed to be

the most highly represented. This may have been due to my limited exposure to these groups. However, many members claimed some "kinship" with Tshiambi Luka, either directly or through marital and village ties. Some Apostles from Demba Territory told me that they had learned about the church through Tshiambi. The Bikuku, Ndesha, Katoka, and Abattoire subkereks all constituted neighborhood groupings, some having had prior contact before their migration to Kananga. Of these, the Ndesha and Katoka groups also contained many persons who claimed direct "kinship" with Tshiambi, while the Bikuku group had its own internal network of families.

Each subkerek consisted of a core of members, meeting regularly several times a week outside of Sabbath services. During the week, these neighbors would work together as tailors, shoemakers, furniture makers, or small merchants in the market, each group sharing goods and services cooperatively. The prophet Tshilumbu and his brother worked together in a furniture business. Another group of young evangelists also ran a furniture business. The baptist Tshitala was a tailor among those who lined the main streets, with several younger members working near him. Other young evangelists worked as assistant tailors and small merchants in the town market. The railroad workers formed another subgrouping of men who worked and worshiped together. Their wives constituted one of the largest women's groupings in the kerek, working collectively as a singing unit in the Sabbath ceremony.

Unlike other independent churches, such as the Apostles of John Masowe, which also originated in Rhodesia, the Maranke groupings did not establish community-wide cottage industries.[7] The Apostles of Masowe, known as the "Hosannas," because of their singing style, and as the "Bas-

[7] For more information on the Masowe groups, see Sundkler 1961: 323–325; Kileff 1973:1–73.

ketweavers," on the basis of their trades of basketweaving
and tinsmithing, live in self-sufficient communities that are
adjacent to those of the Maranke Apostles in Zambia and
Rhodesia. The Masowes share the profits of this work to
buy large communal homes where they live and worship
together. As these communes expand, emissaries are sent
to establish communal quarters in new areas. While a few
of the Maranke Apostles live together on farms in Zambia
and Zaire, outside of Rhodesia their pattern is less communal and blends more easily with the variety of family styles
already found in urban areas.

While the early history of the Maranke church might
suggest that networks of contact and baptism would be
somewhat random, as they were for the earlier members
Nawezi, Kasanda, and Kadima, the Kananga interviews
tended to invalidate this assumption. The subkerek groupings contained family ties, following John's initial pattern
of intrafamilial baptism. In addition, these groups were
crosscut by new neighborhood and cooperative group clus-
terings that drew in members of the entire local congregation on a residence basis. The only group that was isolated
from the central kerek was the Nganza splinter group that
constituted both a subkerek associational group and a small
separate congregation.

From Village to Town: The Rites of Transition

I was interested in assessing the reasons that adult members gave for their residence in town. With the exception
of one 13-year-old, the age range of those interviewed was
17 to 62 years, spanning the adult life of most members of
the congregation. Migration influxes from rural areas to
Kananga correspond to the major periods of church growth
there. Clearly, the urban sample does not indicate parallel
rural growth of the church, particularly in Demba Territory. The data on the whole indicate that the church ap-

pealed to many first-generation citydwellers. I have attempted to trace the relationships between birthdates, arrival in Kananga, and baptism for the members questioned. Most of the men interviewed were born between 1930 and 1939, the women between 1940 and 1949. The mean age of the men interviewed was thirty-eight and of the women thirty, with a total mean age of thirty-six.[8]

From this information, I expected to see a definite pattern of migration to Kananga emerge but did not know what relation this might bear to church membership. Did members join once in town, or were they already members in the rural context? Of the total number interviewed, only four were born in town. The others came from the surrounding territories of the West Kasai, as far as three hundred miles away. Although Apostles place great emphasis on the need for a country environment for prayer, their migration patterns followed those of the general urban influx for the West Kasai.[9] Membership in the church seemed to take place after Apostles arrived in the city. Only one per cent of those interviewed gave reasons connected with the church for their arrival in Kananga. Most men cited the availability of work. Although many family and village connections predate membership, urban associations and marriage alliances seem to grow concomitantly with it.

The table below shows that the majority of respondents

[8] Of the twenty male members whose wives also answered the schedule, I found that the mean age difference between husband and wife was eleven years. These age differences ranged from a wife who was eight years older to a husband twenty-seven years older than his wife. Both of these combinations were for the same husband, an elder of the kerek who also had two other wives fifteen years younger than he. Three of his four wives were widows who had been given to him in marriage as the church's way of providing for them.

[9] On the emphasis on country surroundings for prayer, see Heimer 1970:309. For a detailed study of urban migration patterns into Kananga in the late 1950's, see Lux 1958:820–877.

were baptized after their arrival in town, but that more men than women had arrived before being baptized. This follows a general pattern that researchers have noted in African urban migration: "The men followed the money and the women followed the men" (Little 1973:17). Apostolic women expressed this general assumption by indicating the presence of their families as the reason for their move to town. The pattern of baptism, men first, then women, follows that of migration for my sample. The mean year of arrival of men in town was 1957, and of women 1961, while the men's mean year of baptism was 1962, and of women 1964. The bulk of arrivals and baptisms for both men and women, however, were located in the period from 1960 to 1964. These figures seem to have been influenced by the influx of members immediately preceding and following the 1963 Passover celebration. These also appear to have been the heaviest migration to Kananga as a whole, al-

Table. Number of respondents born, migrated to Kananga, and baptized during five-year periods, 1910–1970, Kasai sample (n=115)

Year	Year of birth			Year of arrival			Year of baptism		
	Men	Women	Total	Men	Women	Total	Men	Women	Total
1910–1914	5	0	5	0	0	0	0	0	0
1915–1919	3	2	5	0	0	0	0	0	0
1920–1924	3	1	4	0	0	0	0	0	0
1925–1929	13	0	13	0	0	0	0	0	0
1930–1934	17	0	17	2	0	2	0	0	0
1935–1939	21	3	24	0	0	0	0	0	0
1940–1944	11	9	20	3	1	4	0	0	0
1945–1949	10	6	16	4	0	4	0	0	0
1950–1954	0	8	8	11	0	11	0	0	0
1955–1959	0	2	2	17	5	22	18	4	22
1960–1964	0	0	0	31	14	45	43	15	58
1965–1969	0	0	0	12	9	21	13	9	22
1970–	0	0	0	1	2	3	7	4	11
Unknown	0	1	1	2	1	3	2	0	2
Total	83	32	115	83	32	115	83	32	115

Note: This table shows the number of respondents in the Kasai sample who were born, arrived in Kananga as permanent residents, and were baptized in each of the five-year periods shown. The peak of activity for both arrivals and baptisms was the period of 1960 to 1964. The preponderance of arrivals and baptisms in young adulthood does not reflect a policy of the Apostolic church against infant baptism, since the church now contains many baptized children of adult members.

though official figures are not available. The men in the sample averaged twenty nine years of age at baptism, older than the women at an average of twenty. The profile suggests that most men arrived in Kananga in early maturity to do unskilled and semiskilled work, in many cases, immediately after completing primary school. A period of stabilization in town followed, after which, in rapid succession, their families joined them and they were baptized as Apostles.

Maps 2 and 3 (below) depict the successive residences, travel, and participation in the church of interview respondents in the Kasai and Shaba provinces. The maps indicate where personal events took place (for example, first reception of the Passover) to provide a travel history of the two samples. The Kasai sample (Map 2) shows extensive travel throughout the Kasai and contact with members in Lubumbashi and Zambia, with less direct contact in the Shaba interior. While most of the church's "net flow" via baptism has been from surrounding territories into Kananga, there were also a number of cases where church participation did not involve geographical movement. People already residing in Kananga were simply baptized by other Apostles living there. Since Kananga has always been a provincial center for the church, I expected a direction of baptism would emerge in which urban residents were increasingly predominant. As Apostles became stablized in urban jobs and in the urban environment, this trend seems to have risen, although the data themselves are admittedly biased toward urban respondents. Reverse movement toward the rural areas is not yet taking place on a large scale in Kananga. On the other hand, among Zambian Apostles, there is a definite reverse migration of citydwellers to the countryside and an increase of rural baptisms. These first generation urbanites are moving not to villages but to communal farms that incorporate some advantages from both

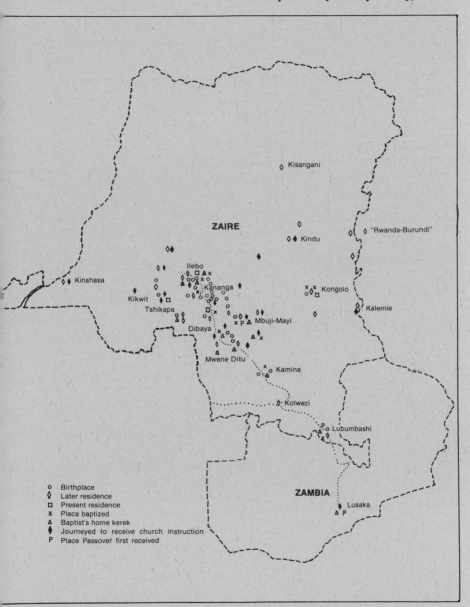

◊ Kisangani

ZAIRE

◊
◊ ◊ Kindu

◊ "Rwanda-Burundi"

◊

◊ ◊

◊
♦

◊ ◊ Kinshasa   Ilebo

Kikwit

Tshikapa   Kananga

Dibaya   Mbuji-Mayi

Mwene Ditu

Kamina

Kolwezi

P o Lubumbashi

ZAMBIA

Lusaka
P

o   Birthplace
◊   Later residence
□   Present residence
x   Place baptized
△   Baptist's home kerek
♦   Journeyed to receive church instruction
P   Place Passover first received

Map 2. Personal participation: Kasai sample

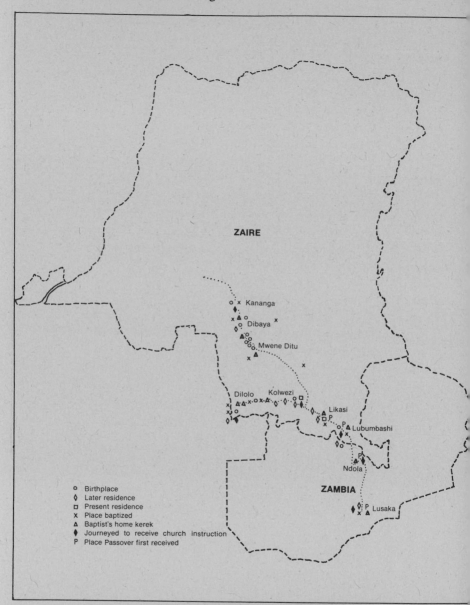

Map 3. Personal participation: Shaba sample

environments. In the Kasai, Demba Territory has grown as a rural Apostolic center and in 1964, was recognized by leaders as a paschal location. Nonetheless, many persons who were not permanent villagers seem to have returned to Demba for the Passover.

The Shaba sample (Map 3) shows strong contact among members from Lubumbashi and southwestern Shaba along the Dilolo railroad and some association with the Kasai. A head baptist in Lubumbashi was born in Kapanga in western Shaba. A major Apostolic farm is located at Dilolo, and contact between Dilolo and Lubumbashi is frequent. Many Kasaian Apostles affiliated with other congregations did not figure in the sample. The expected connection between Kasaian migrants in Lubumbashi and their relatives at home was, therefore, not reflected.

The Influence of General Urban Migration on the Apostles

The Apostles' movements toward Kananga parallel the concentrated urban migration of Kasaians over the past twenty years. Census figures show Kananga with a population of 60,758 at the beginning of 1957; 107,346 in 1958; and 459,960 in 1970.[10] Although several sociologists have viewed the latest population figures as possible exaggerations by local officials, no one denies that the recent migration to Kananga from the surrounding countryside has been extensive.[11] Coupled with heavy migration of Kanangans and rural Kasaians to large cities outside of the Kasai, this urban influx has greatly reduced the population in the

[10] This 1957 figure is taken from TCRB (1957). The AIMO reported the total population of Kananga in 1956, however, as 111,346 (Belgian Congo, AIMO 1956:B.I.). This difference may represent a discrepancy in data collection techniques on the local level, or it may simply reflect different definitions of the extent of the urban area. The 1958 and 1970 figures are given in De Saint Moulin 1970:1.

[11] Haldor Heimer and Daniel Juengst, personal communication.

countryside. As a result, many Apostles periodically farm in their village on a cash crop basis, commuting to town to sell their produce. Apostolic women and children are often sent to dwell in the village for a short period, for members explained that rural life was "cheaper," with food costing less than a third of city prices. Under these temporary arrangements, wives and children are briefly supported by parents or relatives.

Members stated that the former colonial policy of enforced rural residence to maintain high food production resulted in a preference for urban living, once independence ended these restrictions. During the colonial period, persons not employed in town were not allowed to live there. According to the AIMO's figures, the population living outside the traditional milieus, including those in town and in workers' and military compounds, was very erratic between 1947 and 1956. In 1948, it rose by 73 per cent to 169,081, while the total population of the Kasai rose by only 1.8 per cent to 1,878,634. While growth in the province continued steadily, passing the 2 million mark in 1954, the population living outside the village fluctuated several times before rising to 183,315 in 1956. Of this number, 43,341 were listed as urban residents of Kananga, excluding the compounds and suburban villages.[12]

The crowded settlers on the outskirts of Kananga were already considered an administrative problem in 1956.[13] Early 1956 also marked the year that the first Apostolic evangelizing began in Kananga and the West Kasai in general. Within the next year, the percentage of the population outside of the villages had risen to 12.05 per cent, as opposed to 22 per cent for the country as a whole (Young 1965:206).

[12] See Belgian Congo, AIMO 1956:24; the Kananga figure is from AIMO (1957:1).

[13] The AIMO (1956:25) gives the total population of the Kasai in 1956 as 2,074,457.

If the colonial administration's figures do not conflict with those cited in Crawford Young's study, the gain in population was impressive, although the West Kasai remained the most rural province in the country (Young 1965:207).

Migration to Kananga on a larger scale began after independence and still continues. The city now claims a population of over 400,000, making it the second largest in the Zaire. Among Apostles, responses on dates of arrival in Kananga (see above table) showed that the years in which the greatest numbers of members arrived were those immediately following independence, 1960–1964. In keeping with Young's figures on the relatively homogeneous Kasaian origin of Kananga residents, the interviews confirmed my impression of Kananga as a center of regional migration within the Tshiluba-speaking area of the West Kasai. The relative ethnic uniformity of the region dates chiefly from the Baluba-Lulua wars of 1962–1963, when local Baluba fled to the East Kasai (Chomé 1959). Four respondents gave the wars as their reason for migrating to Kananga.

Others not of Kasaian origin were born in Likasi and Kamina, respectively a mining center and a military camp on the railroad between Kananga and Lubumbashi. A full seventy-one per cent of the respondents were born in territories along the railroad line. This roughly supports the common assertions about the church's tendency to proselytize along the railroad and its introduction into the Kasai by this means. Recently, however, overland commuting has contributed to the geographic concentration in Kananga and has decreased the church's dependence on the railroad as the sole means of interregional and rural-urban communication.

What happens to the lives of Apostles when they move from one setting to another? How does religion aid in this transition? It has been stated that traditional tribal and familial solidarity breaks down when people move to an urban area and is partially replaced by Apostolic associational ties (Lanzas and Bernard 1966:190–193). Not specified, however, are the ways in which Apostolic associational ties "substitute" for familial networks as opposed to preserving bonds already in existence outside of the church. It is difficult to determine from the interviews to what extent urban networks are primarily church-linked. In many cases, change to an urban environment in conjunction with the church supplants traditional customs with more flexible ones without a sense of loss. The structure of kinship and of traditional communal life is reinterpreted and to a certain extent retained through Apostolic social organization.

Recent Developments in the Zaire

Both membership and exposure to accounts of church expansion in the sixties changed my interpretation of the AIMO documents when I returned to them a second time. During my travels and while collecting oral histories of the church, I had met several church elders who figured in the documents, including Nawezi, Kadima, Kasanda, and one of my most important teachers, Tshiaba. Kasanda had recounted his experiences in the 1950's, while Nawezi provided me with a copy of his own printed documents. I was now able to look at these documents as part of a continuity that has lasted until the present. Where before, I had implicitly treated the documents as accurate representations of the church, I now saw them as attempts to describe ceremonies familiar to me but confusing to the authorities, who did not accept the grounds on which the events were based.

The year 1972 marked an abrupt change from the country's earlier benevolent tolerance for independent churches. The change may be compared with the church's first years in the Zaire. The context of these developments was the "Return to Authenticity," a program of national unification begun by President Mobutu in October 1971. This program may be characterized as an attempt to reinforce political centralization by strengthening nationalist ideology, extending the influence of the national political party, and bringing other organizations in the country under stringent government controls. Religious organizations, in particular, were asked to prove their contribution to economic development and to consolidate themselves under a few key organizations directly responsible to the government. The law of December 31, 1971 placed all churches, except the Catholic church, the Eglise du Christ au Zaire (a Protestant council of mission churches) and the Kimbanguist church, in a problematic position and required them to submit new dossiers to the Ministry of Justice for reconsideration of their legal status. All churches were to fulfill conditions that included possession of a bank account worth $200,000, a clergy with four-year diplomas in theology, lists of all effective members and leaders, and a plan and budget for educational and economic programs.[14]

While these conditions were feasible for the Catholic and Protestant churches, for a large number of independent groups many were unrealistic and impossible to fulfill. The local leaders of Apostolic congregations considered various alternatives. They desired the freedom to worship even without full recognition and considered claiming privileged status as an international church. Their aim was to convince the government of the validity of Apostolic reasons for failing to meet the requirements. Representatives were sent to Kinshasa from the Apostolic centers in Zaire, each with a dossier constituting its version of the history, doctrine, and organization of the church. In the course of

[14] République du Zaire, Assemblée Nationale, Loi No. 71–012.

compiling the Kananga dossier, a member expressed his hope for official recognition, since the dossier contained records of the church dating from its arrival in 1956. This was my first indication that the church had any of the AIMO records. As a result, I was able to peruse these documents and reflect upon them for the first time as a member of the church.

During the negotiations in Kinshasa, the Ministry of Justice also stipulated that churches maintain schools, hospitals, and downtown offices with paid workers. The Apostles were told that their church was "lazy," having been in the country for so many years without constructing any buildings. Although the commandment against building structures was eventually accepted by administrators as part of the church doctrine, during three months of discussion the requirement to build schools and offices was still upheld.[15] It was rumored that the financial conditions would be waived for some independent groups, while others were able to fulfill them with help from their missionary offices in America and Europe.

The required listing of official church leaders in the Zaire led to some difficulties because of the commensurate status of all Lieb-Umah elders and the presence of diverse congregations. Should a baptist or an evangelist represent a congregation, or should an entirely separate elected official be chosen for one or more groups? Depending on the congregation, different solutions were offered, generally involving the election of the more literate members as representatives, regardless of church position. Listing church leaders in the Zaire also led to difficulties in negotiations, since four representatives from each of the large Apostolic communities were present, each with his own dossier. The

[15] Personal communication, an Apostle in Lubumbashi.

government considered this situation confusing and had difficulty choosing the representative group.

This reaction was in contrast to the earlier Belgian colonial rationale for investigating the independent churches. Where the Belgian government had feared the combined force of independent churches unified into "politico-religious movements," the Zairian government considered the independent churches, officially registered as exceeding three hundred, to be too scattered. Through councils and mergers, the authorities attempted to unify them, creating in essence an enforced ecumenism.[16]

It was felt that the educational and financial qualifications might force the affiliation of the independent churches with those already approved. According to the law, the Catholic church, the Eglise du Christ au Zaire (ECZ) and the Kimbanguist church were exempt.[17] Three other religious communities, the Jewish, the Eastern Orthodox, and the Ishmaelite, Moslems and Arabized peoples of various nationalities, were subsequently added. All other Christian churches were invited to join the ECZ or face dissolution. A rival Protestant body disbanded, leaving the ECZ as the sole Protestant organization with access to legal status. The independent churches had to negotiate with them as well as with the Ministry of Justice.

The ministry later considered waiving the educational requirements, conceding that the Apostolic and similar churches were spiritually inspired. The Apostolic church, however, was not included on an official list of twenty-four approved "spiritual" churches that was broadcast on Zaire radio. An administrator stated that provisional recognition would be given to Apostolic congregations only if they

[16] Such a process of enforced ecumenism contrasts with denominational pluralism that, according to Parsons (1967:413–416), allows various American religious groups to operate on common terms.

[17] République du Zaire, Assemblée Nationale, Loi No. 71–012.

built and staffed offices and schools. After two years, the schools were to be transferred to the government but would continue to be run and staffed at church expense. The church would then be given full recognition, following the pattern of subsidy established by mission schools and related churches.[18]

The possibility of recognizing the Apostolic church as an international organization, since its major leaders were Rhodesians, presented further problems to the Zairian administration. While mission churches were accepted on an international basis, there was no established precedent for according similar rights to relatively new, African-based churches. At one point in the negotiations, some representatives of the Ministry of Justice were reputedly prepared to grant overall recognition to the church on these grounds, but the move was blocked by a decision claiming that the church was a dissident organization from Protestantism and had to be affiliated with the Protestant organization.

Lack of access to a full text of the original law of December 31 affected its enforcement in Kananga, where the church was tentatively outlawed by a decision of the governor's office on January 26, 1972. The local administration decided to interpret the law in the direction of stringent control (*Aurore* 1972:1). This measure was taken despite the fact that Article Three stated that all churches would be free to worship publicly until the March 31 deadline. Tshiambi and Kasanda consulted with their congregations. In early March, they risked open worship, but by the end of March, it was clear that the usual Sabbath kerek would not be possible in Kananga. Some members complained that the truly faithful would worship anyway and risk mass arrest. The surveillance continued, and the plan for mass worship, despite the law, was soon abandoned.

[18] Personal communication, an Apostle in Lubumbashi.

Many members decided to travel south to Lubumbashi for worship. There, temporary freedom for public worship had been granted by the local government. The central government accorded similar freedom in Kinshasa, Bandundu, Mbandaka, and the Lower Zaire. Public worship for independent churches was initially forbidden in the East Kasai and later reinstated. The official rationale for the shift in policy and for the variation between the adjacent Kasai provinces was ambiguous.

The Apostles anxiously awaited March 31, hoping for a favorable decision regarding the independent churches. They felt that the abrupt invalidation of their religious world was surely the result of an error or misunderstanding. They were disappointed. The status quo continued in each province except the West Kasai, where the church was again forbidden to hold services until it had gained official approval. On May 1, 1972, a list of seventy-nine approved churches was published (*Taïfa* 1972:1). The Apostles, however, were not on the general list, although they were promised approval after the final negotiations. They awaited news by letter, radio or formal decree. Silence greeted them, and their uncertainty about worship increased. At the end of my visit in July of 1972, the official policy in Kananga stated that the Apostolic Church was not a church but a "politico-religious movement." [19]

[19] Governor of West Kasai, personal interview, March 26, 1972. In 1974, Apostles reported that public worship had been reinstated in the West Kasai as well.

CHAPTER 8

The Silent Return

My return from Africa and from the protective community of the Apostles is perhaps the most difficult part of the total journey to articulate. It introduced a new testing ground for my own membership and the universality of the Apostles' message. To me, the experiences of conversion were valid and forceful, but responses to my letters from the field showed that they had not been credible to many who knew me before. This doubt stemmed not only from friends' astonishment at my personal choice but also from a bald utilitarian questioning.

Once I explained that I had not joined the group merely for research purposes or to exploit the "real story," the inevitable questions arose: Did membership hurt or distort my research and its possible "objectivity"? If it did not, I must have been deluded, insincere, or, at least, inexperienced in the new beliefs. From the perspective of another world's assumptions, suspending disbelief to approach a new reality was regarded as a source of personal turmoil, especially when the beliefs of science and fundamentalist religion seemed to merge. Yet in moving from one situation to another, it was often possible for me to manage a shift in perspective with relative ease. The dual demands of membership and research made these shifts an integral feature of my daily life.

"The struggle to remain an Apostle will be difficult," prophet Petro predicted, before I left. He stated that I would see visions and report them but would not be a prophetess myself. Despite my acceptance through conversion, I would have to battle for the faith to maintain the

Apostles' vision intact. This particular message recalled the instructions and canons of Apostolic belief that had formed the backdrop of my activities as a new member and transformed observed scenes into meaningful events. The ability to recognize and use instructions was most crucial as part of the vocabulary of membership. Some of these instructions were verbal, and others were not. Some were more explicit than the rest. Ultimately, the specific purpose of each ritual event and the focus of membership developed through participation rather than verbal instruction.[1]

The purpose of instruction was not just to inform me about ritual. It was to instruct me about myself. To distinguish one ceremony from another is a simple selective process. To participate in an event, be judged by it, and glimpse oneself through it is another matter. The coherence with which I categorized my first observations of ritual had been arbitrary. I was unaware that from the earliest meetings with Apostles I was subtly learning new forms of thought. I was collecting a lexicon of events and expectations through which I discovered aspects of an inner self.

The conversion was not an act of grace, or at least not that alone. It offered access to a way of perceiving an inner self and its divisions (cf. James 1958:143). It pointed to fleeting possibilities for unifying that self through interpreting dogma and ceremony, through thought and action. The difference between the scenes that I had witnessed as an outsider and the instruction received as a member was the very sense of spiritual purpose with which I was able to unravel them, not my learning of more intricate labels for them. Apostles did not withhold essential secret informa-

[1] Castaneda (1968:207) stresses specific purposes of "ritual," or understanding the intent of actions personally and in accordance with the system of knowledge, as a key feature of learning an esoteric body of knowledge.

tion from me during the learning process. My own perspective had initially blinded me to what they saw as the meaning of events. What I could not grasp as possible or practical as an outsider could only remain obscure. Nor was the conversion to religion so different from the affirmations of science to which I clung (cf. Polanyi 1962:151; Schutz 1964a:19–22). In each case, a set of unifying themes performed a fundamental transformation, shaping reality for me (cf. Pearce 1973:7). Making the inferences of science and religion involved returning to reaffirm these themes as reality principles.

In the abstract, it seems that the observer's partial blindness might be overcome by an act of will, as if faith in seeing alone would create the very things he or she wished to see. The need to transcend perspectives pushes the researcher to broader and broader conclusions about what are actually unique experiences. These generalizations are set forth as scientific induction and unavoidable comparison. Two British sociologists decided to test the questions of perspective and membership in their joint research.[2] Each assumed a substantially different subjective relationship to the members of the religious sect they studied. One impersonated a committed believer, while the other remained a skeptic for the purpose of observing both his partner and the group more effectively. While the former apparently did not experience any internal change, the latter claimed that he was able to collect much more specific information about the group and its rituals. Objectivity was equated with the lack of group commitment or membership. The overt stranger role allowed legitimate

[2] Assuming the positions of a committed believer and an outsider, Walker and Atherton (1972:362–387) studied an Easter Pentecostal Convention in England and, simultaneously, their own process of research. Neither became a convert or began to learn about the Pentecostal experience as one fully applicable to him as a member.

questioning. In my case, such an experiment was unfeasible.

Apostles were no longer as willing to argue about basic points of doctrine, such as whether cure by faith was actually possible, once I was baptized. By acceptance, I had opened the possibility of a new reality with its own requirements for validation. Pearce describes this process by suggesting that approaching a "crack" between worlds or realities "is neither a 'real world' nor an opening into such—for there is no such thing as a 'real world' other than the one from which one makes such a statement" (1973:138). He refers to the crack as an "ontological function" for passing through many realities without residing in an absolute reality. Yet, as a member, I was in the position of having to defend an absolute. All of my actions were interpreted in terms of dogma, and I had to learn how and why these arguments were made.

Harsh and practical as the circumstances of this learning were in Africa, they prepared me only minimally for the things that happened on my return. As a new Apostle in Africa, it was often difficult to question a shared reality, a special consensus about the world that seemed opaque to me but not others. Nevertheless, it was simple enough to read aloud a biblical passage that someone else found for me or to defend the rejection of Christmas as a pagan holiday to other Apostles assured of this fact. To debunk the pagan festival and its saint when questioned by my own child was considerably harder. In this case, I had both to create and to defend a new reality in the face of old, comfortable assumptions. It was similarly difficult to defend the outward customs that Apostolic women adopted, in the face of their meaning outside of Africa. I soon stopped trying to explain them.

During my visit, I learned far more about doctrine and ritual through active ceremonial participation than I had on most other occasions. This involved a paradox. When I was most immersed in events, my capacities for abstract reflection were far away, and so were pen and paper. The experiences that were central to my eventual understanding of ceremony were the most ineffable and difficult to analyze. The events that could be documented more readily presumed the spiritual experience as a silent grounding. Though I could recall many of these experiences vividly, their impact was lost in recording. The report bore only the strong marks of my own humanity.

Merely observing an activity and attempting to note its parts prior to participating was not enough. Gradually, I became totally dissatisfied with observational descriptions that earlier would have been completely adequate. These descriptions also failed to capture what I later saw as the important aspects of my participation, such as the joy of learning to sing in kerek.

Metzger and Williams (1963:216–234) point to a similar case for members of a southern Mexican community who wanted to learn the practices of faith healing. Acquiring knowledge of the technique through observation was considered dangerous and had to be done in a circumspect manner. Those who merely watched and were not divinely chosen and specifically instructed were considered both vulnerable to illness and likely to cause misfortune themselves. Theirs was considered a lesser version of healing that would endanger others who accepted it. For Apostles, spiritual gifts were similarly considered to be confined to those who had been blessed and confirmed. These gifts could not be learned through observation and were transmitted through prescribed spiritual and moral instruction. A person simply following the healer's routine movements without spiritual preparation would be considered ignorant of the process of cure, and harmful. Imparting specialized knowledge about healing often directly preceded performing the rites and in many cases was not conceivable without them.

My statements suggest that a description from a member's perspective is essential and has a certain privilege over other accounts. They can be misread as saying that there is a single member's perspective. Membership, instead, may be defined as an introduction to the vocabulary and intents of members and to the viability of their descriptions. Insofar as my aims were to uncover how members think and feel about the world, these experiences were the primary data that would have been unavailable without my membership. Another account could only have returned for its auspices to the points of reference of the reporter. The baptism and first Passover constituted a critical turning point, since they involved my subjective participation on grounds requiring me to be fully accountable to other members and to master their expectations. Yet, the momentary, totally absorbing experience of being smothered between an active crowd and the confessional fire did not yield the full insights of a member. Participation could not substitute for reflection and learning.

The possibility of learning through performance developed and was acknowledged by other members only after baptism. The baptism involved a conversion experience that created a change in the underlying themes that I had used to interpret events. Members addressed me in terms of my presumed desire to seek heaven, to learn healing, and to participate in kerek. I found myself through performance and through unraveling instructions. Although similar commitments are not possible or desirable in every study, participation forces the ethnographer to test his skill by uniting perceptions and performance, a process that challenges previous questions and perspectives.

It is not possible to describe exactly how membership is a grounding for perception and description, how experience and assumptions mutually alter each other. For Apostles, however, certain themes did arise as central: self-scrutiny and purity, visionary experience through ceremony. The member of a modern cult in the West might find salvation, or at least solace, in reconciling the findings of science and spiritism.[3] The Apostles struggle to combine fruits of custom and Christianity. If these explanations of themes and convergences do not take place in terms of the doctrine and purposes of a group, however, it is all too simple to impose the assumptions of the observer's perspective upon them. In this way Africanists have found the "distorted" rudiments of Roman law and European philosophy in African religious and social life. There is a point at which divergences in the assumptions of membership and the cultural presuppositions for explanation become too great to bridge.

Members rebuke the outsider who seeks an Apostolic healer, thinking that the healer himself accomplishes the cure. They explain that healing, like compliance with the commandments, is performed only through the Holy Spirit. The healer is merely a vehicle. The explanation that is logical to the outsider, that the act was an individual one, is unacceptable to the member. Translation from one order of understanding to another violates the most basic assumptions of those who hold fast to its tenets. As an ethnographer, I was presented with the ideal that all explanations were equally plausible. As a participant in a healing, however, one explanation took precedence over others. Members were always keenly aware of relativistic positions. They suggested that it was important to learn the Bible to understand religious practices other than those of the Apostles.

[3] Wilson (1970:141–144) discusses "manipulationist sects" as those modern groups that combine aspects of scientific terminology with their own theological interpretations.

Relativistic positions can always be defended intellectually and for the sake of loyalty, but loyalty or advocacy is not to be confused with acceptance. During the first few weeks of my research, I was thrown, like many fieldworkers, into situations that required a personal response. Like the students of asylums who become the patients' advocates, I was already the Apostles' advocate. When the young Director of Cults and Religious Affairs in Kananga asked if I believed that faith healing could restore life to a child, I responded "yes." This was not religious conviction, and it was probably not convincing. I was simply defending my friends. The director admitted that he found the incident "amusing." The Apostles accompanying me smiled benignly, but the questions were not over.

"If you really believe in the Apostolic church," the administrator continued, "how can you wear the jewelry denied their women?" I mumbled in embarrassment, head bowed, already feeling that in some way I represented the church. This incident was echoed again after my conversion, when a market woman predicted that I would soon return to the jewelry that I had cast aside.

The official then questioned my stand on the damaging character of the Apostles' public worship and their failure to use medicines. "These people flaunt the standards of public health. They insist upon worshiping in the rain, while the mothers nurse small babies openly." I continued to defend the Apostles with increasing loyalty, while Tshiambi, the evangelist Marcel, and others nodded in assent and approval. As I left the administrator's office, I was stricken with nausea on the street. Everyone there saw my condition, and workers peered at me from the administrative building. By the following afternoon, rumors filled the town center that the Apostles had fed me local dishes to which I was unaccustomed (presumably a sign of intimacy) and that I, following their rules, had refused medicines. My experience had hardly seemed a spiritual one, and I could not foresee its relation to my later conversion.

The loyalty that I had displayed preceded a glimpse of new realities. To resolve the conflict between their formal models of indigenous beliefs and lived experience, researchers often settle for loyalty. The models are presented as detached from experience and, therefore, can be seen from a relativistic perspective. Through loyalty, researchers appear to provide translations of members' beliefs and categories. These renderings substitute the sympathy of the detached observer for the test of performance and performative description. The turning point of my research, the critical conversion experience, required the step from loyalty to assertion. Ultimately, this step always remained in the making; it was never completed. With a tone of sadness, Apostles occasionally reminded me that I had allowed the faith of science to overshadow membership. The prophet Esau once stated that he saw the church as a tall strong tree to which I was chained. I held a book, and each time that I attempted to stretch the chain, pulling myself and the book away, the chain would bounce back like an elastic, thumping me harshly against the tree. This prophecy has returned to me many times, as both I and this book have wandered far afield.

At the close of my visit, members clamored for my conclusions (*votre synthèse*) about the research I had done. Tshiaba was particularly insistent that I generalize beyond the daily events and ceremonies to evaluate the church's merit and make predictions about its future. This would lend scientific credence to predictions that the prophets had already made. Once I joined the church, many others considered the aims of my work to be even more mysterious. Each new conversation required a balancing of statuses. While every encounter for the researcher may be a potential interview, for the Apostle, each meeting is a time of proselytism and doctrinal discussion.[4] When one is both researcher and member, there is an understandable conflict of interest. I was more confused by members' expectations than by my own resolutions. Some members were bemused by my formal interviews and the constant presence of a tape recorder or still camera. Peter was even referred to as "Mr. Photo." Others expected and encouraged these outward signs of research, because they allowed them to place me in a distinctive status. When I was told by prophets that I was too "cheeky" for an Apostolic woman, the complaint seemed based on my scientific prying and aggressiveness.

Following Tshiaba's suggestion, I attempted to evaluate the spiritual organization of the church in order to present official statements to the Rhodesian center and the local government. In both cases, my testimony as a new convert and researcher was to lend "objective" validation to the church's undertakings and describe its predicament. Once and for all, I would attempt to explain Abel's position to the government and clarify why a single Apostolic leader could not possibly represent all of the Zairian congregations without clearance from the Rhodesian center. My status as a sociologist made me among the first emissaries to be chosen to translate these matters to outside officials.

The report that I wrote for the Kananga Apostles was not a conclusive statement. Each assertion was modified by a sociological generalization and a brief tracing of the historical context in which it was made. I demonstrated that the research had its own legitimate hypotheses and directions. This both pleased and dismayed some of the Apostles who read it. The organization of information about the

---

[4] Cicourel (1964:73) refers to every social encounter as a potential interview situation, based on the way in which the researcher orients to social interaction. Not only the researcher but also any actor operating under the assumptions of a specific body of knowledge or set of purposes may transform interactions into activities with a specific theme and goal.

church was praised. I was merely reminded to stress that all leaders performed their duties only through the powers of the Holy Spirit. My failure to draw from these data and openly assert the "obvious" conclusion, that the Apostolic church was the true, perhaps the only true, Spirit church was considered regrettable. When asked to draw this conclusion in conversation, I would gladly nod in assent, but somehow the scientific perspective of the report could not be temporized.

As a messenger from one congregation to another, it was assumed that I represented the personal viewpoint of each group's leaders. Even at the Rhodesian center, I was treated as a representative of Zairian Apostles, who were considered to be in spiritual trouble because of the absence of the Passover. I was also considered an emissary to a new land. I was ambivalent about these responsibilities. Since I was still learning about the church, I did not think it appropriate to criticize each group's assumptions. The church was, after all, the creation of the African Apostles, and I, as a foreign researcher, should attempt to tamper with it as little as possible. In this situation, I felt that it was most important for me to gather information rather than to express opinions of my own.

The problems arising from the Zairian administration's interpretation of my membership were complex. On the afternoon that the new governor had arrived in the Kasai, I had been among the white-clad Apostles who greeted him. This natural compliance with the Apostles' expectation was a shock to some outsiders. Although there were some precedents in the Kimbanguist church, administrators viewed a Westerner who embraced independency as an anomaly. A Westerner's beliefs could not come out of a nostalgia for the past, since this past is not actually ours. In the official view, these simple churches denied progress. Therefore, an outsider's membership was a puzzle and, worse, was suspect. Research or no research, the only explanation feasible to the authorities was political. I was, logically, there to agitate. Neither sociological statements nor assertions of faith could explain the realities of my research and membership.

Unfortunately, I am afraid that the fulfilling conclusions members desired have never been written for the Apostles of Kananga. Tshiaba, Nawezi, and others continue to produce church histories and sociologies that are of interest in their own right. These statements have been sent to audiences as diverse as the Zairian central government and Pope Paul. Several months after I left Kananga, some of the Apostles with whom I had lived were jailed after being interrogated about the church and the purpose of my stay. My voice was too faint and far away to be heard on their behalf.

Sitting with friends after our return, we discussed the fact that not long ago, none of us had experienced "zeal." Beyond our mundane faiths and our skepticism about science, we had felt little. Even now, for us, it was strange and somehow impolite to talk with zeal of conversion. The reality that had opened for me could never open for them. To suggest that it could, would be too presumptuous, too personal, and wrong for them. Or worse, it would be to proselytize, an act that has a place only for those who count it toward heavenly merit. In mutual tolerance, they would tell others that I had become an "African fundamentalist" and would silently wonder why.

Speaking to my old friends was often like knocking on an invisible wall. I could not open a box, demonstrate the faith of the Apostles, translate it into reasonable terms, and then close the box. While some historical version of the church and the lives of many members might easily bear up under this scrutiny, the depth of my individual experiences could not so readily be translated. Yet, without being able to show it, I continued to claim that these experiences made all else possible. There could be no conclusions without them.

When I left the Rhodesian Passover, my thoughts about the return to America had been optimistic. Thousands of Apostles had shared in the joy of the Passover at John Maranke's home. I was reconfirmed as a healer, and Peter became a baptist. We were sent home with good wishes. These last close experiences with the Apostles were those that lingered most, when I returned. Despite my recurrent doubts and battles of faith, I always emphasized the charismatic powers that I had seen them display—the firewalking, prophecy, exorcism, and inspired singing.

One afternoon, following a lecture on the Apostles in which I had described some of these experiences, I went grocery shopping. A woman stopped me, staring glassily. She asked if I was the one who had walked on coals and cured people in Africa. I replied that members of the group to which I belonged had walked on coals, but I had not. As I continued to say that I had experienced cures that I considered miraculous, she had already turned away, her eyes downcast. In a moment of silence, I thought that I should have said "yes" and taken this opportunity to offer instruction. But in silence I too resisted.

In the absence of an Apostolic community, our worship practices became modified in America. They resembled those used by the African Apostles on a masowe retreat. We held kerek alone, either in our own yard or in a secluded mountain spot, singing, praying, and performing the curing ceremony. Even though Peter had been proclaimed a baptist, we sorely missed the gift of prophecy, so important to Apostolic practice. Despite some of my visions, this absence of confirmed prophecy meant that kerek took place without the prophetic examination as a direct review of our spiritual state. It was our individual responsibility to confess sins to each other and to write to members in Africa, whenever difficulties arose.

Even the matter of individual confession was based on an exception to the Apostolic rule. As a woman and a healer, I would not ordinarily have been permitted to hear confession. In the absence of a large community, the elders had stated that I could hear, but not officially comment on, confessions, until an evangelist of kerek was baptized. We were instructed to begin by searching first for an evangelist and then a prophet. These new members would appear after a divine inspiration. We would recognize them immediately, as Christ had the original twelve.

The prophets had stated that four to ten members were all we would need to establish a full kerek officially recognized by the Rhodesian center as a congregation, but none of these people seemed to be forthcoming. No conscious effort to search for them or to pull them from the network of our friends, relatives, or acquaintances would work. We waited for the seeds that the Apostles had planted in Africa to grow and examined ourselves as the thorny ground on which they had fallen. A year and a half passed, and gradually our enthusiasm in explaining the church to others declined.

Friends asked if our faith, too, was declining, and we answered with despondent silence. We made plans to return to Africa for further research and to discuss the plight of the church in America. At about this time, when we least expected it and had virtually abandoned any overt efforts at proselytizing, Philip came to us. He had learned about the church a year earlier in a lecture and had not been particularly impressed. But something about the talk had remained with him. He wanted to learn more. After attending kerek twice, he requested to be baptized. We were surprised and tried to delay to give him time to reconsider. Baptist William had just sent us a note saying that a tall young man, a "giant," would come to us and request baptism and healing. Philip met this description. In mid-January of 1974, he became the first convert in America.

Like a family welcoming a new child, the kerek had to readjust. Philip assumed my former role of hearing confession and quickly learned the Apostolic style of preaching and some of the songs. We instructed him in lore and ritual as we had been taught, and his questions mirrored ours. Why were there so many rules? When could he expect true vision? I found many points of doctrine difficult to uphold and requested that the format of kerek be modified so that we might discuss them. Although we attempted to change to a more informal structure, the habits of ritual were difficult to break.

The absence of a prophet continued to influence our individual relationships to ceremony. Philip brought a friend with him whose visionary experiences led us to believe that he would become the first prophet of our group. But we curtailed our enthusiasm to watch the unfolding of events. In kerek we now sang as a threesome, and our eagerness to participate together enlivened the ceremony. Other visitors came, and we continued to pray in the manner taught by the Apostles of Africa.

Presenting a description of the Apostles and their ritual has been an account of how I lived with and became a part of them, sharing the hopes and visions of their communities. The story does not end with our return, for many months a silent return, or with the gradual succumbing of zeal to uniformity. As the Apostles parted with us in Zambia and Rhodesia, they had bid us good courage and prophesied of the many converts to come. More than this, they urged us to the new and unaccustomed work of "missionizing in reverse," or, as they put it, "preaching the gospel to the people of my tribe"—the people of America.

This mission was as strange as that of the early European Christians who ventured into Africa. Their message, difficult to communicate to another culture, ultimately found its own roots there, producing a new type of religion. On the other hand, in many ways the message of the Apostles is already well understood in America, to which its history might be traced. Spiritual churches of the Pentecostal type have long practiced faith healing, prophecy, and spiritual inspiration. Millenarian sects and movements are not lacking in the Western Protestant tradition, and many have actually been transplanted from America to Africa. Food taboos, fasting, and spiritual discipline are all part of the Judeo-Christian tradition. Aspects of Apostolic practice can easily strike many chords of Western Christianity and mysticism. Yet, even the black churches of America, whose traditions and contexts of growth have been intertwined with and so closely resemble those of the African independent churches, find their style and form of ritual alien.

Some theologians cry that the churches of the West have become "secularized," that they have lost the sense of the sacred (Needleman 1972:12). Others claim that they are merely becoming relevant, adapting to the other institutions of a contemporary society. Certainly, it is rare to find the forms of concrete thought contained in Apostolic doctrine in much of Western religion. It has been stated that Western religions have now become vulnerable in the "absence of religious techniques and methods and the underestimation of human possibility" (Needleman 1972:20). Among Apostles, these religious techniques are an integral part of forming a community that, as the Kanangan administrators suggested, is absent in its specific form from the American past.

Although they are puzzled about the American case, African Apostles claim to be prepared for expansion across cultures and nations.[5] The autonomy of leadership at the local level is a way of assuring the rapid, fluid growth of the church. This local autonomy is combined with flexibility in ritual and belief. Only after my own experiences in explaining the church in America did I recognize how important this freedom of interpretation is. Members do not consider flexibility heterodox, since a core of shared doctrines and rites remains. Variation and growth rely on sustained community in the midst of rapidly changing societies that tend to destroy customary social relationships. The formation of community is central to the Apostolic message. Without it, the ceremonies would become only a shadow of their promise.

Within Africa, the appeal of biblical utopianism is rising. Ten thousand more Apostles made the journey to the Rhodesian Passover in 1973 than in 1972. The church has also begun to attract a few European members in Rhodesia and Mozambique. Barrett estimates that by 2000 A.D., sub-Saharan Africa will probably be more than 60 per cent Christian—over 350 million Christians—with many of these persons members of independent churches (1970:43). Regardless of one's attitude toward this growth, it indicates a possible combination of cultural forms, including ritual innovation and the development of new types of communities. Religion in Africa is never divorced from community, but these new combinations are already encountering opposition from outside religious and political institutions. In the Zaire, and in other parts of the continent, their position is likely to change in the near future, as their influence increases in urban areas and new alliances arise.

[5] In the late 1960's several other independent churches also began to expand their scope outside Africa. The Nigerian Aladura church opened a branch in London (Moorhouse 1973:319). The Kimbanguists were admitted to the World Council of Churches in 1969 and announced several Europeans within their ranks.

Despite a variety of speculations from outside sources, Apostles are confident that their organization is a true and universal church that will grow throughout Africa and the world. As I returned home, with the church's struggle and message silently in mind, members were convinced that yet another of the founder's prophecies had at long last been fulfilled.

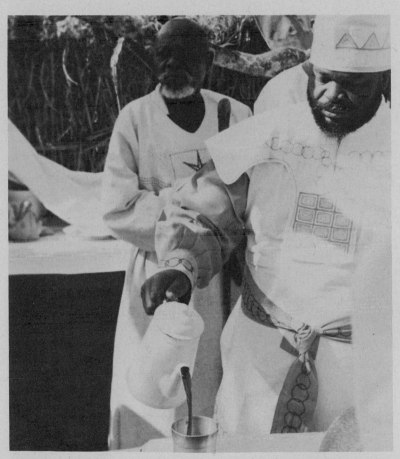

Plate 14. Abel Sithole, John Maranke's son, administering the Passover at Maranke Reserve, July 17, 1974.

Songs, Sermons, and Kerek Excerpts

The excerpts presented here show the basic format of kerek. The ceremony proceeds as follows once the prophetic examination is completed:

I. Opening Hymns: "Kwese, Kwese" and "Mwari Komborera Africa"
II. The Lord's Prayer
III. Preaching and Song in Kerek
IV. "Pa Ku Denga": Closing the Kerek
V. Prophetic Testimony
VI. "Ndo Famba": Ending the Ceremony
VII. Songs of Prophecy, Curing, and Prayer Sung outside of Kerek

I. Opening Hymns

"Kwese, Kwese" [Chishona]

Kwese, kwese, tinovona vanhu hamuzivi Kristu [1]
Vakarasikirwa nediko
Vanomutadza muponesi

Refrain: *Mwari wedu wemasimba*
          Tinzwe tinomukumbira
          Tumai mweya mutsvene
          Kuno kune vamwe vasinawo

[1] As sung by Rhodesian Apostles in Lusaka, Zambia.

Vatumei mangwanani
Vatumei pamauro
Vatumei masikati
Kune misha yavo yose

Asi isu Baba wedu tine basa rokuita
Tine hama nesha Mwari ti
Tumei kuna ivo

Everywhere, everywhere, we see people who do not know Christ
They have lost the time
Because of sins

Refrain: Our God of strength
            Hear us, we beg you
            Send us the Holy Spirit
            Here, there, where they do not have it

Send them in the morning
Send them in the evening
Send them in the midday
To all their villages

But we, our Father, have work to do
We have relatives and friends, Lord
Send us to them

"Mwari Komborera Africa" [Chishona]

Mwari Komborera Africa, Alleluia [2]
Chisua yemina matu yedu
Mwari Baba Jesu utukomborera
            (Utukomborera)
Jesu, turi baranda bako

Refrain: *(Uya mueya)*
O mueya, hosanna mueya, utukomborera
            (Hosanna mueya)
O mueya, hosanna mueya, utukomborera
            (Utukomborera)

[2] As sung by Rhodesian Apostles in Lusaka, Zambia.

O mueya, mueya
Mwari Baba Jesu, utokomborera
          (Utukomborera)
Jesu, turi baranda bako
Aridzi mzitwe zhitarako, Alleluia
Chisua yemina matu yedu, etc.
               (Uya mueya), etc.
Mwari fungeni Africa, Alleluia
Chisua yemina matu yedu, etc.
               (Uya mueya), etc.
Turi pano pa rusambo rako.

God save Africa, Alleluia
Hear our prayers
God, Father, Jesus, bless us
          (Bless us)
Jesus, we are Your servants

     Refrain: (Come Spirit)
O come Holy Spirit, bless us
          (Hosanna Spirit)
O come Holy Spirit, bless us
O Holy Spirit, God, Father, Jesus, bless us
          (Bless us)
Jesus, we are Your servants

Let Your name be exalted, Alleluia
Hear our prayers, etc.
          (Come Spirit), etc.
God remember Africa, Alleluia
Hear our prayers, etc.
          (Come Spirit), etc.
We are here to meet You

II. The Lord's Prayer [Tshiluba]

Tatu wetu udi mu diulu, banameke dina diebe. Bukelenge buebe bulue.
Benze ha buloba mudi musue bu mûdibo benza mu diulu. Utuhe tshituha
tshia bidia bietu bia buatshia-buatshia a lelu. Utulekelele mabanza a
malu mabi etu bu mutuakumana kulekelela, kabidi badi n'etu mabanza
a malu mabi. Kutufikishi hadi mateyi, kadi utusungile kudi bubi.

III. Preaching and Song in Kerek

The following excerpts will present: (a) song texts in the original and in translation and (b) portions of kerek in translation showing the articulation of preaching and song.

Song texts

"The Baptism of John" [Tshiluba]

Dibatiza dia Yona ndia bualu bukole
Satana muimana Yesu muimana belangana mpata
Buloba bujima butukonka bua Nyuma wa Nzambi

Mikenji kayena mu diulu, kayena dishiya dia mayi
Mikenji bakayifunda mu Mukanda wa Nzambi
Wayenza ne wayilama neasungidibue

Mambo wa Mambo, midimu ya kubuikila buloba bujima we
Munya wakatemena bakamuibabeya, O Baba
Bakadia mubidi ne mashi bia mfumuetu Yesu

The baptism of John is difficult
Satan stands here, Jesus there, they are fighting
The whole earth asks us about the Holy Spirit

The laws are not in Heaven nor on the other bank of the river
The laws are written in the Bible
He who does and keeps them will be saved

Lord God, the darkness was spread out over the whole earth
Light was revealed to those who believed, O Father
Those who ate the body and blood of our Lord Jesus

The "baptism of John" refers to the Holy Spirit baptism brought by John Maranke in the name of the Trinity rather than the baptism of John the Baptist (Acts 19:1–7).

"Preacher tell the people" [Tshiluba]

Muvangeri ambile bantu, buloba budi bupia (2)

Refrain: *Tuakabambile, bakabenga*
            Bua kulomba Nzambi (2)

Anania ne Sabila bakashina Nzambi (2)
Sala wakalela mwana bua kulomba Nzambi (2)
Chakazunkano wakalela muana wa mulayi (2)

Preacher tell the people
The earth will be burned (2)

    Refrain: We told them, they refused
                to pray to God (2)

Ananias and Sapphira
Tried to fool God (2)

Sarah bore a child
Because she prayed to God (2)

Chakazunkano bore
The child of the promise (2)

    The Tshiluba translation is presented above, since a
fuller version was collected of it than of the Chishona original. Verses 2 and 3 refer to the biblical stories of Ananias
and Sapphira (Acts 5:1–11) and the birth of Isaac (Gen. 21:1–5).
Verse 4 refers to the Apostolic account of the descent of
John Maranke from Chakazunkano, who is said to have
hosted the infant Jesus and his family for three years in
Egypt.

"John has gone to Jerusalem" [Chishona]

Jonyi waenda Jerusalema, Osana
Pa tyenda ku Jerusalema uko
Pa Maranke pa Jerusalema, Osana
Pa Maranke muno Jerusalema, O
Maranke warari Jerusalema
Waenda pa Jerusalema
Tichamona pa Jerusalema

John has gone to Jerusalem, Hosanna
When we go to Jerusalem up there
In Maranke is Jerusalem, Hosanna

In Maranke here in Jerusalem, O
Maranke is lying down in Jerusalem
He has gone to Jerusalem
We come from Jerusalem

This song is dedicated to the founder's death and ascent
to Heaven.

"Sodom and Gomorrah" [Tshiluba]

Solo: *Bantu, luayi ku tshiondo tshia muoyo, mu buloba mu
         So—*

All: *Mu Sodomo ne Gomorrah
         Mu buloba mu Sodomo ne Gomorrah
         Mu buloba mu Sodoma*

Solo: *Jehovah Nzambi utubuikidile, mu buloba mu So—*

All: *Mu Sodomo ne Gomorrah
         Mu buloba mu Sodomo ne Gomorrah
         Mu buloba mu Sodomo*

         (Similarly)
         *Kumuedi kabobo, kena kule
         Umuele kabobo, yeye apa
         Muoyo wanyi wakujinga
         Nzambi wetu musela nzala*

Solo: People, come to the drum of life, on earth is So—

All: In Sodom and Gomorrah
         On earth is Sodom and Gomorrah
         On earth is Sodom

         (Similarly)
         Lord God pardon us
         If you call Him, He is not far
         If you call Him, He is there
         My heart is longing
         Our God sought in fasting

"We have gathered" [Tshiluba adapted from the Chishona]

Taunga, taunge, taungane, Mambo wa ku denga
Tuimbayi, tuimbayi, taungane, Mambo wa ku denga
Tuakengi, tuakengi, etc.
Osana, tuakengi, etc.
Balunda, tuimbayi, etc.
Baprofete, imbayi, etc.
Bavangeri, imbayi, etc.
Bamama, imbayi, etc.
Bapostolo, imbayi, etc.
Yezu katshia waya, etc.

We have gathered, we have gathered, Lord in Heaven
Let us sing, we have gathered, Lord in Heaven
Let us learn, we have gathered, Lord in Heaven
Hosanna, let us learn, etc.
Friends, let us sing, etc.
Prophets, sing, etc.
Evangelists, sing, etc.
Mothers, sing, etc.
Apostles, sing, etc.
Since Jesus departed, etc.

Preaching and song

Sermon: The True Baptism [Demba Territory, 1969]

(Greeting)
Speaker: Children of God, life to you. (Response.)
             Peace be with you. (Response.)
(Topic introduction by speaker)
Speaker: The Bible says that we should not hate each other. Our
    brothers showed us that the Bible unites us. But we have found
    out that those who possess the Bible are those who destroy
    others. The name of Apostles: we find that Jesus was an Apos-
    tle, and He was a Saviour. We are the Apostles of Jesus Christ

and we are the Saviours of our land. That's why they say that
if God is in Africa, the land of the devil, [then] these are the
words I have prepared for you. I have prepared other words
besides these, but the main subject is the subject of baptism.
Children of God, life to you. (Response.)
(Reference to previous speaker's topic)
When our Kimbanguist brothers came, they read a letter to us,
and they showed us that everyone should know where he
stands; that everyone should know the tools with which he is
doing his job, what his foundations are, and what his job is.
(Break in transcription)

Song: We are passengers, we are passengers
            Refrain: I put my heart in God
                      I put my heart in God
                      I put my heart in God
        We are not baptized from the cup
        (Refrain)
        We are sons of Heaven
        (Refrain)

(Topic integration of song by speaker)
Speaker: The singer just told us that you [nonmembers in the
audience] are baptized from the cup. It's astonishing to see that
such a big man can be put into a can like canned beef. We can't
find a glass of water showing a whole body. The singer says
that you are baptized from the cup. But I still doubt that a man
can be washed from the cup.
(Speaker selection)
Speaker: Let's hear what the Bible says.
Reader: Today we are going to read Psalms, chapter 124, verse
1. The title says that if God is not on our side, Israel may say—
(Management of reading by speaker)
Speaker: Go on.
Reader: —that when people rose against us, that when they per-
secuted us alive, when they directed their anger towards us—
Speaker: Skip to verse four.
Reader: Then water passes over our heads, water of disdain.
Rivers were stronger than our hearts.
(Topic elaboration by speaker in antiphonal preaching)

Speaker: Children of God, life to you. (Response.) The Bible says that Jesus was baptized with the baptism of the river. The preacher taught us that after the baptism, He got the Holy Spirit. The act of getting the Holy Spirit made Him know what was inside the Jews. Then this water gave them strength. What did they call this water?

Reader: The fifth verse says that afterward the water of disdain was stronger than our hearts.

Speaker: Children of God, life to you. (Response.) This water from the cup, the water of disdain. When the Europeans saw that there were no useful tools for our jobs, they gave you the water from the cup, the water of disdain. Our forefathers said that the hero was bought when there was water [i.e., surrendered from thirst]. . . .

(Responsorial preaching with audience)

Speaker: Let us be aware that there is no other church under the sun, even where the Pope lives, but we cannot name it. Children of God, life to you. (Response.) There is under the sun only one [true] church, one God, one book—

Congregation: —One.

Speaker: There is no other church under the sky from the time of Israel until this time I am addressing you. There is only one church because there is one God, one book—

Congregation: —One.

Speaker: They do not know which one it is; neither do I. . . .

IV. "Pa Ku Denga": Two Versions of Hymn Closing the Kerek (Chishona)

Pa kudenga kuna Baba [3]	Pa kudenga kuna Baba [4]
Kwakanaka kwazwo	Kwakanaka kwazwo
Pa kudenga kuna Baba	Pa kudenga kuna Baba
Kwakafara kwazwo	Kwakafara kwazwo

[3] Reprinted by permission of the Methodist Church, Salisbury, Rhodesia.

[4] As sung by Rhodesian Apostles in Lusaka, Zambia.

Hakupindi chakaipa	*Hakupindi chakaipa*
Kanachiri chimwe	*Kanachiri chimwe*
Hakupindi zwo kurwara	*Hakupindi chakurwadza*
Ne chimwere chimwe	*Nechimwere chimwe*
Ndabatswene ibo bose	*Ndevatsvene ivo vose*
Banogara iko	*Vanogara uko*
Banokuda banamate	*Vanokunda vanamati*
Iwe Mwari wabo	*Iwe Mwari wavo*
Bakawana musha wabo	*Vakavona musha wavo*
Musha wakagara	*Musha wakanaka*
Bakawana no upenyu	*Vakavona neupenyu*
Bgusingabfubure	*Bwuzinazoperi*
Ndiri mwenyi pane nyika	*Ndiri mwenyi paneino nyika*
Ndinosuba denga	*Ndinoshuwa kudenga*
Ngandipinde newe Jesu	*Ngandipinde newe Jesu*
Ndiende kudenga	*Ndiendewo kudenga*

These are two of the many variations in which this hymn is sung. A translation follows.

> In Heaven near the Father
> It is a good place
> In Heaven near the Father
> It is a happy place
>
> Nothing which is bad can enter there
> Nothing, even one
> Nothing painful can enter
> Nor any sickness
>
> They are all holy,
> Those who stay there
> They surpass even those who pray
> You are their God
>
> They have found [bakawana] their home
> They have seen [vakavona] their home
> Their home to stay [wakagara]
> Their good home [wakanaka]

They have found everlasting life
Which will never end

I am a stranger on this earth
I am longing for Heaven
Let me enter with you, Jesus
Let me go to Heaven

V. Prophetic Testimony in Kerek (Kananga, 1969)

I saw in a vision an angel with a big basin. Inside this basin was a serpent. It had its head extended inside this basin. There was no water in the basin. The angel made a turn of all the four cardinal points. When he had finished, he stood in the middle of the earth, and the snake was still inside this basin. On its turn around the world with the angel, the serpent was drinking the blood that was in the basin. When the angel stopped in the middle of the earth, I saw the serpent fall to the ground, thus causing a strong dusty wind. When I asked God what all that meant, God referred me to Ezekiel 40. This is what would happen in the seventies. There will be incessant wars all over the world, in white man's country as well as black. This war will not respect border lines between countries. This war will even spread to the countries bordering the Congo. The serpent symbolized the refusal of God to send destructive war in the Congo. He does not agree that Congolese blood be spilled once more. But the famine will take over, beginning in the 1970's. Rains will change the calendar. People will not be able to grow anything in their fields. People will trade their children against fortune so that they can survive. Then God asks you to find the means to store so that you will not be in misery. God is with you. This is according to the Spirit of God. [Formulaic closing for all prophecies.]

VI. "Ndo Famba": The Hymn Ending the Ceremony [5]

Ndo famba, ndo famba	I am leaving, I am leaving
Ndoshuwa kudenga	I am longing for Heaven

[5] As sung by Rhodesian Apostles in Lusaka, Zambia.

Kunyika ya Tenzi	To God's land
Isina nenhama	Where there are no sufferings
Famayi vatendi	Go along, those who pray
Kunyika kureyo	There is a land
Inoda vasimbi	It needs those who are strong [in praying]
Kusvikayo nyika	To reach that land
Upfumi uriyo	The riches are there
Hakuna murombo	There is no one poor
Hakuna neumwe	There is no one
Neumwe hakuna	Not one
Madzinza ariyo	The forefathers are there
Kunyika ya Tenzi	In God's land
Havachazo chemi	There will never cry
Havana rushuvi	There will never be sad

Vatsvene ariyo
Votara zvikuru
Kuvona iyo nyenye
Mufiri wavose

VII. Songs of Prayer, Curing, and Prophecy Sung outside of Kerek

"Nditungambira Jehovah"

There are many variations in the way in which this song of prayer and supplication is sung. After the principal verse, "Nditungambira Jehovah," it may take any combination of two or three of the verses presented here. Members kneel and face the east, arms extended. Men hold their staffs in one hand or rest them on their shoulders. All prayers are performed barefoot.

Nditungambira, Jehovah (3) [6]
Une wa masimba, Jehovah
Sandisiye, Jehovah (3)

[6] Chishona verses as sung in Lubumbashi, Zaire.

Tikale newe, Jehovah (3)
Hosanna, hosanna, hosanna (3)
Kumpala kuetu ndianjila, wewe Nzambi (3)[7]
Tulombayi Jesu Munazareta (3)
        Mambo wetu mudi mudenga (3)
Tulombayi Nzambi netubande (3)

Appear before me [lead me], O God
You have all the power, O God
Do not leave me alone, O God
Be always with me, O God
Hosanna, hosanna, hosanna
Appear before me, O God
We pray to Jesus of Nazareth
Our God in Heaven
We pray to God we shall rise

"Ndirapire we Mambo mudi mudenga"

This basic curing song, which appears in many different versions, is sung after kerek or in private healing settings. The patient sits on the ground with legs extended and hands in the lap, palms upward. Women patients remove their veils. The healer kneels behind the patient and prays while touching the patient's head, shoulders, back, stomach, arms and legs in a prescribed manner. Women healers use a short stick, corresponding to the man's staff, called a karapi or healing stick that they apply to the patient's body during healing. Other members stand around and sing the healing song continuously during the ceremony. The healer may also pray over a small bottle of water for drinking or washing or over a small jar of oil to be rubbed on the patient.

Ndirapire we Mambo mudi mudenga (3)[8]
Munganga mukuru Jesu Munazareta (3)

[7] Further verses sung by Tshiluba speakers.
[8] Chishona verses as sung in the Zaire.

Masama etu onso mu bianza biebe (3) [9]
Masama neashike mu dina diebe (3)
Ndire rapire Mambo ku mu deng [10]
Alleluia ku mu denga, Mambo ku mu deng

I heal in the name of God in Heaven
The great doctor is Jesus of Nazareth
All our sicknesses are in your hands
The sicknesses will end in your name
I heal in the name of God in Heaven
Alleluia in Heaven, God in Heaven

[9] Further verses sung by Tshiluba speakers.
[10] As sung in Blantyre, Malawi.

Documents and Accounts of Apostolic Social Organization

Excerpt from "History of the Appearance of the African Apostolic in the Democratic Republic of the Congo" (Tshibangu 1970)

In effect, in 1950 there lived in the Congo in the Province of Katanga near the District of the Lualaba, a humble Pastor named Nawezi Petro and his dear wife Tshibola Marie-Therèse. This woman fell gravely ill. After three unsuccessful operations in the hospitals of Dibaya (Province of Kasai), Kolwezi and Sandoa (Province of Katanga), the unhappy family turned toward Northern Rhodesia (Lusaka) to be cured there by British doctors.

The first part of the history narrates the difficulties of Nawezi's journey and the worsening illness of his wife.

After all these burdensome thoughts, the Pastor was visitied by a certain man by the name of Tshibasu cha Kasanda of the Apostolic religion. . . . This person asked him to bring his wife to be miraculously healed there. . . . [A] Congolese woman who was a prophet of their religion consulted the word of God and then told them that this illness could be cured. He who was chosen to pray for the sick was the Reverend Pastor Baptist Kazimil: "Invoke the name of God and of his Holy Spirit while you are with Him on the mountain which the Saviour has shown you, who will pity this prayer and the illness will be healed by the good Lord."

On the evening of March 24, 1953, the Pastor was taken into the bush, on the mountain which the Lord had showed them, where there were other sick people who had come from South

Africa. . . . At eight o'clock that night, the Reverend Pastor Kazimil ordered some Apostles who had accompanied the sick people to light a fire with the tree trunks which lay around the mountain. After having lit the fire, everyone came to sit around it, the men toward the sunrise and the women toward the sunset. After the Pastors Kazimil and Tshiwaya sat among the others, they began to sing divine songs and to preach the Gospel. Here are several chapters of the Gospel that the men announced to the audience: Daniel 3:1–24, 27–35; Matthew 8:1, 6:5; Mark 16:15–18, 3:1, 5:2; Luke 8:26; John 4:46–54, 9:1; Acts 15:1–20, 20:9–12; I Cor. 2:16–34; Galatians 2:16; James 5:11–18; Matthew 8:22 and 8:28. Such were the chapters that were given them that day.

From that time on, Pastor Nawezi was convinced that it was the religion of God. After all this, the Reverend Pastor Kazimil prayed for all the sick people. He took water, blessed it and then gave it to the sick people who drank it without any difficulties in a moment. The cripple Ngombe Katataka received the Holy Spirit which shook him with great force, extended all his limbs including his arms and hands and both his legs [which were both stuck to his chest], threw them in the fire, and he climbed tall trees all night. The next day he was cured. . . . He spoke a mysterious language which no one could understand. Everyone was astonished and glorified God. The same night, the two sick people vomited all night and had diarrhea until the morning of the following day, when all of them were cured. Following that, Pastor Nawezi accepted to enter into this religion and was baptized by the Baptist Kazimil. The two Reverend Pastors of Lusaka prayed very much that Pastor Nawezi would announce this news to the Congolese people; they gave him courage and promised him that if he did it, he would be the first Archbishop of the Congo.

After all these events, the Reverend Pastor and his following took the road to return to the Congo. They arrived in Lubumbashi on August 22, 1953. He preached there several days and baptized a total of twenty Apostles.

Apostolic Regulations in Kananga (Tshiaba 1971)

The Sabbath Day

1. The Sabbath is the most holy day for Apostles, according to the Prophet John Maranke. It begins Friday at exactly 6:00 P.M. It ends Saturday at exactly 6:00 P.M.

2. The Sabbath is violated:

—If an Apostle works, even if he buys or sells something, even if he buys or sells something for someone else;

—If an Apostle eats something offered to him the Sabbath day, or before the day is over;

—If an Apostle takes off his holy garment to wash himself with the whole body nude on the Sabbath day;

—If an Apostle kills and eats a chicken on the Sabbath day, or before the end of the Sabbath;

Whoever violates the Sabbath sins against the law of God. And so in order to worship he must first confess his sin.

[Note: To wash oneself on the Sabbath day, one washes only the face and the feet. To wash the whole body, one should wash on Friday before sundown.]

Passover

1. It is not to be bought or sold; that is a sin.

2. Any man having bought or sold the Passover, or the work of God, or the maka, has sinned. He must confess in front of everyone in witness of his sin. He must give back any money given to him by fraud.

3. No one may suppress any Passover celebrated by St. John or by his son St. Abel. Whoever does so, sins.

In the Service

1. "Kwese, Kwese" is only for the baptists.

2. The teaching of the word of God is only for the evangelists. If a holder of another gift wants to teach, if he is not a baptist Lieb-Umah, a prophet Lieb-Umah or a murapi Lieb-Umah, let him preach in the second person's place. At the end an evangelist should finish the preaching, because it is his gift. [This ruling has been questioned in some congregations.]

Prophetic Examination

1. Only the prophets shall do it.

Marriage

1. An Apostle shall not marry the wife of another, or a woman who was in another marriage. Whoever does so, sins, and should give her back to her former husband. Even if he will have borne one thousand children with her, they belong to the first husband.

2. An Apostle who removes his daughter from her marriage to marry her to another man with greed for goods, or else in bad faith, is no longer an Apostle. He cannot carry the robe, the mutambo, or the staff. He should shave his beard.

3. An Apostle who marries his daughter to a pagan cannot worship. He can no longer be an Apostle. He cannot carry any sign of the apostolate on him.

4. If a pagan has daughters already married before his conversion into the Apostolic Church, and when he enters the church, he must also convert his daughters and his sons-in-law. If they refuse, he dissolves their marriage, because it is pagan.

5. If an Apostle sleeps with another's virgin daughter, he must marry her. If he should refuse, he is no longer an Apostle; he is an adulterer.

6. If an Apostle is divorced, the husband cannot reclaim the brideprice, to escape being guilty toward the chief of divorce.

It is the same for the parents of the Apostle's wife. They should not give back the brideprice to escape guilt before the chiefs of divorce.

If the wife has left the husband's house, and if she has borne many children, if her husband wants to take her back or else to repudiate her, that is their business alone.

Adultery

1. If an Apostle commits adultery he sins. Let them do to him according to the laws of the church for adulterers, after he has confessed publicly.

Glossary

This glossary includes the most frequently used African and French expressions dealing with Apostolic ritual and social organization. It does not include all such terms that appear in the study.

AIMO: Affaires Indigènes et Main d'Oeuvres: The Indigenous Affairs and Labor Department of the Belgian colonial administration. Part of its work was the recording of all activities of political and sect groups among African inhabitants.

akamira (Chishona): Standing aside. This term has much the same sense as the Tshiluba *mulenduke* or Kiswahili *alienduke*. It refers to members who have left the church, whether temporarily or permanently.

Aladura churches: Spiritual churches in West Africa, particularly Ghana, that emphasize faith healing and spiritual communication.

AMS (barani, mabarani): Church scribe, secretary, and historian.

baba (Chishona): Father. Term of address used for male Apostles in the Zaire and in Zambia.

Bapostolo (Tshiluba) or *Vapostori, Wapostori* (Chishona): Apostles of John Maranke.

Bapostolo, muoyo wenu (Tshiluba): Apostles, life to you. Muoyo is the Tshiluba greeting that is translated literally as life. This greeting is used rhetorically and as a way of making transitions from one worship event to another in Apostolic preaching.

Bena kuitabusha (Tshiluba): Apostles (those who believe).

bwanga (pl. *manga*) (Tshiluba): herbal or patent medicine.

Chibemba: Language of the Bemba people of Zambia.

Chikwambo spirit (Chishona): Spirit that causes illness.

Chishona: Major African language spoken throughout Rhodesia. It has various dialects, including those spoken by the Manyika and Zezuru people.

chomeur (French): unemployed.

Conseil Supérieur des Sacrificateurs (French): Supreme Council of Priests, an organization uniting thirty-seven independent churches in Kananga. It was founded by Kadima Marc in the mid-1960's.

dare (Chishona): Literally an open space. The church court at which a council of Apostolic judges *(vatongi)* and elders hears cases.

Demba (or *Ndemba*) Territory: Territory in the West Kasai, to the northeast of Kananga. This area was evangelized by Apostles quite early and has a paschal site of its own at Tshibambula.

Ditalala ku tudi (Tshiluba): Peace to you. This is an Apostolic greeting used rhetorically in kerek and at other times of meeting.

Do Famba (or *Ndo Famba*) (Chishona): Our prayer has ended. The hymn that closes each Apostolic kerek.

ECZ: Eglise du Christ au Zaire: Council of Protestant churches in the Zaire, successor to the Eglise du Christ au Congo, presently under the leadership of Rev. Bokeleale.

Eglise Apostolique Africaine: The African Apostolic church: refers to the branch of Maranke's Apostles that was founded by Nawezi Petro in Lubumbashi in 1953.

Eglise Apostolique au Congo (Eglise Apostolique au Zaire): The Apostolic church in the Congo (Zaire). The branch of Apostles headed by Musumbu Pierre in Lubumbashi.

Eglise Apostolique de Jésus-Christ par le Prophète John Marangue: Tshiambi Luka's Kananga branch of the Apostles.

Eglise de Jésus-Christ sur la Terre par le Prophète Simon Kimbangu: The Kimbanguist church. This independent church was founded in the early 1920's by the prophet-messiah Simon Kimbangu. Its largest following is in the Lower Zaire. It also has several regional groupings in other provinces.

Eglise des Ancêtres: Church of the Ancestors: A small "church" in Kananga in which members from various Lulua villages unite for traditional worship practices. It is headed by a single "prophet" who provides spiritual communications that are translated by other members.

Harikros (pl. *maharikros*): Literally high cross, taken from English. Master singers of a congregation.

Hosannas (Apostolic Sabbath Church of God): A spiritual church begun by John Masowe in the Rusape District of Rhodesia, 1932.

Jerusalem: Symbolically titled encampment for the Passover.

Jordan: Any body of water used for Apostolic baptism.

Kananga: Capital of the West Kasai, Zaire.

karapi: Healing stick used by women in prayer and in healing ceremonies.

Katoka: Commune (neighborhood) of Kananga where the central Apostolic kerek was held, 1971–1972.

kerek (or *kireke*): Full worship service of the Apostles, held on Saturday afternoon and often on other days

keti: Gate or *enquête* (inquiry). The barrier or gate that prophets form in order to examine members before they enter each public worship service or partake of the Passover.

Kiswahili: Language employed as a lingua franca among the Apostles of Zaire and Zambia.

Kitawala: An independent church movement in Zaire related to the Watchtower movement in Zambia. It came to a head in a revolt in the Kumu District in the northeastern Congo, then Belgian, 1944.

konto, dikombo (Tshiluba): Apostle's staff.

kubvumira (Chishona): Answer, trust, join in singing. The enrichment of musical themes by the performers.

kuitabusha (Tshiluba): Believe, accept. The implication here is the acceptance of Christ.

kuteererana (Chishona): Listen to each other. The following of a call-response pattern in music.

kutendelela Nzambi, kulombela Nzambi (Tshiluba): To worship God, pray.

"Kwese, Kwese" (Chishona): Everywhere, Everywhere. The opening hymn of the Apostolic kerek. It encourages members to evangelize and invokes angels to guard the place of worship.

Lieb-Umah (pronounced rabba-umah): A holy word revealed to John Maranke. It has been translated as "he who speaks with God," or "priest," and refers to the twelve heads of each Apostolic community.

Lopasa, (LPZ): The baptist who prepares the vessels for the Passover and who is charged with the washing of the feet.

mafundu (Chishona): The teachings of the church.

maka: Taken from the English "marks." Insignia of office worn by members of the Apostolic church who have been confirmed in a spiritual gift. Men generally wear the insignia on their chests and women on their headscarves. The term is also occasionally used to refer to a sign of symbol in general.

mama (pl. *bamama*): Term of address for female Apostles.

Maranke: A reserve and chiefdom in northeastern Rhodesia. John Maranke's family name by marriage.

mashave (Chishona): Spirit causing illness.

masowe (Chishona): Literally, wilderness. The mountain prayer retreats of the Apostles.

matimana (Chishona): Journey that Apostles make for the purpose of doing missionary work, taking anywhere from a few weeks to a year away from the home area.

mikenji (sing. *mukenji*) (Tshiluba): The commandments of the church and the Bible.

muanza (pl. *mianza*) (Tshiluba): Grade or rank in the church, e.g., L-U, Lieb-Umah.

mubaptizi: Baptist, in charge of baptizing members.

muena buloji (Tshiluba): Medicine man, sorcerer.

muena diabolo (Tshiluba): Pagan, unconverted person.

MRP (Muganga Rapa Preacher): Doctor Healer Preacher: Apostolic healer.

Mukanda wa Nzambi (Tshiluba): Bible, God's Book.

mukishi (Tshiluba): Ancestral spirit.

mulenduke (Tshiluba): Used to a refer to members of the church who have transgressed the church's commandments.

munganga (Tshiluba): Doctor.

muprophète: Prophet.

musankano (Chishona): Church conference.

mushecho (Chishona): Apostolic virginity examination administered at church conferences and just before the Passover celebration.

mutambo: Man's undercloth worn by Apostles for prayer, retreats and public worship.

mutendi kudenga (Chishona): Holy man, one who seeks Heaven.

mutongi (Chishona): Apostolic judge chosen from among the evangelists.

muvangel, muvangeri: Evangelist, teacher. One of the four spiritual gifts in the church.

Mvidye Mukulu (Tshiluba): God.

Mwari (Chishona): God.

"Mwari Komborera Africa" (Chishona): God Save Africa. Hymn sung at the opening of each kerek.

Ndi rapirire Mambo (Chishona): I heal in the name of God. Song of curing.

Ndi tungambira Jehovah (Chishona): Appear before me, O God. Song of prayer.

nganga (Tshiluba): Witch doctor.

ngoma (Tshiluba): Drum with membrane head. The term is used by Apostles to refer to their technique of imitating the sounds of instruments with the voice during singing.

Nyuma Muimpe (Tshiluba): Holy Spirit.

Nzambi, Kabezya Mpungu (Tshiluba): God, Great Spirit.

"Pa Ku Denga" (Chishona): Toward Heaven. The penultimate hymn sung in kerek.

Pasika (Pascah): The Passover ceremony, which also commemorates the Last Supper for Apostles. This sacrament can be administered only by Abel Sithole and Makebi Sithole, the eldest sons of the church's founder.

Rugare (Chishona): Peace: Apostolic greeting used both within and outside of worship settings.

shakena (Tshiluba): Namesake. The term implies a tie similar to that between godparent and godchild in Western society.

tshibanda (Tshiluba): Demon.

tshibindi (Tshiluba): Incest by marriage within one's own clan.

tshijila (Tshiluba): Holy, taboo.

tshikumbula (Tshiluba): Sin, punishment. To have a tshikumbula is to be in sin.

Tshiluba: Language spoken by the Luba, Lulua and related peoples from the Kasai province of Zaire.

tshilumbu (Tshiluba): Discussion, case, palaver.

tshimanyinu (Tshiluba): Symbol.

Tshina Lunda: Language of the Lunda people in southern Zaire and northern Zambia. Some members of this group are Apostles including Nawezi Petro, the first Congolese Apostle.

Tshindembu: The Ndembu language, spoken in southern Zaire and in Zambia. The Ndembu were a part of the Lunda Kingdom, and their language is closely related to Tshina Lunda. There are Ndembu Apostles in Shaba, Zaire, as well as in Zambia.

tshiota (Tshiluba): Clan.

tshipedi (Tshiluba): Gift of the Spirit.

tshipostolo (Tshiluba): Apostlehood, the Apostolic church.

tshitambala (Tshiluba): Woman's veil or head scarf worn for worship.

uroyi (Chishona): Sorcery.

vadzimu (pl.) (Chishona): Clan or family spirits.

varoyi (pl.) (Chishona): Evil spirits causing illness and death.

Varoyi wedzima (Chishona): Witchcraft.

Bibliography

Albert, Ethel M. 1964. " 'Rhetoric,' 'Logic,' and 'Poetics' in Burundi: Culture Patterning of Speech Behavior," *American Anthropologist* 66:-35–54.

Andersson, Efraim. 1958. *Messianic Popular Movements in the Lower Congo.* Uppsala: Almqvist and Wiksells.

Anyenyola, J. O. 1972. "A propos du vandaisme et de son fondateur," *Extrait du Bulletin Trimestriel du CEPSI: Programmes sociaux et économiques* 94–95: 57–88.

Aquina, Sister Mary, O. P. 1966. "Christianity in a Rhodesian Tribal Trust Land," *African Social Research* 1:1–40.

——. 1967. "The People of the Spirit: An Independent Church in Rhodesia," *Africa* 37:203–219.

Arnols, H. J. 1958. "Rapport sur le fonctionnement de la secte 'Apostolic Church' en Territoire de Dimbelenge." No. 15/M.4, Mar. 21. Archives of the Apostles of John Maranke, Kananga.

Aurore. 1972. "Une décision salvatrice pour le Kasai Occidental." Jan. 20–25:1.

Banda-Mwaka, Justin L. 1972. "Le Kimbanguisme en tant que mouvement prépolitique chez les Kongo," *Extrait du Bulletin trimestriel du CEPSI: Problèmes sociaux zaïrois,* No. 5:92–93.

Barrett, David B. 1968. *Schism and Renewal in Africa: An Analysis of Six Thousand Contemporary Religious Movements.* Nairobi: Oxford University Press.

——. 1970. "A.D. 2000: 350 Million Christians in Africa," *International Review of Mission* 59:39–54.

——, ed. 1971. *African Initiatives in Religion: Twenty-One Studies from Eastern and Central Africa.* Nairobi: East Africa Publishing House.

Barrett, William, ed. 1956. *Zen Buddhism: Selected Writings of D. T. Suzuki.* Garden City: Anchor.

Bateson, Gregory, 1972. "A Theory of Play and Fantasy." In *Steps to an Ecology of Mind.* New York: Ballantine.

Belgian Congo. AIMO (Affaires Indigènes et Main d'Oeuvres). 1956. *Rapport annuel.* Province du Kasai.

——. AIMO (Affaires Indigènes et Main d'Oeuvres). 1957. *Enquêtes démographiques.* Province du Kasai.

——, Governor General. 1957. Letter No. 211/23194, July 26. Archives of the Apostles of John Maranke, Kananga.

Bellman, Beryl L. 1974. "The Hermeneutics of Fala Kpelle Secret Society Rituals." Paper presented at the Third Triennial Symposium on Traditional African Art, Columbia University.

Biebuyck, Daniel. 1957. "La société kumu face au Kitawala," *Zaire: Revue congolaise* 11:7–40.

Bittner, Egon. 1963. "Radicalism and the Organization of Radical Movements," *American Sociological Review* 28:928–940.

Blum, Alan F., and Peter McHugh. 1971. "The Social Ascription of Motives," *American Sociological Review* 36:98–109.

Castaneda, Carlos. 1968. *The Teachings of Don Juan: A Yaqui Way of Knowledge.* New York: Ballantine.

——. 1971. *A Separate Reality: Further Conversations with Don Juan.* New York: Simon & Schuster.

Chomé, Jules. 1959. *Le Drame de Luluabourg.* Brussels: Editions de Remarques Congolaises.

——. 1959. *La Passion de Simon Kimbangu.* Brussels: Les Amis de Présence Africaine.

Cicourel, Aaron V. 1964. *Method and Measurement in Sociology.* New York: The Free Press.

——. 1973. *Cognitive Sociology.* London: Penguin.

Coetzee, Abel, ed. 1969. *Woordeboek Afrikaans-Engels   Engels-Afrikaans.* Johannesburg: William Collins.

Colson, Elizabeth. 1969. "Spirit Possession among the Tonga of Zambia." In John Beattie and John Middleton, eds., *Spirit Mediumship and Society in Africa.* New York: Africana.

Crawford, J. R. 1967. *Withcraft and Sorcery in Rhodesia.* London: International African Institute.

Créspy, Georges. 1952. *La guérison par la foi.* Cahiers Théologiques, Séries 30. Neuchâtel: Delachaux et Niestlé.

Daneel, Marthinus L. 1970. *The God of the Matopo Hills: An Essay on the Mwari Cult in Rhodesia.* Leiden: Africa Study Center.

——. 1971. The Background and Rise of Southern Shona Independent Churches. The Hague: Mouton.

De Craemer, Willy, M. de Wilde D'Estmael, and G. Noirhomme. 1963. "Analyse sociologique de la Jamaa," *Rapport du Centre de Recherches Sociologiques.* Mimeographed. Léopoldville.

De Saint Moulin, Léon. 1970. "RDC: La population en chiffres," *Congo-Afrique* 47:377 ff.

Desmedt, R. J. A. 1958a. "Apostolic Church." Mimeographed. Archives of the Apostles of John Maranke, Kananga.

———. 1958b. "L'organisation de l'Apostolic Church." Mimeographed. Archives of the Apostles of John Maranke, Kananga.

Douglas, Mary. 1966. *Purity and Danger: An Analysis of the Concepts of Pollution and Taboo.* New York: Praeger.

———. 1967. "Animals in Lele Religious Thought." In John Middleton, ed., *Myth and Cosmos.* Garden City: Natural History Press. Pp. 231–247.

———. 1968. "The Social Control of Cognition: Some Factors in Joke Perception," *Man* 3:361–376.

———. 1970. *Natural Symbols: Explorations in Cosmology.* New York: Pantheon.

———. 1972. "Deciphering a Meal," *Daedalus* 101:61–81.

Durkheim, Emile. 1965. *The Elementary Forms of the Religious Life.* Trans. Joseph Ward Swain. New York: The Free Press.

Essor du Congo. 1956. "Interdiction d'une sect indigène au Katanga," Nov. 12.

Fernandez, James W. 1964. "African Religious Movements: Types and Dynamics," *Journal of Modern African Studies* 2:531–549.

———. 1972. "Persuasions and Performances," *Daedalus* 101:39–60.

Fetter, Bruce Sigmund. 1967. "The Luluabourg Revolt at Elisabethville," *African Historical Studies* 2:269–277.

Firth, Raymond. 1973. *Symbols: Public and Private.* Ithaca: Cornell University Press.

Fitzgerald, Dale K. 1970. "Prophetic Speech in Ga Spirit Mediumship." Unpublished Working Paper, No. 36, Language-Behavior Research Laboratory.

Foss, George. 1973. "The Transcription and Analysis of Folk Music." In Roger Abrahams, ed., *Folk Song and Folk Song Scholarship: Changing Approaches and Attitudes.* Warner Reprint 609. First Published 1964.

Garfias, Robert. n.d. Liner notes, "The African Mbira: Music of the Shona People of Rhodesia." Nonesuch H-72043.

Garfinkel, Harold. 1959. "Aspects of the Problem of Common-Sense Knowledge of Social Structures," *Transactions of the Fourth World Congress of Sociology* 4:51–65.

———. 1963. "A Conception of, and Experiments with, 'Trust' as a Condition of Stable Concerted Actions." In O. J. Harvey, ed., *Motivation and Social Interaction.* New York: Ronald Press.

———. 1967. *Studies in Ethnomethodology.* Englewood Cliffs: Prentice-Hall.

———, and Harvey Sacks. 1970. "On Formal Structures of Practical Actions." In John C. McKinney and Edward A. Tiryakian, eds., *Theoretical Sociology*. New York: Appleton-Century-Crofts. Pp. 338–366.

Geertz, Clifford. 1965. "Religion as a Cultural System." In William A. Lessa and Evon Z. Vogt, eds., *Reader in Comparative Religion*. New York: Harper and Row. Pp. 205–215.

Gelfand, Michael. 1967. *The African Witch*. Edinburgh and London: E. and E. Livingston.

Goffard, J. 1958. "Compte rendu de la réunion tenue le 30.8.58 au Bureau de Territoire entre M. l'Administrateur de Territoire Pepin et Kasanda Vincent, Prophète de l'Apostolic Church." Archives of the Apostles of John Maranke, Kananga.

Goffman, Erving. 1959. *The Presentation of Self in Everyday Life*. Garden City: Anchor.

——. 1967. *Interaction Ritual*. Garden City: Anchor.

——. 1971. *Relations in Public*. New York: Basic Books.

Gurwitsch, Aron. 1964. *The Field of Consciousness*. Pittsburgh: Duquesne University Press.

Hayward, V. E. W. 1963. *African Independent Church Movements*. London: Edinburgh House.

Heimer, Haldor. 1971. "The Kimbanguists and the Bapostolo: A Study of Two African Independent Churches in Luluabourg, Congo, in Relation to Similar Churches and in the Context of Lulua Traditional Culture and Religion." Ph.D. dissertation, Hartford Seminary Foundation.

——. 1971. "A Church Suited to Home Needs: A Look at Two Churches in Luluabourg, Congo." In Robert T. Parsons, ed., *Windows on Africa*. Leiden, J. Brill.

Hentgen, E. F. 1958. Letter No. 46, April 17. Archives of the Apostles of John Maranke, Kananga.

——. 1959. Letter No. 26/31, April 20. Archives of the Apostles of John Maranke, Kananga.

Heynen, G. 1958. Letter No. 3187/k.03, Oct. 30. Archives of the Apostles of John Maranke, Kananga.

Holleman, J. F. 1969. *Shona Customary Law*. Manchester: Manchester University Press.

The Holy Bible. 1952. Revised Standard Version. New York: Thomas Nelson.

Husserl, Edmund. 1964. *The Phenomenology of Internal Time Consciousness*. Bloomington: Indiana University Press.

——. 1970. *The Crisis of European Sciences and Transcendental Phenomenology*. Trans. David Carr. Evanston: Northwestern University Press.

James, William. 1956. *The Will to Believe and Other Essays in Popular Philosophy.* New York: Dover.

———. 1958. *The Varieties of Religious Experience: A Study in Human Nature.* New York: Mentor Books. First published 1902.

Jones, A. M. 1969. *Studies in African Music.* Vol. I. London: Oxford University Press.

Jules-Rosette, Bennetta. 1974. "Ceremony and Leadership: The Influence of Women in African Independent Churches." Paper presented at the UCLA African Studies Center Colloquium, "Women and Change in Africa, 1870–1970."

Kasanda, Vincent. 1959. Letter to Governor of Kasai, Aug. 4. Archives of the Apostles of John Maranke, Kananga.

Kileff, Peggy. 1973. "The Apostolic Sabbath Church of God: Organization, Ritual, and Belief." Unpublished ms., University of Tennessee, Chattanooga.

Kilson, Marion. 1971. *Kpele Lala: Ga Religious Songs and Symbols.* Cambridge: Harvard University Press.

Kuper, Leo. 1971. *An African Bourgeoisie: Race, Class, and Politics in South Africa.* New Haven: Yale University Press.

Lanternari, Vittorio. 1965. *The Religions of the Oppressed: A Study of Modern Messianic Cults.* Trans. Lisa Sergio. New York: Mentor.

Lanzas, A., and G. Bernard. 1966. "Les fidèles d'une nouvelle église au Congo," *Genève-Afrique: Acta Africana* 5:189–216.

Leach, Edmund. 1967. "Magical Hair." In John Middleton, ed., *Myth and Cosmos.* Garden City: Natural History Press. Pp. 77–108.

Lemborelle, J. 1957. Province du Kasai. Draft ordinance, June 8. Archives of the Apostles of John Maranke, Kananga.

———. 1958. Letter from Governor of Kasai, No. 221/00833, Feb. 26. Archives of the Apostles of John Maranke, Kanaga.

Lévi-Strauss, Claude. 1966. *The Savage Mind.* Trans. anon. Chicago: University of Chicago Press.

Linton, Ralph. 1953. "Nativistic Movements," *American Anthropologist* 45:230–240.

Little, Kenneth. 1973. *African Women in Towns.* Cambridge: Cambridge University Press.

Littlejohn, James. 1967. "The Temne House." In John Middleton, ed., *Myth and Cosmos.* Garden City: Natural History Press.

Lomax, Alan. 1970. "The Homogeneity of African-Afro-American Musical Style." In M. E. Whitten and J. F. Szwed, eds., *Afro-American Anthropology.* New York: The Free Press.

Lux, André. 1958. "Migrations, accroissement, et urbanisation de la population congolaise de Luluabourg," *Zaire: Revue congolaise* 12:675–724, 819–877.

Maranke, John. c. 1953. "The New Witness of the Apostles." Mimeographed. Bocha.

Martin, Marie-Louise. 1971. "The Mai Chaza Church in Rhodesia." In David B. Barrett, ed., *African Initiatives in Religion*. Nairobi: East Africa Publishing House.

Mayer, Philip. 1961. *Townsmen or Tribesmen*. London: Oxford University Press.

Mbiti, John S. 1969. *African Religions and Philosophy*. New York: Praeger.

Merleau-Ponty, Maurice. 1962. *Phenomenology of Perception*. Trans. Colin Smith. London: Routledge & Kegan Paul.

Metzger, Duane, and Gerald Williams. 1963. "Curers and Curing in Southern Mexico," *Southwestern Journal of Anthropology* 19, 2:216–225, 228–234.

Middleton, John, ed. 1967. *Myth and Cosmos*. Garden City: Natural History Press.

Minon, Paul. 1960. *Katuba: Etude quantitative d'une communauté urbaine africaine*. Lubumbashi: CEPSI, Collection de Mémoires, No. 10.

Moorhouse, Geoffrey. 1973. *The Missionairies*. New York: Lippincott.

Moriame. 1956. Province du Katanga. Arrêté No. 21/149 du 30 novembre 1956 interdisant l'activité de la secte "Apostolic Church," *Bulletin administratif*.

Mukenge, Léonard. 1968. "Croyances religieuses et structures socio-familiales en société luba." Extract from Ph.D. dissertation, McGill University.

Murphree, Marshall W. 1969. *Christianity and the Shona*. London: Athlone.

———. 1971. "Religious Interdependency among the Budga Vapostori." In David B. Barrett, ed., *African Initiatives in Religion*. Nairobi: East Africa Publishing House.

Needleman, Jacob. 1972. *The New Religions: The Teachings of the East—Their Special Meaning for Young Americans*. New York: Pocket Books.

Oesterly, W. O. E. and T. H. Robinson. 1961. *Hebrew Religion: Its Origin and Development*. London: Society for Promoting Christian Knowledge.

Oosthuizen, G. D. 1968. *Post-Christianity in Africa*. Grand Rapids: William B. Eerdmans.

Parsons, Talcott. 1967. *Sociological Theory and Modern Society*. New York: The Free Press.

———, and Robert F. Bales. 1955. *Family, Socialization, and Interaction Process*. New York: The Free Press.

Peacock, James L. 1968. *Rites of Modernization: Symbolic and Social Aspects of Indonesian Proletarian Drama.* Chicago: University of Chicago Press.

Pearce, Joseph Chilton. 1971. *The Crack in the Cosmic Egg: Challenging Constructs of Mind and Reality.* New York: The Julian Press.

Perrin Jassy, Marie-France. 1970. *La communauté de base dans les églises africaines.* Bandundu: Centre d'Etudes Ethnologiques. Série II, Vol. 3.

Polanyi, Michael. 1962. *Personal Knowledge: Towards a Post-Critical Philosophy.* New York: Harper Torchbooks.

Pollner, Melvin. 1970. "Working Notes on Ad Hocing in a Self-Explicating Field." Unpublished paper, UCLA.

République du Zaire. Assemblée Nationale. 1971. Loi No. 71–012 du 31 décembre 1971 réglementant l'exercice des cultes. Mimeographed. Author's archives.

Robertson Smith, William. 1889. *Lectures on the Religion of the Semites.* Edinburgh: Black.

Royers, Charles. 1956. Province du Kasai, Administration de la Sûrêté. Bulletin d'information, Oct. 30. Archives of the Apostles of John Maranke, Kananga.

Rutten, M., Gouverneur Général. 1926. Ordonnance du 11 février 1926 No. 14/Cont. relative aux associations indigènes dans les centres européens. *Bulletin administratif.*

Sacks, Harvey, Gail Jefferson, and Emanuel Schegloff. 1975. "A Simplest Systematics for the Organization of Turn-Taking in Conversation." To appear in *Semiotica.*

Schegloff, Emanuel. 1968. "Sequencing in Conversational Openings," *American Anthropologist* 70:1075–1095.

Schutz, Alfred. 1964a. *Collected Papers,* Vol. I: *The Problem of Social Reality.* The Hague: Martinus Nijhoff.

——. 1964b. *Collected Papers,* Vol. II: *Studies in Social Theory.* The Hague: Martinus Nijhoff.

Shepperson, George. 1962. "Nyasaland and the Millennium." In Sylvia Thrupp, ed., *Millennial Dreams in Action: Comparative Studies in Society and History.* Supplement II. The Hague: Mouton. Pp. 144–159.

The Shona Methodist Hymnal: Nziyo Dzemethodist Neminamato. 1969. Salisbury: The Methodist Church.

Shor, Ronald E. 1972. "Hypnosis and the Concept of the Generalized Reality Orientation," and "Three Dimensions of Hypnotic Depth." In Charles T. Tart, ed., *Altered States of Consciousness.* Garden City: Anchor.

Siman, Emmanuel Pataq. 1971. *L'expérience de l'esprit par l'église.* Paris: Beauchesne.

Sundkler, B. G. M. 1961. *Bantu Prophets in South Africa.* London: International African Institute.

Taïfa. 1972. "79 communautés religieuses reconnues au Zaire," May 2:1.

Tart, Charles T., ed. 1972. *Altered States of Consciousness.* Garden City: Anchor.

Thilmany. 1959. Province du Katanga. Arrêté No. 221/124 du 25 août 1959 portant dissolutions de certaines associations indigènes compromettant ou menaçant de compromettre la tranquillité ou l'ordre publics. *Bulletin administratif.*

Tshiaba, Daniel. 1970. "Eglise Apostolique par le Prophète John Marangue: Mikenji Ya Tshipostolo: Instructions Apostoliques." Mimeographed. Kananga.

Tshibangu, Georges Thimothée. 1970. "Histoire de l'apparition de l'église Apostolique Church africaine dans la République Démocratique du Congo." Mimeographed. Lubumbashi.

Touring Club Royal du Congo Belge. 1959. Carte routière du Congo Belge.

Turner, Victor W. 1967. *The Forest of Symbols: Aspects of Ndembu Ritual.* Ithaca: Cornell University Press.

——. 1969. *The Ritual Process: Structure and Anti-Structure.* Chicago: Aldine.

Van Caeneghem, P. R. 1956. *La notion de Dieu chez les Baluba du Kasai.* Brussels. Académie Royale des Sciences Coloniales.

Van Gennep, Arnold. 1909. *Les rites de passage.* Paris: E. Nourry.

Van Holsbeke, C. 1959. Untitled report and projected reply to Kasanda Vincent, Aug. 25. Archives of the Apostles of John Maranke, Kananga.

Vansina, Jan. 1965. *Introduction à l'ethnographie du Congo.* Brussels: CRISP.

——. 1970. "Cultures through Time." In Raoul Naroll and Ronald Cohen, eds., *A Handbook of Method in Cultural Anthropology.* Garden City: Natural History Press. Pp. 165–179.

Walker, Andrew B. and James S. Atherton. 1971. "An Easter Pentecostal Convention: The Successful Management of a 'Time of Blessing,'" *Sociological Review* 19:367–387.

Wallace, Anthony F. C. 1957. "Mazeway Disintegration," *Human Organization* 16:23–27.

——. 1966. *Religion: An Anthropological View.* New York: Random House.

Weber, Max. 1958. *The Protestant Ethic and the Spirit of Capitalism.* Trans. Talcott Parsons. New York: Scribner's.

Welbourn, F. B. and B. A. Ogot. 1966. *A Place to Feel at Home: A Study of Two Independent Churches in Western Kenya.* London: Oxford University Press.

Wilson, Bryan. 1970. *Religious Sects.* London: World University Library.

Yezi, C. 1970. "La structure du mariage coutumier des Luba," *Extrait du Bulletin trimestriel du CEPSI: Problèmes sociaux congolais* 82:3–92.

Young, Crawford. 1965. *Politics in the Congo: Decolonization and Independence.* Princeton: Princeton University Press.

Zimmerman, Don H., and Melvin Pollner. 1970. "The Everyday World as a Phenomenon." In Jack D. Douglas, ed., *Understanding Everyday Life.* Chicago: Aldine.

Index

AFRICAN APOSTLES

Designed by R. E. Rosenbaum.
Composed by Kingsport Press, Inc.
in 11 point RCA VideoComp Janson, 2 points leaded,
with display lines in VideoComp Eterna.
Printed offset by Kingsport Press
on Warren's Number 66 text, 60 pound basis.
Bound by Kingsport Press
in Columbia Bayside Linen
and stamped in All Purpose foil.